THE DOW JONES-IRWIN GUIDE TO PROPERTY OWNERSHIP

How to Understand, Control and Protect Your Assets

THE DOW JONES-IRWIN GUIDE TO PROPERTY OWNERSHIP

How to Understand, Control and Protect Your Assets

MARGARET B. SCHULMAN

DOW JONES-IRWIN
Homewood, Illinois 60430

© DOW JONES-IRWIN, 1986

All rights reserved. No part of this publication may be
reproduced, stored in a retrieval system, or transmitted,
in any form or by any means, electronic, mechanical,
photocopying, recording, or otherwise, without the prior
written permission of the publisher.

This publication is designed to provide accurate and
authoritative information in regard to the subject matter
covered. It is sold with the understanding that the
publisher is not engaged in rendering legal, accounting, or
other professional service. If legal advice or other expert
assistance is required, the services of a competent
professional person should be sought.

*From a Declaration of Principles jointly adopted by a Committee
of the American Bar Association and a Committee of Publishers.*

ISBN 0-87094-662-5

Library of Congress Catalog Card No. 86-070512

Printed in the United States of America

1 2 3 4 5 6 7 8 9 0 B 3 2 1 0 9 8 7 6

PREFACE

Certain aspects of property ownership should be known by anyone who owns or *expects to own* property, real or personal; either as a place in which to live, a possession to have, an investment for potential growth or earnings, a source of income, a business to operate, a nest egg for retirement, or a foundation on which to build an estate. This book covers the significance of particular types of property ownership arrangements (taking into account various family and other relationships and life situations) and points out the reasons for and advantages of having *advance* knowledge in acquiring, transferring, or preserving property. After reading this book, or referring to it on a topic that might affect your personal, business, or investment planning, you will be in a better position to utilize, understand, and benefit from the services of professional advisers. On the other hand, the information and explanations alone may provide instant answers and enable you to act on your own.

Much that is crucial to property ownership planning is not common knowledge. Important legal information that could affect decisions on how to title or transfer property should not be a mystery to the layman. You are entitled to know the *meaning of the labels* attached to various forms of ownership. Such words have tremendous import. After reading this guide, you will understand the labels and avoid mistakes in titling *your* property.

This book will take you, step by step, through various aspects of property ownership. Part One deals with the significance of ownership. Chapter One covers concepts that may introduce you to an entirely new way of looking at ownership. Chapter Two explains the Internal Revenue Code's effect on property transactions, and Chapter Three discusses the effect of state laws. Part Two deals with types of planning for various life situations. Part Three contains Appendix I, a brief chronological listing of federal tax laws from 1913 to the present (including proposed laws) as such laws might affect property ownership, and Appendix II, a summary of state laws affecting property as covered by this book.

Sprinkled throughout are samples of documents that might be used in different life situations. They are *not* intended to be taken from the text and used as such. In fact, there are countless variations, and any document relevant to your own situation must be tailored specifically by your own lawyer. Nevertheless, it is useful to know what these writings might contain.

This is not a legal reference book and should not be treated as such. It is, rather, a guide to *understanding* ways of owning property. The premise of the book is that understanding the evolution of property law and knowing the impact of applicable federal and state laws are prerequisites to intelligent planning and to dealing with the currently evolving changes in our property laws, concepts, and mores. The goal is to prevent the lament, "I wish I had known!"

ACKNOWLEDGMENTS

The valuable critiques and suggestions of the following individuals are gratefully acknowledged: David Weaver, Professor of Law, National Law Center, George Washington University; Elizabeth J. Weisberg, Attorney at Law, specialist in family law; and Ronald Posner and Warren Davis, Certified Public Accountants. Any errors, of course, are my own responsibility. William Kramer, President of Sidney Kramer Books, Inc., deserves special mention for his involvement as a reader and adviser and for urging the project forward. My sister Henrietta Pincus assisted in many ways, and my husband Cy provided continuous encouragement and support.

Margaret B. Schulman

CONTENTS

Agreement Necessary? A Different Arrangement.
Qualified Terminable Interest Property Trust. See
Your Lawyer. Other Uses of QTIP Trusts. Why
Discuss This Complicated Device? Let the Lawyers
Handle It! Notes.

Junior Grows Up. Gifts. Tapping the Unified Credit.
When a Lifetime Gift Becomes Part of Your Estate.
Joint Tenancies—A Solution or an Added Problem?
JTRS with Grandchild. "Lifetime" Gifts with
Retained Interest. Joint Bank Accounts. U.S. Savings
Bonds. Securities. Securities in a "Street" Name.
Importance of Basis. Care of an Elderly Parent. Equity
Sharing. Notes.

Life Insurance. Ownership of a Business. Partnership.
The Closely-Held Business Corporation: *Shares of
Stock as Property*. Professional Service Corporation.
Family Businesses. Sample of a Revocable Living
Trust. Using the Revocable Living Trust. Is There
Anything Else? Notes.

Some Conclusions. Tax Laws that Did Not Work (Or
May Not). Will "Tax Simplification" Work?

In the Beginning. The Income Tax. The Estate Tax.
The Gift Tax. The Marital Deduction. The
Withholding System. Marital Deduction Reenacted in
1954. Equalization of Tax on Lifetime and
Testamentary Gifts. Joint Interests of Spouses: Farm
or Business Property. 1981-Year of Changes. Fiscal

Responsibility Returns. Tax Reform and Deficit
Reduction. Retirement Equity Act of 1984. Are
We Any Closer to Simplification?

Introduction to Appendix II. Topics Covered in the
Appendix. How to Use This Appendix.

PART ONE

Significance of Ownership

CHAPTER ONE

What Do You Own?

AN IMAGINARY CONVERSATION

"I own my car, my condominium, furniture, clothes, some stocks and bonds, a bank account, shares of a mutual fund, and a mobile home in the trailer park at the beach near my home."

"All of those items are owned by you alone?"

"No, of course not. My wife and I own the condominium and the mobile home jointly and the stocks and bonds and the mutual fund. I guess you might say the bank owns part of the condo, car, and mobile home. It holds a mortgage on the condo and mobile home, and the car is financed too."

"That just means it has a lien until those debts are paid. You say, though, that you and your wife own certain things jointly, right?"

"What's wrong with that?"

"Nothing, so long as you understand it. What *you* own is merely an expectancy that you will be the survivor and then the sole owner. Of course, you each have many valuable rights during the joint ownership. Each joint owner, for example, has the right to possession of your jointly owned real estate; each may write checks (usually) on a joint bank account; each (usually) may instruct a broker with respect to securities in your joint brokerage account. Of course, when a dividend check comes in made out to joint owners' names, such as 'Bill and Mary, JTRS,' both will have to sign in order to *cash* it (but it may be deposited by either)."

Except in states that have a special kind of joint ownership for marrieds (known as a 'tenancy by the entireties') and if your property is held that way, any joint owner may have an attorney file an action in court requesting dissolution of joint tenancy and conversion into a 'tenancy in common,' thus destroying the survivorship. There are many aspects of joint ownership, pro and con. Married people favor joint ownership. There are many good reasons for owning property jointly. What you should understand is that your relationship to ownership of the *whole* is merely an *interest*. In law, it is called a 'survivorship interest.' "

"What difference does it make? If she dies, I get the whole thing. If I die, she gets everything. That is what we both want."

"True. However, has it ever occurred to you that if you want to deal with the *entire* property that you hold in joint ownership with another, such as sell it, give it away, or the like, *you* would be unable to do so. Those acts that require dominion or control over the whole property would be impossible for the holder of a mere survivorship interest."

"That's no problem. I would simply ask my wife to join in such action."

"Ah—exactly. What if she refuses?" (End of conversation.)

"PROPERTY" AND "OWNERSHIP"—SOME BASIC CONCEPTS

The point of the above imaginary conversation is to draw attention to a key element in property ownership, the element of control. Without it, the totality of your ownership is diminished. You may still have valuable rights and interests in property, but you will not have *sole dominion*. Note the emphasis on the concepts of control and exclusivity in the definition of property in *Black's Law Dictionary* (rev. 4th ed., 1968):

> PROPERTY. That which is peculiar or proper to any person; that which belongs exclusively to one; ... more specifically, ownership; the unrestricted and exclusive right to a thing; the right to dispose of it, and to exclude everyone else from interfering with it.... The exclusive right of possessing, enjoying, and disposing of a thing.... The word is commonly used to denote everything which is the subject of ownership, corporeal or incorporeal, tangible or intangible, visible or invisible, real or personal; everything that has an exchangeable value or which goes to make up wealth or estate.

What kinds of things constitute "property"? The term *property* encompasses both what we commonly think of as real (estate) property and the kind of property known in law as "personal property." The latter is sometimes difficult to define. Real property generally refers to land and buildings and things permanently attached to them. In a legal sense, personal property is essentially everything else. Personal property may be tangible or intangible. Jewelry, furniture, and automobiles are examples of tangible personal property. Intangible personal property includes such things as contract rights, employee benefits, business interests, bank deposits, security rights, and perhaps a valuable professional education.

Sometimes the distinction between real and personal property is blurred. If you own an office building, you own real property. If you own a certificate of a limited partnership interest in an office building, your certificate is personal property. If you own shares of stock in a real estate investment trust, your shares of stock are personal property. Dealers in real estate can get very precise as to what is or is not real property. For example, a fixture has been defined as an article that was once personal property but that has been installed in or attached to a building in a permanent manner so that it is regarded as part of the real estate. This has a practical application for tenants. A tenant's temporarily attached fixtures, such as bookshelves or a washing machine, are personal property and may be removed when the tenant leaves. However, a kitchen sink that has been attached rather permanently is real estate and belongs to the landlord-owner and not to the temporary tenant.

When real estate is sold, ownership is transferred by means of a deed. Articles of personal property can be sold and ownership transferred without a writing, but for certain purchases a bill of sale is required to evidence the transfer of ownership.

As a matter of fact, insofar as wealth is concerned, the distinction between real and personal property is no longer significant. You would be just as wealthy owning $50 million worth of stock (personal property) as you would owning a shopping center (real property) worth $50 million. At one time in history, however, land was regarded as the principal true measure of value. Since many of the concepts regarding property law in this country evolved from centuries-old English land law, reference to this background is an appropriate starting place.

FEE SIMPLE

The most extensive estate in land in ancient England was an *estate in fee simple*. This language describes the totality of rights in land that can be owned. The holder of a fee simple estate may sell it, give it away, convey it to anyone of his choosing, and will it to his beneficiaries. In England, it was necessary to include *words of inheritance* to indicate that a fee simple estate was being conveyed. Such words were something like these: "To Barnstable and his heirs." The words *and his heirs* indicated that Barnstable received the entire estate. Barnstable was free to convey that estate to anyone of his choosing *or* to his heirs.

The American states dropped the need for words of inheritance. Here is a definition of fee simple in American law:

> An absolute or fee-simple estate is one in which the owner is entitled to the entire property, with unconditional power of disposition during his life, and descending to his heirs and legal representatives upon his death intestate. (*Black's Law Dictionary*, rev. 4th ed.)

"Intestate" means "without a will." "Power to dispose of" means that the holder of a fee simple estate may make a will and designate whomever he wishes to inherit the property so held. This is not dead or incomprehensible language. We deal with fee simple estates every day and should not be mystified by the terminology. When you buy a condominium and receive a deed with the words *in fee simple* as part of the description of the conveyance, you know that you are getting the best ownership of the real estate.

SOMETHING LESS THAN FEE SIMPLE

The word *estate* is used to express the "degree, quantity, nature, duration, or extent of an interest." If we are dealing with real property, the maximum possible ownership is an *estate in fee simple*. There are also other types of estates, such as *life estates* and *leasehold estates*. These terms indicate that the holder of such an estate has an *interest* that is not as complete as *fee simple title*. Having a life estate means that the holder can only use and enjoy (this means live on or receive the income from) the *land* (or property) during his lifetime. A life estate ends with the holder's life. Life estates exist today, and since many other forms of wealth are equivalent to land, a life estate can exist in any kind of property. We will be discussing life estates more fully in Chapter Eight, when we tackle "second marriages." A *leasehold estate* is an estate whose terms are spelled out in a lease, and of course a lease is an agreement between a landlord and a tenant. The holder of a leasehold estate is a *tenant* who pays rent to the *landlord* during the term of the lease. No one has to be told where the term *landlord* came from. Now you know that when you rented your apartment and signed a lease for a year, you became the owner of a leasehold estate. If you pay your rent regularly, you cannot be removed during that year (except for some other cause written into the lease). Your leasehold estate is a valuable property interest!

WHAT IS AN "INTEREST?"

According to *Black's Law Dictionary*, an interest is a "right to have the advantage accruing from anything; any right in the nature of property, but less than title. . . . The terms 'interest' and 'title' are not synonymous." A survivorship "interest" means the right to own the given property if you outlive the other joint owner or owners (who also have the same survivorship interest). If your cotenant survives you, your "interest" is extinguished as swiftly and completely as an electric light goes out when someone touches a switch.

There are, of course, types of "interests" other than survivorship interests. For example, as we have seen, there are leasehold interests and life estate interests. Each of these interests can be of great value. Depending on the circumstances, it is possible to sell and convey some types of interests. Leases are frequently sold in the commercial world. Life estates are usually specific for the life of the holder. But a survivorship interest can never be conveyed away. It ripens into full ownership in the survivor by operation of law on the death of the first of two joint owners (as, for example, in the case of husband and wife owners). If there are more than two owners, then the remaining cotenants share the joint tenancy on the death of one (of multiple) joint owners. Concepts of joint ownership and the various forms of joint ownership will be discussed fully in succeeding chapters.

LIST *YOUR* PROPERTY

Make a list of all the properties you alone own. Then make a list of the properties that you own together with someone else. It is not as simple as it sounds. Don't forget to include all manner of items and "interests" that you may not have thought of before as constituting "property." Have you listed your pension benefits? Your valuable professional education? Other intangible items? If you are married, have you listed your dower, curtesy, or statutory rights in your spouse's property? Perhaps not, but in later chapters the nature of these various property "interests" will be explained. If there is any real estate, who has title? Now, perhaps, you can see that making a list of the property you own is a far from simple exercise. If you think this is complicated, though, look at the next chapter, where we learn that the Internal Revenue Service attaches its own labels to our property and our property transfers.

CHAPTER TWO

What Does Internal Revenue Think You Own?

THE EFFECT OF FEDERAL TAX LAWS ON PLANNING

The material in Appendix I will give you a capsule history of our tax laws. The frenetic changes of recent years have made it imperative for the property owner to follow trends in tax law. For starters, it is interesting to note that there has been a tendency to reduce estate and gift taxes. The income tax picture is, as always, complicated and confusing. The first income tax law, which was passed in 1913 and levied a percentage tax on income, did not at first give rise to any questionable practices as to compliance. By 1920, however, taxpayers began to arrange to have income that did not fit in with the statutory definition of "income" (see Appendix I), and this was when the period of tax avoidance began. Understand: Tax *avoidance*, if legal, is acceptable. Tax *evasion* is not, and sometimes the distinction between the two is blurred.

You may feel that the interpretation and applications of tax law are of no concern to you because: You don't own all that much; you have no desire to violate the law; you are not a tax avoider. Maybe not. Nevertheless, you might: Inherit a house from someone who did have a sizable estate; you could inadvertently be in violation of the law; you are, too, a tax avoider (we all are).

DO YOU HAVE A TAXABLE ESTATE?

Two terms of significance in understanding the federal estate tax laws are: "unified credit" and "exemption equivalent." In the tax legislation of 1976, Congress equalized the tax on transfers of wealth during life or at death. The way this operates is by computing the tax on a transfer (lifetime gift or transfer in an estate at death) according to tax rate tables and then applying a *credit*, which is called a "unified credit" (because it applies equally to the tax on lifetime gifts and the tax on death transfers). This reduces the tax and thus results in an exemption from gift or estate taxes. The credit, first enacted in 1976, was phased in over a five-year period. The effect was to eliminate transfer taxes on an increasingly large amount of wealth being transferred. The unified credit was again increased by the tax legislation passed in 1981, which provided for a new phased-in period that is to end in 1987, when the highest unified credit amount will be $192,000, resulting in an estate exemption of $600,000.

THE UNIFIED ESTATE AND GIFT TAX TABLES

The following table shows the phase-in of the 1981 law:

(a) Year of Death or Lifetime Gift	(b) Unified Credit	(c) Exemption Equivalent
1981	$ 47,000	$175,625
1982	62,800	225,000
1983	79,300	275,000
1984	96,300	325,000
1985	121,800	400,000
1986	155,800	500,000
1987 and thereafter	192,800	600,000

Since the law first became effective in 1981, the entire table is included. Also, since the settling of some estates may go on for several years, the figures might apply to estates that came into being in earlier years. For estates that predated 1981, reference to the Tax Code tables would be necessary.

EXEMPTION EQUIVALENT

To use the table, first refer to column (a). A lifetime gift is valued as of the date it is made. The valuation of assets in an estate is made as of the date of death (or the executor may elect to choose six months after the date of death as the valuation date). Thus, the value is ascertained for a gift or an adjusted gross estate (the gross estate minus debts and liabilities and certain allowable expenditures, such as administration costs), and the tax for that value is determined by reference to tax tables for estates and gifts and a "tentative tax" arrived at. From this tentative tax, the unified credit—see column (b)—is subtracted. The result of this arithmetic—tentative tax less unified credit—equals column (c), "Exemption Equivalent."

Here is an example, with figures:

Mr. Gotrocks dies in 1986 with a taxable estate of $1 million. (See also column listing estate as $500,000.) During his lifetime he did not make any gifts that were subject to gift tax. (If he made any gifts, they were within the $10,000 annual exclusion and so it was not necessary that they be reported.)

Taxable estate	$1,000,000	$500,000
Tax on $1,000,000 (from tax tables)	345,800	
Tentative tax	345,800	155,800
Less: Unified credit	155,800	155,800
Estate tax	$ 190,000	0

This is, of course, a very simplified description of a highly complicated subject. Nevertheless, it serves to show the reader just when thoughts about estate taxes and estate planning might reasonably be expected to enter his head. If for the years 1986 or 1987 your assets are less than the amounts in column (c) above, breathe easier. You do not have an estate tax problem. Of course, no one knows what Congress will do after 1987. For the time being, we must assume that the unified credit amount will remain $192,800. However, if the trend toward relieving ever greater estates from the burden of taxation continues, then your estate might escape taxation even if it is greater than $600,000.

WHAT IS PART OF YOUR ESTATE?

Here are some items that you may or may not have thought of as being includable in your estate:

Real estate.

Jointly held property to the extent that you contributed to its acquisition (only one half if spouse is co-owner but no tax because of tax-free transfer to spouse).

Bonds and stocks plus dividends or interest due to date of death.

Cash and bank accounts.

Flight insurance.

Joint and survivor annuity.

Refund annuity.

Insurance proceeds (if you held "incidents of ownership").

Lump-sum distributions from pension plans, Keogh plans, and IRAs.

Furniture, jewelry, automobiles, art.

Transfers with retained interest.

The above list is incomplete. It merely suggests some of the kinds of items that could be included in your estate. You are richer than you thought!

TRANSFERS WITH RETAINED INTEREST

This topic is selected from the list in order to illustrate the basic premise of this chapter, namely, that taxpayers should learn some of the little-known provisions of the Tax Code that might affect their planning. If you are wondering how you are expected to know about these complex provisions, the answer is: Read on. You will be alerted to some items that you should know about. *At the very least, you will know when to seek professional advice.*

A common planning device engaged in by elderly persons is to transfer property to loved ones in order to (they think) save estate taxes. It is completely possible, for example, to have a title company or an attorney prepare a deed conveying your home to your daughter. Title to the home will then be in her name even if you continue to live there rent-free. The title can be recorded, and she will be the new owner—to the entire outside world. But there can be trouble if, when you depart this world, you have a taxable estate.

Here is what could happen: A federal estate tax return is filed by your executor, and it may be selected for audit. In fact, if a large item such as a home you lived in is shown to have been excluded from your estate because it was given away (this will show up on the return as a "transfer"), that will almost guarantee that your return will be selected for audit—which means that all items will be gone over with minute attention. Suppose your adviser had filed a gift tax return evidencing the transfer at the time it was made. This will show up on the estate tax return on Schedule G—"Transfers during Decedent's Life," House and Lot, 1900 Vista Lane. The Internal Revenue Service can claim that the house was yours and part of your estate if you had *retained the right to live there* without paying rent.

This seems to be completely inconsistent. The house is your daughter's. She received good title and is the new owner. The house was not part of your *probate* estate. Your *taxable* estate, however, is another matter. The Service has a blind spot when it comes to accepting your executor's opinion that you gave the house away. The Service interpretation is that the home at 1900 Vista Lane was *your* home and includable in your estate because you continued to live there after "giving" it away.

Here is an explanation: Section 2036 of the Internal Revenue Code requires inclusion in an estate of "transfers with a retained life interest." If a person at any time during life transfers property for less than full consideration (that is, "makes a gift" of the property) but *retains a life estate* or the use of the property until death, the law is clear that retaining such an interest nullifies the lifetime completion of the transaction—*for estate tax purposes.* The life interest does not have to be specified in terms but can be implied from the circumstances.

As we saw in Chapter One, an "interest" is property. Here is a reference to interest as property in the Estate Tax Regulations:

> If the decedent retained or reserved an *interest* or right with respect to all of the property transferred by him, the amount to be included in his gross estate under section 2036 is the value of the entire property." (Emphasis added.)[1]

Suppose your daughter accepted the gift of the house, thereafter "fixed it up," paid the real estate taxes, and did all the things a house owner does in connection with property. Nevertheless , if a federal estate tax auditor finds that by your retention of a life estate (you lived in the house), 1900 Vista Lane is includable in your estate, you may have placed a "cloud" on the title your daughter received. The cloud has been created by virtue of the lien for federal estate taxes due on the inclusion of the house in your estate for federal estate tax purposes. What have you done? Instead of making it easier for your daughter to take possession of your house, you have saddled her with problems that neither of you ever contemplated! (Of course, such a lien can be discharged by paying the tax liability.)

This does not mean that one should never engage in such a transfer. There might be many reasons for doing so. Since a taxable gift transfer and a taxable transfer through the estate are taxed under identical rate tables, no federal taxes are saved by making a transfer of this kind. However, there are some savings. The appreciation between the date of the gift and the later date of death does save the estate the value of the appreciation. The transfer during life removes the asset from the need to be included in the probate estate. This means that the daughter has the house—and has title. She does not have to wait until a probate court says that she may claim the asset. However, for the transfer to stick without hazarding the label "estate asset" from the IRS, the gift must be complete and not a possible target for inclusion in the category "transfers with retained interest." Possible techniques could be: Pay rent to your daughter or have documentation that the "forgiven" rent is less than $10,000 a year and thus is a gift from your daughter to you (but she may have to report the forgiven rent as income to her). The significant point is that there are correct ways in which to make a lifetime gift, if that is your wish. The goal is to avoid having Internal Revenue negate your act. The best approach would be to seek tax advice from an experienced tax specialist, especially when the property is something as valuable and important as a house. Awareness of the Service's definition of taxable estate creates enlightenment not to be denied. We now have an added dimension to our concepts of ownership.

It should be pointed out in passing that if property is included in the estate of the donor at the insistence of the Internal Revenue Service, all is not lost even if some dollars must be paid to the estate tax collector. The more favorable result that is possible has to do with *basis*. This tax planning concept will be discussed in future chapters. Here it should be noted that the seemingly harsh result of IRS meddling in the affairs of parent and daughter in the example above is ameliorated by the fact that the daughter will receive a stepped-up *basis* (value as of date of death or alternate valuation date) in the value of the house at 1900 Vista Lane.[2]

Therefore, if she sells the house after the death of the parent donor, her income-taxable gain on the transaction could be less than it would be if the lifetime-gift nature of the transfer had been allowed to stand.

GIFTS AND "NONGIFTS"

The discussion with regard to "transfers with retained interest" applied to situations where the donor may have *thought* that a gift to a particular donee was being made and completed. Later, the *donee* finds out that *for tax purposes* the gift was not made during the donor's life at all but ended up as part of the donor's estate—with possible tax consequences never contemplated by either party to the gift. In that case, estate taxes were involved. Here is another situation where an incomplete gift may involve *income tax* consequences.

TRANSFER TO A LOW-BRACKET TAXPAYER

A father establishes a joint bank account for himself and his minor son. He gives the bank the son's tax ID number so that income when earned will be reported to that number. The son has no other income and pays no income taxes. The father's *intention* is that the bank account savings will be a nest egg for the son's college education. The father retains the savings statement, adds money occasionally, never withdraws. The earnings compound. In this situation, on an audit the father will be found to have been the true earner of the income. The reasoning is based on the element of *control*. Remember the significance of *control* as described in Chapter One. The father has not relinquished control—even though he thinks he has. The *possibility of control* is there. The father *could* withdraw the entire amount and apply the funds to his own use. The income is the father's income for income tax purposes. Despite his good intentions, he did not make a gift to his son. He says, "I'll never be audited for that piddling amount." Don't count on it. The Random Compliance Audit procedure is a snare applicable to all.

How to avoid this? Easily. Do it right! The father should acknowledge that he is making a gift of the money in the account to the son. He does this by making the account read: "Bill Jones, Custodian for Billy Jones, a minor under the Uniform Gifts to

Minors Act of (State)." The gift is then complete, and the father's transfer to the son will not incur IRS inquisitiveness. (For more safety, a gift tax return may be filed to document a gift even if it is valued at less than $10,000.) "But," you are saying, "the father is still in control." True. But now the father is *custodian*. This has a fiduciary quality. Custodianship is a simplified trust for a minor. Furthermore, the law is clear that the income from property held by a custodian is includable in the gross income of any person (the father) who is legally obligated to support the minor donee if used for items of "support." Some advisers, in fact, recommend that the custodian be someone other than a parent, who has just such a legal duty according to most state law, in order not to create a possible situation in which the custodian-parent has access to the funds and might use them for items included in the legal duty to support.

PROBATE AND NONPROBATE TRANSFERS

Here is a situation in which the donor understands that the income tax obligation remains with the holder of a jointly held bank certificate of deposit but gives little thought to possible estate tax consequences. Don't forget, even if the federal estate tax is not a hazard, there might be state inheritance taxes to consider (see Appendix II).

A grandmother buys a certificate of deposit, listing herself and her grandson Michael as JTRS owners. She keeps the CD, receives the income from it, but tells herself and Michael's parents that if she should die during the term of the CD, Michael will automatically receive it ("The bank clerk told me so"). What she doesn't know is that if she should die, the value of the CD will be considered a part of her estate for estate tax purposes. She owns it and will continue to own it, if she holds it, until the day she dies. The only comfort one can derive from this kind of transaction is that the certificate of deposit will automatically be transferred on death to the listed co-owner and so will pass outside the *probate* estate. This may not be a small advantage.

Suppose Michael is waiting in the wings to get his hands on the money as politely and quickly as possible because college tuition is due. The transfer can be immediate to Michael, the surviving joint owner. But the executor of Grandmother's estate will have to include the value of the CD on the estate tax return (if her estate is large enough to require filing of a return) even if the money has already been spent by the time the tax return is prepared and Michael is halfway through his sophomore year at college!

In this situation, the IRS was not after the income tax on the earnings of the CD while Grandmother received those earnings. She dutifully reported the earnings and paid income taxes on that income. The inclusion of the value of the CD in Grandmother's estate has to do with the rules relating to estate inclusion of JTRS property. IRS Code Section 2040 states that there is a presumption that all jointly owned property was owned by the first of the joint owners to die. (Different rules apply to married joint owners.) The other surviving owner or owners may come forward and rebut this presumption with proof of their monetary contribution to acquisition of the jointly owned asset(s), but unless such proof is forthcoming, the estate of the first joint owner to die will include the jointly held property. If the estate of that individual is large enough to incur a federal estate tax, the value of the jointly owned asset will be included along with other assets and taxed accordingly. This means that unless a surviving joint owner had made such a contribution (and grandson Michael certainly had not), the joint property is considered by the IRS as having belonged to Grandmother (in the example). Grandson received the CD, and now it may have matured and the money may have been passed along to the college bursar, but somewhere along the line taxes may have to be paid on the transfer. What can happen is that the *estate* pays the taxes (executor) using other assets that either are liquid or can be made liquid, thus depleting other inheritances. Michael's inheritance got to him outside the tax bite. That may be just what Grandmother wanted. Her will may have delineated that wish. The point being made here is just that she has a right to know—while alive and planning.

RELATIONSHIP BETWEEN FEDERAL TAX LAW AND STATE LAW OR INTERPRETATIONS BY STATE COURTS

Very often the regulations implementing the Internal Revenue Code and changes in the Code as enacted by Congress ("Tax Reform Act of [year]") will contain references to specific tax provisions at the federal level that will depend on state statutes or interpretations of state statutes by state courts. Here is an example: A short-term trust in which the income from trust property is given to a beneficiary for a period of at least 10 years may be taxed to the beneficiary instead of the donor. This is a codification of a controversial court case, and it has resulted in the commonly mentioned "Clifford Trust" (more fully discussed in Chapter Six). The Clifford Trust is used in tax planning where the desire is to shift income from a high-bracket taxpayer to a low-bracket taxpayer, the beneficiary, without permanently losing the asset that produces the income. If the beneficiary is a minor to whom the donor owes a duty of support and the trustee uses the funds for that purpose, those funds will be taxed to the donor and not the low-bracket beneficiary.

What is "support"? Here the crucial determination depends on state law. In the case of *P_____* v. *P_____*, a divorce case in State X, the court held that *support* could include private school tuition (where the father was wealthy and had previously sent his child to a private school). Consequently, in State X a wealthy father-donor who attempts to establish a Clifford Trust so as to use its income for private school tuition for its minor beneficiary (while asking the Treasury to consider the income the minor's and not the father's) is quite likely to lose! That is what is meant by the Code reference to "obligations of support."[3] In a controversy as to what support is, the lawyers will seek out local law interpretations, as in the case above.

State laws affect both nontax planning and tax planning in a multitude of ways. The next chapter will deal with variations in state law concepts of property ownership so that you can know in what ways a reference to state law, either statutory or judge-made, can be an important adjunct in your property-ownership planning.

NOTES

[1]IRC Reg. Sec. 20.2036-1(a).
[2]IRC Sec. 1014(a).
[3]IRC Sec. 677(b).

CHAPTER THREE

What Does Your State Think You Own?

Since these pages cannot include all the information available in a standard law library on state concepts of property ownership as reflected in laws and their court interpretations, what this chapter presents is a discussion of highlights and points of reference. Attention is drawn to some of the ways in which state laws might affect your property planning. The presumption is that you will view this material as a summary and not as an all-inclusive manual. This chapter may serve to answer some of your questions, add a dimension to your planning, and, most of all, provoke your inquisitiveness as to ways in which state laws could be of particular interest to you—perhaps because you live in one state and own property in another or because your employer has transferred you to another state or because you are going to Nevada to get a divorce or because you have decided to retire in Arizona.

SEPARATE PROPERTY IN "COMMON LAW" STATES

The states that adopted the English common law system of property ownership are sometimes known as "separate property" states or "common law property" states. As we will see, these are all of the states except the eight "community property" states of Arizona, California, Idaho, Louisiana, Nevada, New Mexico, Texas, and Washington. (Puerto Rico also uses the community property system.) Although most of the common law states now tend to minimize certain historic distinctions between real and personal property, in the days when the common law states were establishing legal systems under the influence of old English law, property meant mostly land and its crops. Therefore, it seems appropriate to begin the discussion of state concepts of property ownership with the topic of real property.

In approaching a real estate venture, you will first be faced with the question of form of ownership. There are state law considerations. There are tax and nontax aspects. There are marital (or divorce) planning aspects. These various considerations should enter into your selection of the form of ownership. If you are buying property in your own name alone, in fee simple, with title in "John Jones," Life can be Beautiful (perhaps). What if John Jones gets married? Complications!

19TH-CENTURY MARITAL PROPERTY

If we could turn the clock back to the 19th century, perhaps married men would be much happier. At that time, as a holdover from English common law, states in this country still clung to the common law doctrine that marriage suspended a *woman's* property rights. *She* could not own property outright in her name while married. *He* could. As a matter of fact (and law), if a woman owning property in fee simple married, upon her marriage the law gave her husband a life estate carved out of *her* estate. This meant that he was entitled to the rents and profits of the property, free from the claim of his wife. He could convey this life estate without his wife's consent, and the life interest could even be pledged to pay his debts. He could sell his wife's interests in land, and whatever remained became his upon her death. If, however, the husband died first, then she finally became owner of those interests in her land that he had not dissipated. Essentially, when it came to ownership, the wife during marriage was a nonperson. As the price of marriage, she gave up her property rights.

DOWER

There was, however, one benefit of marriage for a widow with relation to property. In order to avoid becoming liable for the support of indigent widows whose husbands had squandered their fortunes, states adopted the English common law concept of dower. This was an interest in the real estate of the late husband that state law gave to a widow to provide her with a means of support after her husband's death. It was originally a life estate, which, as we now know, was an *income interest* for her life. It only referred to real property (the early form of wealth); usually it was a life interest in one third of the real estate owned by the husband at any time during the marriage. Of course, the husband was free to will his entire fortune to his wife, but if he chose not to, he could not disinherit her.

STATUTORY SHARE

Is this dead law? By no means. Some states have abolished the concept of dower, but in practically every state a surviving wife who has been left out of her husband's will may "elect to take [her "statutory share"] against the will." The statutory share is no longer merely a *life income interest* in the lands or real property of the husband but is usually an *outright ownership* of the prescribed share (such as one third) of *all* of her late husband's wealth.

CURTESY

In some states there are also laws that provide a surviving husband with a similar life estate in the wife's real estate if she chooses to disinherit him. This is called "curtesy." There were some differences between a widow's dower and a widower's curtesy. In the latter, it was required that a child be born for the interest in land to arise. In the states that followed the old English law, a widower's curtesy was a life estate in *all* land owned by the wife during the marriage, as contrasted with the one third allowed the widow as dower. In those states that still have curtesy, the widower's share has been reduced to a fraction similar to a widow's. Statutory election to take against the will applies to both spouses.

EFFECT OF THESE CONCEPTS ON PLANNING

How will all of this affect you if you are planning to buy a farm that you hope to have rezoned so that you can lease it to a McDonald's that is looking for a spot next to the miniature golf course going up on the state highway near the "wild animal preserve"? Well, it will affect you if you have, or later acquire, a wife and the state in which the farm-to-become-a-McDonald's is located has some form of dower on its statute books. If dower has been abolished in that state, you are home free. Don't forget, however, that should you ever plan to leave your wife out in the cold as to inheriting the fantastic wealth the farm is going to bring you, if she becomes your widow she can still take her statutory share (if you disinherit her in your will) or the state-provided "intestate" share (because you didn't make a will).

The effect that state dower laws may have on your purchase is to put a lien on your title. The lien is by virtue of the "inchoate" right to dower in your wife. Depending on the nuances and variations in the law of State X, *where the real property is located* (not necessarily the state where you are domiciled), your wife's dower right may be extinguished if you convey away your real property while you live since the widow's statutory share may be limited to land that the husband owned at his death, or, conversely, the widow may be *entitled* to her ownership share in any land conveyed by the husband in his lifetime without her signature. In some states the wife's signature on a deed is unnecessary if she is a nonresident. In states that give the widower an ownership share in lieu of curtesy, he is entitled to his ownership share in any land owned by and conveyed by the wife in her lifetime without his signature.

Suppose you decide that you will take title in joint tenancy with your wife; you will need to know that in some states a joint tenancy with a wife can create a form of ownership known as a "tenancy by the entirety." This type of ownership is a form of property linkage that makes one think of the traditional marriage vows, "Till death do us part." In most states, divorce causes the partition of a tenancy by the entirety and also extinguishes any lingering rights of dower or curtesy. Of course, if the two of you take title as joint tenants with right of survivorship, dower will not apply to that piece of property because if your wife is the survivor she will get the entire piece. Depending on state law, this type of ownership can apply to personal property as well as real property.

Suppose that when you are making the purchase of a farm titled in the name of the farmer alone, the farmer's wife (who is opposed to the sale) refuses to sign the deed conveying the farm to you? If State X still has some form of dower on its statute books, you will not get good title, because she has a lien, namely, the inchoate right of dower. Even if dower has been abolished, most purchasers would feel more comfortable if the wife's signature were on the deed. If the farm is titled in the names of the farmer and his wife, then both signatures are necessary to convey title.

If the farm is located in State Y and that is a community property state, a different set of considerations will color your decision.

COMMUNITY PROPERTY STATES

Although the property notions in most states have been derived from English common law, in a number of states the property concepts are of Spanish or French origin. Napoleon established a civil code in France that was adopted by the French settlers in the Louisiana Territory, part of which eventually became the state of Louisiana. Other states in our American West took over the community property system from the Spanish. The states of Arizona, California, Idaho, Louisiana, Nevada, New Mexico, Texas, and Washington and the jurisdiction of Puerto Rico have adopted versions of community property law. In these states, each spouse has a present, vested, undivided, and equal interest in the property of the married couple that is classified as community property. In common law states, property may belong to one spouse or the other as separate property. Even though there can be various forms of joint ownership, such *ownership interests* are still the *separate property* of the spouses. In general, in a community property jurisdiction the separate property of either the husband or the wife is what he or she owned at the time of their marriage and what he or she acquired during the marriage by inheritance, will, or gift (from another—not the spouse). The separate property of each spouse is free from all interest or claim on the part of the other and is entirely under the management and control of the spouse to whom it belongs. All other property is community property.

The theory of community property is that the husband and wife should share equally property acquired by their joint efforts during their marriage. Each spouse is also deemed to be entitled to share equally in acquisitions of the other spouse during the marriage, and each spouse owns one half of all that is earned or gained. Property *purchased* with separate funds is the *separate* property of the purchaser spouse. Property purchased with community funds is community property. It is deemed desirable, however, to document the intent that a spouse's purchase of separate property be considered the separate property of that spouse. In some community property states, a husband and wife may by agreement change the status of property from separate to community or the reverse. Income tax returns have been accepted as evidence of such agreements. When dealing with real estate, property acquired by purchase during marriage with marital funds is ordinarily presumed to be owned by the husband and wife as community property, regardless of the grantees named in the deed, and so in the community property states the ownership of real property does not depend on the naming of the grantee in the deed.

SEPARATE PROPERTY, COMMUNITY PROPERTY, AND FEDERAL LAWS

Interaction between the separate property states and the community property states has resulted in an intermingling of marital property systems in this country. What is community property in one state may be separate property in another. If you buy a retirement home in Nevada and you want it to remain your separate property, since you have always lived in a non–community property state, you should have that intention clearly spelled out and you and your spouse should have a signed agreement documenting it. Most of all—you should see a real estate attorney well versed in the property systems of both separate and community property states. A perusal of the state law summaries in Appendix II will provide a background but checking with a local expert would be imperative *prior to taking action or signing any documents.*

There is a curious aspect of community property law that is not yet ancient history. In community property states, the husband was by law the manager of the property. Although most of the community property states have eliminated this requirement, the concept lingers on. As recently as March 1982, the Social Security Administration had to make an explanation to Social Security recipients whose income accounts over the years had reflected lowered income because of the presumption that the husband was the operator of the trade or business that had produced the income of the married couple. This, of course, was reflected in the income credits accruing to the wife. Here is an enclosure that went out with Social Security checks in March 1982:

New Rule for Community Property Business Income

The Social Security Administration has changed the rule regarding treatment of income from a trade or business in community property States to eliminate the presumption that the husband is the operator. Recent court decisions have held that such income may not be presumed to be the husband's income. The old community property rule was used in Puerto Rico and the following States: Arizona, California, Idaho, Louisiana, Nevada, New Mexico, Texas, and Washington.

As a result of the decision in *Edwards et al.* v. *Schweiker* (U.S.D.C., N.D., California, Civil Number C–80–3959 MHP), the changed rule applies to persons reporting income earned in calendar year 1980 or later or fiscal years beginning November 1, 1979, or later. However, the changed rule is not intended to limit the years for which earnings may be computed or recomputed for benefit purposes. A person whose application for benefits was reduced by reason of this presumption is entitled to recomputation of past earnings and reconsideration of his application. The Government may appeal the Edwards decision.

If you believe that you are affected by this changed rule, you should contact a Social Security office.

The belatedness of this new rule is an example of the lag that exists between the changed mores, customs, and even laws of today and the earlier customs and mores that we have become used to.

Another example of this lag is the slowness with which married women living in non–community property states accepted the status accorded them when the onerous common law doctrine that marriage suspended a woman's property rights was relegated to history as the states passed, one by one, what came to be known as "Married Women's Property Acts." Although this reform was completed by the 1900s, many married women are still reluctant to be separate property owners. Outdated customs also linger in our very documents. In certain states, a deed of real estate to a married woman might contain this language: "To Jane Brown, as femme sole, to acquire, hold, use, control, and dispose of said property *as if she were unmarried.*"

The purpose of this chapter is to point out that state labels are significant. The large subject of marital property will be covered fully in Chapter Seven, "Divorce." In enacting the domestic relations provisions of the Tax Reform Act of 1984, Congress took note of the various statutes through which several states had attempted to grant each (divorcing) spouse certain ownership rights in marital assets. The House committee report complained: "The tax treatment of divisions of property between spouses involving . . . [other] various types of ownership under the different State laws is often unclear and has resulted in much litigation." Consequently, Congress has created a uniform system for viewing the tax effect of a transfer of property incident to a divorce. Under former law it was crucial to determine whether a divorcing wife had an ownership interest in the property that was purportedly being transferred to her in exchange for the release of marital claims. The Tax Reform Act of 1984 has made this determination less crucial because it provides that in such a transfer no gain or loss will be recognized for income tax purposes. The interplay between federal and state law has been resolved with the application of federal law and doctrine to an area of confusion because of state law variations.

IMPRINT OF STATES ON "JOINT"

The state law effect on joint ownership can relate to specific types of property, can color creditor's rights, can deter (or encourage) would-be litigants who would like to sue one joint owner, can determine state inheritance taxes, can be the determining factor in federal tax decisions as to the consequences of joint ownership, and can in a multitude of ways be a significant consideration in property ownership planning. Here are some things to think about.

In some states, laws spell out the legal consequences of joint bank accounts. Other states allow the deposit agreement with the bank to define the rights of the joint holders of the account. In most instances, the account will provide for payment to and allow withdrawals by any of the joint owners of the account. Upon the death of one of the joint owners (and proof by means of a death certificate), the bank will usually reregister the account in the names of the survivor or survivors.

In some instances, a joint account may be a "convenience account." In such cases, one person deposits all the funds and has the sole right to them while alive. The other joint owner acts only as "agent" for the depositor of the funds. Some elderly people engage in this type of "agency" with another adult or with an adult child, reasoning that this is a simple way to satisfy that gnawing question, "Who will take the money out and pay bills if I am incapacitated?" The unintended consequence may be that if the deposit agreement and local law unrelentingly provide that the survivor (a son, for example) is the owner upon the death of the depositor (a parent), a less conveniently located daughter living across the country will be left out in the cold. An equally effective way to provide for an agent to act in case of emergency is to execute a "power of attorney." Most banks have a simple form for this, but it will be restricted to use with a specific bank account.

INTENT AS A FACTOR

There are traps for the unwary. A recent court decision involved a set of facts in which a resident of State Y asked his landlady whether she would mind being a cotenant with him on his bank account for the sole purpose of withdrawing money for him if he became ill or incapacitated, since he had no relatives or close friends. (Obviously, he trusted the landlady.) After he had changed the bank account to read "Joe Smith and Mary Bell, JTRS," Mary Bell, the landlady, had the temerity and lack of consideration to contract an illness and die. The State Y inheritance tax law demanded a tax on assets passing to a survivor of joint tenancy, regardless of which of the prior joint tenants had put up the money! Alas, Joe Smith had to pay a tax on his own money when he became the surviving joint tenant. Federal law also would have required that he pay federal estate taxes (if any were incurred) because of its rule that the first joint owner to die is presumed to be the owner. In the latter situation, Joe could have easily proved that he provided the total "contribution" to the bank account monies. At the local level, however, Joe's attorney must have earned a pretty penny while helping him prove that he *did not intend* to give Mary Bell a real survivorship interest. There are situations in which what one "intended" can be the decisive factor, but in such situations, as in the case above, it might take a lawsuit to prove a certain intent or lack of intent. The Superior Court of D.C., Tax Division, was more sympathetic to the cause of the taxpayer in a case decided in 1979 on similar facts to the fictitious one just described. That Court held that proof of lack of intention to make a gift of the survivorship interest would be controlling.[1]

In most states, there is a way in which one cotenant acting alone can sever the joint tenancy. Assume that Bill and Sam, brothers, own property as joint tenants with right of survivorship. Bill decides that this is a poor arrangement and that he no longer wants his cotenant to "inherit" from him. Furthermore, he wants to sell his share, which, as was pointed out earlier, merely represents a "survivorship interest." The only way this can be done amicably is to have Sam join in the transfer. This Sam refuses to do. Bill files an action in court requesting partition. In order to avoid having a new potential "heir" step into Bill's shoes, the court action and sale to buyer X by one JTRS owner (Bill) immediately *severs* the joint tenancy and turns it into a *tenancy in common*.

Tenancy in common essentially removes the *survivorship feature* from joint ownership. Each of two tenants in common owns a separate portion, and each may will, convey, give, and exercise unrestricted control over his portion, just as in sole ownership. Where state law allows one joint tenant to sever the joint tenancy by acting alone, a creditor with a judgment against one joint tenant *may* attach that joint tenant's interest to satisfy the judgment. The theory behind this seemingly impossible act is that since the joint tenant can sell and convey away his interest by virtue of the fact that such a sale and transfer will convert the joint tenancy into a tenancy in common, then *so can his judgment creditor.*

POTENTIAL HAZARD IN "JOINT"

Suppose that you established a joint tenancy in a piece of investment real estate and that you paid all of the money yourself but listed your adult son, Richard, as JTRS co-owner. You figure that Richard will inherit the property anyway and that with this survivorship interest, the property will avoid probate and go to him directly on your death. Something unexpected happens. Richard is driving his Cadillac one day, and there is an automobile accident. The other party is slightly injured, but the sight of the Cadillac causes the whiplash pain to become very severe. Witnesses are on hand to testify that Richard went through a red light and is at fault. The whiplash plaintiff secures a judgment, and a lawyer discovers that the only thing of real value that Richard has (since the Cadillac is financed up to the hilt) is his joint tenancy interest in *your* investment real estate. Can that interest be attached? If the state law provides that during a joint tenant's life his undivided interest can be reached by his creditors on the theory (outlined above) that each joint tenant can sell or transfer his interest during his life, thus substituting a tenancy in common for the previous joint tenancy, then Richard's interest may also be reachable by a judgment creditor who can step into Richard's shoes and sell that interest to satisfy the judgment.

Already you are crying "Foul! It is my property, not Richard's. I only wanted him to get it on my death. It is his inheritance. I never intended to give him a present interest in the property." A lawyer will be happy to bring an action seeking to prevent Richard's judgment creditor from attaching Richard's interest in the property. Alas, the lawyer may not win. Your admirable plan to enjoy the property today and let Richard receive it tomorrow without probate and its attendant delays and costs has gone awry! Hindsight says: "I should have kept the property in my name and avoided this entanglement! Now I will lose part of *my* property to pay Richard's debt!"

HUSBAND AND WIFE AS "ONE"

In some states, joint tenancy with right of survivorship where the joint tenants are husband and wife can create a form of joint tenancy known as "tenancy by the entirety." This type of ownership is a holdover from the days when the legal fiction existed that husband and wife were one and that that one was the husband. This is not stated facetiously. Rather, it is a reflection of the common law doctrine that when property was transferred to husband and wife, ownership was regarded as being by the *entirety*, meaning not two people but *one person*, namely, the unity created when the parties were married. One could say that this was a romantic notion. If you examine this doctrine more minutely, however, you will learn that under the common law a wife was legally merged with her husband so that her identity, her *legal* identity, was in limbo during the marriage.

The theory was that a wife needed protection from mishandling her wealth due to her inexperience and from foolishly attempting to convey it away and that the possibly improvident and erring husband needed to be restrained from pledging certain assets (those held in this manner) as collateral for a debt. The distinguishing difference between a tenancy by the entirety and a joint tenancy with right of survivorship is that in the latter, as we have seen, any one co-owner can cause a severance and thereby undo the survivorship aspect, whereas in the former it takes *both* tenants to end the joint tenancy (and thus the survivorship interest). *One* tenant (husband *or* wife), acting alone, *cannot.* Originally, a tenancy by the entirety related only to land and real property. States that still have some form of tenancy by the entirety usually apply it to personal property as well as real property. A number of states regard tenancy by the entirety as an archaic form of ownership and have abolished this category of ownership. If tenancy by the entirety still exists, however, and the couple holding property in that manner is divorced, that will sever the tenancy by the entirety. As to the *division* of such property and its distribution to the divorcing parties, a variety of factors enter. These will be covered in Chapter Seven.

EFFECT ON CREDITORS OR LITIGANTS AND WOULD-BE LITIGANTS

In general, a creditor may obtain a court judgment and endeavor to place a lien or attachment on the property of a married person who holds it as a joint tenant with a spouse in a state that recognizes tenancies by the entireties, but the creditor may have to wait and hope that the spouse who is liable on the debt outlives the spouse who is not liable. If the judgment debtor dies before his spouse, the judgment creditor can forget about collecting. Suppose that Dr. and Mrs. A live in a state recognizing tenancies by the entireties, and suppose that all of their property is held in this manner. Dr. A has been the defendant in a malpractice lawsuit attempting to claim damages of $10 million. The judgment against him is for $3 million, but Dr. A's liability insurance stops at $2 million. He still owes $1 million on the judgment, but all of his property is tied up with his wife's in tenancies by the entireties. If the wife dies, Dr. A becomes the sole owner of their joint tenancy property. The creditor can then attach the property to satisfy his claim. Alas, poor Dr. A! However, if Dr. A (fortuitously) dies and his wife is the survivor, the creditor's claim is extinguished as to *that* property. Mrs. A takes possession and control of the property free of the lien and the claim. Poor judgment creditor!

This is not a fictitious scenario but a real-life one. Doctors are plagued today with astronomical malpractice claims. Some potential malpractice plaintiffs or some claimants' appetites for million-dollar-plus claims for damages might, just might, be deterred by an awareness that the form of ownership of the defendant's property will present an obstacle to collection.

Suppose that a doctor faces a malpractice lawsuit and then suddenly decides to transfer his separately owned property into joint ownership with his wife or into *her* separate ownership. That would be an action to defraud potential creditors and would be voidable. *But* suppose instead that the couple has always retained assets in separate ownership. Here is how that might be of use in thwarting would be litigants: If the doctor's creditors try to take possession of his jointly owned property, as we have seen, they would probably be unsuccessful so long as the doctor's wife is alive. The creditors gamble that one day she will predecease the doctor and that he will then become owner of the *entire* property (by his survivorship interest) so that it will *all* be reachable to satisfy the judgment lien. Thus, the patience of the creditors would be rewarded. In some states, a judgment lien may remain viable for as long as 20 years. How, then, would separate ownership work? Since no one knows how the gamble on survivorship will be resolved (until it is), owning property *separately* enables the husband and wife to assure themselves that at least *some* of their assets (those owned by the nonsued party) are totally insulated from attack by a judgment creditor.

AVOID BEING A TARGET

High-income professionals are indeed targets. In fact, this is the motivating force behind their purchase of "umbrella" liability insurance policies and behind the promotion of such policies by insurance companies. The argument is unassailable: "You, Dr. (lawyer, corporate president, big-name athlete, actor, etc.), are a target. Let your car touch another's, let your teenage driver have an altercation with another driver, let your dog bite a passerby, let a passenger on your boat fall into the water and get hurt, and you might be slapped with a huge lawsuit. Protect yourself with this dandy policy with lots of coverage." These arguments make sense. At the same time, attending to your form of property ownership also makes sense and is a type of preventive planning in which you can engage. A word of caution: Large transfers of property from one form of ownership to another should be undertaken only with the advice and assistance of your legal adviser. In some states, property transfer from one spouse to joint ownership or the reverse requires a middleman or a "straw." It is not a do-it-yourself activity.

DISCOVERY OF NET WORTH

One more disquieting word should be added with regard to lawsuits or potential lawsuits against wealthy defendants. One of the modern concepts of litigation is the pretrial use of "discovery" techniques. A trial is supposed to represent a test of legal issues and a determination of the facts in a controversy. Elements of "surprise" are for movie and television versions of a trial. Therefore, facts that are "discoverable" prior to trial encompass a wide area. In many states, when the claim for damages is based on the defendant's alleged negligence and a case can be made out for "punitive" damages, the defendant's net worth is discoverable. Here is what one writer said about punitive damages:

> The defendant's wealth is irrelevant if punitive damages are viewed solely as compensatory. Since almost all jurisdictions use punitive damages to punish and deter, however, any award of punitive damages must be measured relative to the defendant's net worth in order to ensure that the judgment is large enough effectively to achieve these goals.[2]

The significance of this type of thinking is a chilling recognition that if you face the potential hazard of being a defendant and *whether or not* a charge of gross negligence against you is proved at trial, in some jurisdictions a lawyer can ascertain your net worth *in advance of the trial* by means of written questions called "interrogatories." True, the lawyer has to show some basis for an allegation of gross negligence, but the allegation can sometimes be made with relative ease.

What can a potential defendant do? Of course, insurance purveyors want you to insure, insure, insure against potential liabilities. Nevertheless, claims made in the millions cannot, in all practicality, be insured against by buying more liability or malpractice insurance. In fact, there is today a reversal of the trend to urge purchase of more insurance. Insurers are limiting the sale! Here is one possible answer for the married high-risk individual. Share the wealth. Transfer wealth to your spouse. Split your assets down the middle, or even transfer a greater proportion to the spouse who is not at such high risk of a lawsuit. As stated before, this can never be done after the occurrence of the events that might give rise to a claim. It has to be a customary way of life. Something to think about.

"SEPARATE OWNERSHIP"—WAVE OF THE FUTURE?

Are we still bound by the holdovers of ancient English common law? To a certain extent, yes. In one vague way, we are influenced by the past, both distant and more immediate. It bears repeating that married women are reluctant to be sole property owners. The Married Women's Property Acts, which gave married women the right to own separate property, have been held in some states to conflict with tenancies by the entireties. Consider also the Equal Rights Amendment, which has been passed by some states (but has not been sufficiently ratified at this writing to have become a constitutional amendment). Massachusetts has adopted the Equal Rights Amendment. Does this conflict with the still viable doctrine of tenancy by the entireties in Massachusetts, since the latter seems to *restrict* women's property rights? New laws in states that have abolished the estate of tenancy by the entireties as outmoded apply, in general, only *prospectively* and do nothing to change the inequities (favoring the husband) of the *existing* tenancy-by-the-entirety mode of property ownership. This is an evolving area of law. Simultaneously, but perhaps at a slower pace, women are fitting themselves into the changed laws and customs affecting their property ownership rights—at a slower pace because women have really just recently moved into today's world from the era when the husband was deemed to be the financial provider and the wife the economic dependent.

NOTES

[1]*Novak v. D.C.*, CCH Inheritance, Estate and Gift Tax Reporter 21027 (February 13, 1979).

[2]Debra Dison, "Pretrial Discovery of Net Worth in Punitive Damages Cases," 54 *Southern California Law Review*, 1141–66 (July 1981).

PART TWO

Planning Your Property Ownership

CHAPTER FOUR

Single—Now and Forever, or Single Again?

SINGLE NOW AND FOREVER

This topic heading refers to those who prefer their bachelorhood or career-woman status and have made a planned and considered decision to maintain that status. Of course, once the status changes and property decisions become important in the changed status, other chapters might apply.

For the moment, we will stick to the concept of single bliss as the desired state of life for many people. Single people, of course, invariably have relatives, friends, a favorite niece or nephew, and the like to help out, so that the comments on gifts already set forth would be applicable to them. It is not likely that the young, able-bodied, mentally alert single person will devote much time to considering the eventuality of disability or incapacity. At some point in time, however, when one is alone or almost alone, this possibility will receive some consideration, particularly after assets have been acquired that must be managed during the owner's temporary (or permanent) incapacity. The thoughts of the person who has never married will not, then, be very different from those in the minds of individuals who are once again single through the loss of a spouse.

SINGLE AGAIN

Whether one is single as a widow or widower or a busy, active career person who has never married, the prospect of losing control over one's assets and affairs is a disheartening one. The goal is to maintain control as long as possible and to make one's own plans for the eventual transfer of authority and responsibility if necessary.

WHO WILL HANDLE MY PROPERTY
IF I AM INCAPACITATED?

Agency—Power of Attorney

One caution is that you not be like the fellow described as Joe Smith in the last chapter, the one who listed his landlady as cotenant of his bank account for mere "agency" purposes. Assuming that you have eschewed "joint" and have only your name on your bank account, the simplest method of providing for a temporary period of incapacity is to ask a trusted person to act as your "attorney in fact" with regard to just that bank account. Banks can usually provide a simplified form of "power of attorney," in which you name that trusted person to act with regard to that bank account for a limited period of time.

A more extensive power of attorney may be drawn up by your attorney, using some or all of the clauses set forth in the following sample, but *you*, in your conference with your attorney, have every right to specify that your agent's duties, as spelled out in the document, be as inclusive or as *limited* as you wish.

SAMPLE OF A GENERAL POWER OF ATTORNEY
(from the author's files)

Here is a sample of a power of attorney so that you can see just how inclusive such a document can be, provided it is in accord with state law.

GENERAL POWER OF ATTORNEY

KNOW ALL BY THESE PRESENTS: That I, _____, of the City of _____, State of _____, do hereby make, constitute, and appoint and have made, constituted, and appointed _____, of the City of _____, State of _____, my true and lawful attorney in fact for me and in my name, place, and stead, and on my behalf, effective from the date hereof:

1. To exercise or perform any act, power, duty, right, or obligation whatsoever that I now have, or may hereafter acquire the legal right, power, or capacity to exercise or perform, in connection with, arising from, or relating to any person, item, transaction, thing, business property, real or personal, tangible or intangible, or matter whatsoever;

2. To request, ask, demand, sue for, recover, collect, receive, and hold and possess all such sums of money, debts, dues, commercial paper, checks, drafts, accounts, deposits, legacies, bequests, devises, notes, interests, stock certificates, bonds, dividends, certificates of deposit, annuities, pension and retirement benefits, insurance benefits and proceeds, any and all documents of title, choses in action, personal and real property, intangible and tangible property, and property rights and demands whatsoever, liquidated or unliquidated, as now are, or shall hereafter become owned by me, or due, owing, payable, or belonging to me, or in which I have or may hereafter acquire interest; to take all lawful means and equitable and legal remedies in my name for the collection and recovery thereof, and to adjust or compromise and agree for the same; and to make, execute, and deliver for me, on my behalf, and in my name, all endorsements, acquittances, releases, receipts, or other sufficient discharges for the same;

3. To receive and receipt for any and all sums of money or payments due or to become due to me; to continue, to modify, and to terminate any deposit account or other banking arrangement made by me or on my behalf prior to the creation of this instrument; to open deposit accounts of any type with any banking institutions, wherever located, and to make such other contracts for the procuring of services by any banking institution as my attorney in fact deems to be desirable; to make, to sign, and to deliver checks or drafts for any purpose, to withdraw by check, order, or otherwise any funds or property of mine deposited

with, or left in the custody of, any person or banking institution, wherever located, either before or after the creation of this instrument, to receive statements, vouchers, notices, or other documents from any person or banking institution and to act as may be deemed appropriate with respect thereto; to have free access at any time or times to any safe-deposit boxes or vaults to which I might have access, if personally present;

4. To deal in, sell, assign, transfer, and purchase any and all securities, capital stocks, bonds, or indentures on my behalf and in my place, stead, and name;

5. To make, receive, sign, endorse, execute, acknowledge, deliver, and possess such contracts, agreements, options, conveyances, security agreements, leases, mortgages, assignments, insurance policies, documents of title, bonds, debentures, checks, stock certificates, proxies, warrants, receipts, withdrawal receipts, and deposit instruments relating to accounts or deposits in, or certificates of deposit of, banks, savings and loan, or other institutions or associations and such other instruments in writing of whatsoever kind and nature as may be necessary or proper in the exercise of the rights and powers herein granted;

6. To conduct, engage in, and transact any and all lawful business of whatever nature or kind for me, on my behalf, and in my name; to act for me in any business, corporation, partnership, limited partnership, joint venture, or any other enterprise in which I am or have been engaged or interested or have any investment, rights, or participation, hereby giving to my attorney full power and authority to exercise any and all rights, privileges, and/or decisions, including the right to vote with respect thereto to the same extent that I am possessed; and to execute any and all instruments required in connection with or incident to my interest therein;

7. To pay, to compromise, or to contest taxes or assessments of all kinds and to apply for refunds in connection therewith;

8. To execute, acknowledge, and deliver in my name any and all deeds, deeds of trust, notes, including promissory notes, necessary or desirable, to convey, encumber, or otherwise,

affecting any real estate, or interest therein, now or hereafter owned or held by me, including the right, power, and authority to execute, acknowledge, and deliver assignments, sales agreements, leases, and other agreements relating to real estate or interests therein as aforesaid;

9. I grant to said attorney in fact full power and authority to do, take, and perform all and every act and thing whatsoever requisite, proper, or necessary to be done, in the exercise of any of the rights and powers herein granted, as fully to all intents and purposes as I might or could do if personally present, with full power of substitution or revocation, hereby ratifying and confirming all that said attorney in fact, or his substitute or substitutes, shall lawfully do or cause to be done by virtue of this power of attorney and the rights and powers herein granted.

10. This instrument is to be construed and interpreted as a general power of attorney. The enumeration of specific items, rights, acts, or powers herein is not intended to, nor does it, limit or restrict, and is not to be construed or interpreted as limiting or restricting, the general powers herein granted to said attorney in fact.

The rights, powers, and authority of said attorney in fact herein granted shall commence and be in full force and effect on _____, 19____, and such rights, powers, and authority shall remain in full force and effect until terminated by me in writing.

IN TESTIMONY WHEREOF, I have hereunto set my hand and seal this _____ day of _____, 19____.

WITNESSES:

_____   _____
                                                              (SEAL)
_____
(Notarization)

Formerly, a curious anomaly existed with regard to a power of attorney, depending on state law. Normally, a power of attorney is automatically revoked on the mental incapacity of the principal inasmuch as a power of attorney is an agency designation and an agency presumes a principal with capacity to appoint an agent. If this rule applies, the agency contract is revoked just at the point when the principal may most need an agent to act in his behalf. Consequently, all states (not the District of Columbia) have enacted provisions for a "durable power of attorney." This means that the agency transcends the incapacity of the one who appointed the agent. There are variations in the state statutes, but there is usually language providing that a durable power of attorney contain a phrase such as "this power of attorney shall not be affected by my subsequent disability or incapacity." The purpose of the wording is to show the principal's intent that the authority conferred be exercisable notwithstanding the principal's subsequent disability or incapacity.

Conservator

If you become mentally incapacitated and have made no provision for appointment of an agent, it is likely that someone will petition a local court for appointment of a conservator (also called "guardian" or some similar name). You then become a ward of the court, usually a branch of the probate court of your state. The need to ensure that those who conduct business with you (in your incompetent state) do not do so at their peril is as great as the need to ensure that unscrupulous people do not take advantage of you with regard to your property. Presumably, courts have a tendency to be very suspicious of caretaking relatives. A businessman who had acted for years as the agent of his 92-year-old mother was deemed unsatisfactory to act in that capacity when the mother became incompetent. Instead, he had to shed his "agent" (power of attorney) authority and don the mantle of court-appointed "conservator" so that his acts would be scrutinized by the conservator division of the probate court.

USE OF A REVOCABLE LIVING TRUST

How can you avoid becoming a "ward of the court," which is what happens when a conservator is appointed to handle your assets? One available technique is to establish a revocable living trust. Using this method, you, the creator or grantor, transfer your property to a trustee to manage, maintain, invest, and reinvest and to generally do all things with regard to your property that you would do yourself. Those who recommend using a living trust point out various advantages: On your death, the property in the trust goes to your named beneficiaries without having to go through probate; there is no publicity of your affairs (as in probate); a trustee has already been appointed *by you* so that if you become incompetent, the mechanism is in place.

What is not pointed out by those who recommend a living trust is that it is cumbersome (your assets in the trust are thereafter owned by XYZ Bank and Trust Company, as trustee, or, if the trustee is an individual, by Amos Rich, as trustee), that preparation of the document itself costs you a bundle in legal fees, and that yearly fiduciary income tax returns must be filed (in addition to your own tax returns). The transfer of assets should not be a problem, because you as a single individual no doubt own everything yourself and not in joint ownership with another. That is necessary if you are going to transfer property to a trust, and if there are joint ownership arrangements, they will have to be dismantled. The problem of joint ownership is most often encountered when the wealthy family man becomes convinced that a living trust is the right way for him to handle his affairs. He may have an elaborate trust document drawn up, but when the time comes to "fund" the trust (transfer property to the new ownership of the trustee), it may be found that all of his property is in joint ownership. One cannot act in *control* of property that is not separately and individually owned.

(See Chapter Ten for a sample of a revocable living trust.)

TYPE OF OWNERSHIP IN A TRUST

The concept of a trust, like so much of our law, is traceable historically to ancient English law. The significant feature of a trust is that the "trustee" has *legal* ownership of the property in the trust, whereas those who are named as beneficiaries have *equitable* ownership. The latter would even include you, although you might also be the trustee. All business is conducted with the trustee, who has *legal* title to the property in the trust. Just as in the case of a court-appointed conservator, care is taken to protect those who deal with the trustee by making sure that the trustee's transactions will be legally binding. Where a transaction is significant, there will be a request to see the trust document.

JOINT OWNERSHIP

For some propertied individuals, joint ownership is a preferred way of dealing with incapacity. Joint ownership, particularly of a liquid asset such as a bank account, can provide the convenience of immediate access to funds by the nonincapacitated joint owner. The important thing to remember is that the other named joint owner or owners should be individuals whom you would want to inherit the funds anyway—because that is what will most probably happen if you do not survive your incapacity.

OTHER METHODS

"Peace of mind" investments might be an alternative or concurrent way of preparing for the eventuality of being cared for physically or mentally, and financially, by another. Caretakers and agents could do little to interfere with a preplanned periodic income coming to you, such as an annuity or interest on government bonds or Treasury notes. However, having someone manipulate your investments from time to time to keep up with changing circumstances in the financial markets might be more valuable than the feeling of security that you would obtain from a nonfluctuating (but lower-yielding) annuity. These are factors that should be weighed by a competent single individual who wishes to remain on top of his investment decisions. Incompetency may never occur, but if it does, having, insofar as possible, minimal-risk investments would be desirable for the individual who abhors turning over investment decisions to others.

CHANGING LIFESTYLES

At this moment in your life, incapacity may be the thing farthest from your thoughts. You may be enjoying single bliss and the feeling that your property is unquestionably yours. You may also feel that if you choose you can alter your lifestyle temporarily while not altering dominion over your assets. If that is so, perhaps the next chapter will be an eye-opener or, at least, will point out a few hazards to contemplate.

CHAPTER FIVE

Cohabitation

Not too long ago, "cohabitation" was viewed as a union based on meretricious behavior or at least having meretricious overtones. Whatever was a "meretricious" arrangement for living gained the condemnation not only of society but also of courts, because the latter would not lend their dignity to settling disputes between parties who engaged in a lifestyle founded on something akin to prostitution.

MARVIN v. MARVIN

Marvin v. Marvin changed all that. This famous California case opened the door to the *possibility* that the time had come for a changed attitude toward these new-style living arrangements. In the *Marvin* case, Michelle Marvin and Lee Marvin lived together, unmarried, for six years. When the relationship ended, Michelle sued, claiming property rights based on an oral agreement that the parties would pool property and earnings and that she would provide household services and he would provide support for her life. The California Supreme Court held that an agreement to pay money or transfer property where sexual services are the consideration can be enforceable even though sexual relations are involved. The Court enumerated other possible theories as a basis for granting relief to the presumed wronged party. The trial court, to which the case went back for determination as to whether a contract existed, found no contract but gave the defendant an award of $104,000, $1,000 a week for two years (the award was based on what she had been earning before the relationship), as a kind of rehabilitative "alimony." The significant thing about the *Marvin* case is that it occurred in a *community property* jurisdiction. Under community property law, had a marriage existed, either spouse would have been entitled to share in the earnings of the other during the marriage. Michelle Marvin's attorney sought, by analogy, to place the imprint of community property reasoning on nonmarried cohabitants.[1]

TYPES OF AGREEMENTS

In states that recognize common-law marriages, either in state law or in court decisions establishing precedents, one may attempt to prove that either or both of the parties regarded (or did not regard) a particular relationship as a common-law marriage. A common-law marriage is one in which the parties agree to live together in a marriage-like relationship but do not solemnize the marriage in a legal manner. If a common-law marriage is proved (by various types of evidence, such as using "Mr. and Mrs.," having joint bank accounts, and "holding out to the public as a married couple"), then the question of rights in property that one or the other of the parties claims is decided on the same legal principles on which the rights of legally married people are decided. If one of the parties in a cohabiting relationship can convince a court that he or she *believed* a marriage existed, and if the relationship is found to be a marriage, a conflict between the parties might in some states be decided on traditional principles relating to settling property conflicts between partners to a marriage, as in divorce. However, most jurisdictions do not now recognize common-law marriage. That is one of the hazards of cohabitation. In fact, in the *Marvin* case the trial and intermediate appellate courts had the added problem that the oral agreement between the parties was alleged to include among its provisions a plan that the parties would hold themselves out as husband and wife.

In general, the property rights of cohabitants, in states where courts will consider the settlement of claims based on dissolution of cohabitation, are determined on the principles of contract law.

Courts have enforced three types of express agreements: agreements to pool earnings and share in acquisitions, agreements of partnership, and agreements to function as a joint venture.

POLICY CONSIDERATIONS

In some states, if the state views any part of the consideration for an agreement as meretricious (sexual) relations, then the entire agreement is invalid and will not be enforceable. *Black's Law Dictionary* defines consideration as follows: "The inducement to a contract. The cause, motive, price, or impelling influence which induces a contracting party to enter into a contract." Therefore, "legal consideration" is consideration that is "recognized or permitted by the law as valid and lawful; as distinguished from . . . illegal or immoral."[2] In legal terms, consideration is presumed to be something of value. People may have different opinions as to whether meretricious behavior is valuable, but legislatures and courts have a public-policy attitude against encouraging contracts based on such consideration. There was a case in Georgia, for example, in which a woman who for 18 years had cooked, cleaned, and cared for a man and had also contributed money for purchase of the home in which they lived, could not recover anything from his estate when he died, because sexual relations had formed part of her "consideration" for the nonmarital oral agreement.[3]

Court cases along these lines have been categorized as decisions espousing the "Illegal Consideration Doctrine." In one case, for example, a married woman lived with the defendant for six years. She alleged that she had been involved in the defendant's work and that an oral agreement existed to share the assets acquired by him. The court held that the agreement was void because the relationship had been one of adultery.[4]

SEVERANCE DOCTRINE

Some states have imprinted a "Severance Doctrine" on the Illegal Consideration Doctrine to sever the "tainted" (illegal) part from the balance of consideration recited for the cohabitation. This has been done in order to grant relief to a party whose property rights were endangered by strict adherence to the view that the contract was entirely unenforceable, partly because of sexual factors.

State courts' attitudes have changed in some instances. In 1952 a California court refused to find an agreement severable, so that the tainted part (sexual relations) could be separated from the valid consideration. A woman had assisted the defendant (now a deceased defendant) in running a rooming house and a hamburger stand and had also contributed wages that she had earned in outside employment. She claimed that this was sufficient consideration to enforce a promise he had made to provide for her in his will aside from the promise she had made to live with him and bear his children. Not so, said the court. The sexual services negated the whole agreement.[5] But in 1978 a New Jersey court allowed a woman cohabitant of 15 years to recover $55,000, based on actuarial estimates, thus affirming her claim that she had proven an express contract providing that the man she lived with would support her for the rest of her life. The Supreme Court of New Jersey stated that society's morals had changed and that "an agreement between adults living together is enforceable to the extent it is not based on relationship proscribed by law or on a promise to marry."[6]

In 1982 the Maryland Court of Appeals ruled favorably on the claim of the plaintiff that the defendant had promised to give her 1,000 shares of stock, holding that there was no proof than an illicit relationship was part of the consideration for the contract of cohabitation.[7] The trend has been to separate a contractual promise to engage in sexual conduct from other, more acceptable promises (working together, sharing earnings, etc.) wherever possible in order to uphold a contract otherwise unenforceable. The court that recognized that society's morals had changed summed it up. Still other courts find no violation of public policy even if the contract recites the tainted (illegal) consideration.

Today's legislatures have, in general, taken nonmarital sexual activity out of the criminal lexicon. Just to be on the safe side, however, unless you are perfectly sure of the law in your state (and whether that law is well settled and not still evolving), if you plan to enter into a nonmarital relationship, be sure that any agreement you make (preferably written) is founded on contract law and that the consideration is *other than sex*! This would be particularly important where the cohabitants are members of the same sex.

STATE STATUTES OF FRAUDS

The English Statute of Frauds, passed in 1677, has been adopted in some form in nearly all of the states in this country. The object of these state statutes of frauds is to prevent frauds and perjuries, and so the requirement in these statutes is that certain transactions are unenforceable if they are not in writing. Among these transactions are contracts that cannot be performed within one year and agreements affecting ownership of real property. The argument has been made that this technical requirement of contracts applies to the commercial world and should not be strictly applied to oral or implied agreements between parties in noncommercial living-together arrangements and that difficulties of proof (because of no writing) should not prevent or interfere with enforcement on some equitable grounds.

You should know about the statute of frauds because some states still apply it to living-together agreements. In a New York case, for example, a New York appeals court held that a woman could not recover against a man's estate for work, labor, and services in his bar and grill and for her services in domestic ways over a period of seven years. The *oral* promise the man had made to her to compensate and care for her was held void under New York's statute of frauds, which required such agreements to be in writing.[8]

Court decisions have varied widely on whether the statute of frauds applies to cohabitation agreements. In another New York case, it was held that the statute of frauds was inapplicable because the oral contract *could* be performed within one year.[9] In a Wyoming case, the state Supreme Court rejected a woman's claim to a portion of the man's estate that he acquired during their cohabitation. The woman claimed that there was an oral agreement to combine their property. The court held that this oral agreement was unenforceable under the statute of frauds.[10] In another Wyoming case, an oral agreement was upheld because both parties stipulated that an oral agreement existed.[11]

IMPLIED AGREEMENTS

Sometimes actions of the parties are such that the court can infer an implied agreement. What can be implied, if the facts warrant it, is that the parties acted as partners, so that earnings or property can be allocated without regard to sex or marital-nonmarital status. However, it is difficult to prove an implied contract for a partnership-like arrangement if one of the parties is contributing household services and the other is providing or promising money or property. This was essentially the theory on which the *Marvin* case turned.

Another theory, which has been put forward by disappointed plaintiffs (who are almost always women), is that the evidence shows that the parties intended property to be held by one of them (the defendant) in trust for the other, thus establishing a "resulting" or "implied-in-fact" trust. (Oversimplified.) The difficulty that plaintiffs have with proving a resulting trust is that *intent* must be established by clear and convincing proof and that the plaintiff (who hopes to be the beneficiary) must have provided *value* for use (by the defendant) in acquiring the property, which would then be the trust property. An argument has been made that if the household services *contributed* by the plaintiff eliminated the defendant's need to *purchase* those services, then the wealth of the defendant was enhanced, thus enabling him to acquire the property. The key to this argument is to prove the marketplace worth of domestic services contributed on an around-the-clock basis by someone standing in the shoes of a wife.[12]

There are other nuances and arguments, and many of them are related to equitable distribution theories in dividing the marital property of divorcing spouses. Listing some of the theories that have been put forward and that have been analyzed by state courts has been intended as an eye-opener to the innocent and un-initiated cohabitant. The law is not as settled as one might wish. If any sizable property is at stake, you will want to protect and preserve what you consider yours. One method is to write out an agreement.

WRITTEN NONMARITAL PARTNERSHIP AGREEMENTS

The chief reason for entering into a written nonmarital agreement is to negate any inference that an oral agreement exists. If you are the owner of property that you wish to remain your property, you will want to assure that a claim is not made against it or you at some future date. Possibly your about-to-be partner will not like the idea of a written agreement. If there is any under-the-surface mistrust or doubt about the purpose to be served by entering into a written agreement setting forth the respective property rights of the parties, *or* if you don't like the idea of disclosing too much about your wealth, maybe the idea of cohabitation will require a second look.

Here are some things to think about: What you are about to enter into is a contract. You intend that the provisions of the contract will be enforced, if necessary, by a court of law (but you hope such a test never occurs). One of the crucial parts of the agreement may be a recital in some form of your present financial position. Are you prepared to disclose these financial facts about your net worth? An alternative might be a waiver by both parties of this disclosure. Of course, if your net worth is a beat-up old jalopy and your college dorm bed and desk, you have no problem. In that case, you won't be going to a lawyer to have him or her prepare a nonmarital partnership agreement, will you?

If this is your *first* cohabitation, you may just be that carefree fellow, but if you own property and you want to continue owning it, you might give some thought to the requirements of a contract in which each party will have a duty of disclosure (or specific waiver) of his or her financial situation. You may "hedge" a bit by stating that the financial statement was prepared informally (and not, for example, by an accountant), but an obvious effort to hide or gloss over sizable assets might negate the whole thing. Is your cohabitant employed, and does she or he expect to remain employed? Do you want your separate property to remain separate? How will you both pay for living expenses? What about investments that you later acquire? Do you own a condominium or home? If so, and someone moves in with you and does not pay rent, IRS may, on an audit, impute the rent. If the nonowning party does not pay rent, you are making a gift of the rent-free use of the space to your cohabitant. Is it within $10,000 a year? If it is over that amount, you will have to file a gift tax return. Don't forget that although the law of your state may require you to support a spouse, there is no duty of support for a live-in "friend."

A SAMPLE AGREEMENT

The following is a sample of a nonmarital partnership agreement from the author's files. It is not intended to be used per se. It is provided for information only. No agreement of this type has yet stood the test of time, and such agreements may be totally unacceptable in your state. The sample will show you some of the perhaps negative aspects of entering into such a written-down formality. Nothing of this sort should be entered into without the advice and assistance of your lawyer *before* anything is signed.

NONMARITAL AGREEMENT

Date _____

THIS AGREEMENT, made between the following persons, on the terms and conditions set forth below, is for the purpose of defining their property rights, both now and in the future, and various other terms relating to their agreed-upon life together.

(John)	
Name of Partner	Present Occupation

(Helen)	
Name of Partner	Present Occupation

(1)   The life-together began (will begin) on _____.
This Agreement shall be effective as of _____
and shall continue until terminated by one of the following events:
  (a)   Death of either partner.
  (b)   Marriage of John and Helen or marriage of either of them to another.
  (c)   An agreement in writing to terminate their life-together.

(2)   A reasonably accurate and complete list of the capital and assets of each partner is listed below:
  John: Helen:

(3)   The property listed as belonging to each of the partners in Clause (2) above is to remain the separate property of each. Any income earned from separate property is to remain the income of the owner of that property. Each partner is responsible for maintaining records relating to his/her own property.

(4) Any debts outstanding, credit card balances, and other liabilities owed by each partner individually shall remain the obligation of that individual.

(5) Any property acquired by either partner by gift or inheritance, and income from such property, as well as appreciation in value, shall remain the separate property of that partner.

(6) For purposes of providing funds for living expenses, rent, food, entertainment, and the like, each partner shall contribute a proportionate percentage of his/her income from work (but not from investments) to a common fund.

(7) If a home or condominium is purchased by one of the partners and that partner is obligated on the mortgage, the other partner shall pay a reasonable amount of rent. [This would apply also if one partner is already an owner.]

(8) If a home or condominium is purchased jointly by John and Helen, they shall take title as Tenants in Common. [Note to reader: See sample agreement for tenants in common.]

(9) All investments made by either partner from his/her own earnings or profits shall remain the property of that partner.

(10) Any investment properties acquired after the date of this agreement which are impractical to acquire separately shall be owned by John and Helen as tenants in common. The share of each shall bear the same proportion to the whole as the contribution of that partner bears to the total cost of the property. For tax and accounting purposes, the income or tax advantages of the investment property shall be similarly distributed.

(11) Either partner may make gifts to the other, which gifts are agreed to be permanent.

(12) Neither partner looks to the other for inheritances. Each partner is free to transfer assets owned by that partner either *inter vivos* or by will to other family objects of his/her bounty, or, if he/she desires, to the other partner.

(13) Both partners acknowledge that a life-together arrangement based on the terms of this agreement does not constitute a common-law marriage, and if such marriage were valid according to the laws of any state where the partners reside or might in the future reside, they agree not to claim marital status based on this agreement (provided this clause does not contravene the state law).

(14) The consideration for this agreement is the promise of each partner to contribute homemaking services and companionship for their common good.

(15) Each partner acknowledges that he/she has consulted with his/her own attorney prior to signing this agreement and that the legal significance of the provisions herein have been fully explained in accordance with the laws of the state where the partners reside.

(16) If any controversy arises with regard to the terms of this agreement, the partners agree to first seek the assistance of a mediator to resolve such conflict.

(17) Recognizing that tasks, responsibilities of daily living, personal habits, and the like are impossible to regiment by agreement, all reference to such minutiae are deliberately eliminated from this agreement.

IN WITNESS WHEREOF, this Agreement is signed on the date of _____ in the State of _____.

_____
JOHN

_____
HELEN

(Notarization)

Attorney's Certification: Words to the effect that the above agreement has been executed in his (her) presence and that the terms and significance have been explained by him (her) to the above partners to the agreement and that they have indicated full understanding.

Caveat: The above agreement is a creative document that might be compared with the poetic marriage "ceremonies" that some young brides and grooms devise today to supplant the cliché-laden preacher-made wedding language of yesteryear. If a controversy arises (when the honeymoon or life-together is over), the very terms of the agreement might provide the basis for a solution. If such an agreement is entered into, it should be studiously drafted and understood and not taken lightly. Furthermore, and this cannot be overemphasized, nonmarital partnership agreements are a new area of law. No agreement of this kind is to be found in a form book. Each partner should consult a lawyer well versed in family law if such an agreement is being considered.

ALTERNATIVE METHODS OF HANDLING YOUR PROPERTY

Suppose that after reading the above, you decide that cohabiting property entanglements are not for you. You are progressing rapidly in your firm. You have made a sizable down payment on your condominium. You own your car. You have the shares of stock that you received as a present when you got your MBA. You are thinking of buying a Treasury bill because you know the interest will not be taxed by your state. You have your eye on an Oriental rug because your tastes are becoming rather exotic—you are bargaining and you may be able to swing it. What to do?

The obvious answer is: Nothing. All of the above are presumably owned by you in sole and separate ownership. The friend with whom you are closely allied has few personal assets and a terrific position with a law firm. You move in together. Both of you contribute toward household expenses. Something has to be decided about the rent. You own the condominum, don't forget. If your friend pays, you report the rent payments to IRS (and can take some deductions—see your accountant). If your friend does not pay—you consider the rent-free use of the space a gift (assume it is within the $10,000 annual gift-tax-free exclusion).

What else can you do? One possibility: Share ownership of the condominium. You would take title as tenants in common. The distinction between this and joint tenants with right of survivorship is very important. In the latter type of title, there is a built-in inheritance feature. The survivor takes all on the death of the other joint tenant. If you take title and you each contribute 50 percent, as tenants in common each of you owns an undivided one half. You may exercise complete dominion and ownership over that half. You may sell it, convey it away, will it, give it, and so forth. This is similar to individual ownership. It is an appropriate way to own property on a small scale where unrelated people are the co-owners and where each co-owner has suitable heirs *other than* the other co-owner. For example: Two sisters inherit a piece of real estate. They are tenants in common, and each sister may provide that her husband or children, and not the other sister, will inherit her assets. In that case, even though the co-owner is related, there are other, more suitable heirs. In fact, state laws often provide that, unless otherwise designated, a devise to two or more beneficiaries is deemed to create a tenancy in common. (See Appendix II.)

In having the condominium conveyed to you as tenants in common, whether you are cohabitants of opposite sexes or of the same sex or whether you are siblings or just two people working in the same office who happen to have a mutual interest in home ownership, you should treat the arrangement as a partnership. A very sketchy outline is offered here merely to indicate some of the items you should be thinking of:

OUTLINE OF POSSIBLE AGREEMENT FOR TENANTS IN
COMMON TO OWN AND OCCUPY REAL ESTATE TOGETHER

This agreement is made by and between A and B.

A and B intend to purchase Unit 500 in the condominium at 100 South Street in the City of Northside. The price is $_____.

It is intended that A and B will pay the cash down payment as follows:

Share of A = $ Share of B = $

Mortgage payments will be paid monthly in accordance with the same proportion. Therefore,

A will own _____% share, and
B will own _____% share.

All other monthly payments will be paid equally, including home-owners insurance, condominium fees, and expenses of upkeep, repairs, and maintenance.

Real estate taxes will be paid in proportion to ownership.

If A or B desires to sell his (her) share, it shall first be offered to the other co-owner. [Establish terms for agreement on price, such as appraisal.]

No party shall have the right to assign any or all of the rights under this agreement.

This agreement shall be binding upon the heirs and personal representatives of the parties.

Witnesses:

_____   _____
                                                   A

_____   _____
                                                   B

Date of agreement: _____

You alone will have to face up to the problem of whether it is simpler to be married after all. Some commentators, according to one expert in the field of property rights in marital and nonmarital relations, would like to restrict the role of the courts in evaluating nonmarital relationships and thus to encourage a return to traditional marital status and marital responsibilities.[13] Suppose you give up and say, "Let's get married!" See the next chapter.

NOTES

[1]134 *Cal. Rptr.* 815, 557 F.2d 106 (Cal. 1976).

[2]*Black's Law Dictionary*, rev. 4th ed.

[3]*Rehak v. Mathis*, 239 Ga. 541, 238 S.E.2d 81 (1977).

[4]*McCall v. Frampton*, 5 *Fam. L. Rep.* 3015 (N.Y. Sup. Ct. 1979).

[5]*Hill v. Westbrook's Estate*, 312 P.2d 727 (Cal. 1950), 247 P.2d 19 (1952).

[6]*Kozlowski v. Kozlowski*, 164 N.J. Super. 163, 403 A.2d 902 (1978).

[7]*Donovan v. Scueri*, 51 Md. App. 217, 443 A.2d 121 (1982).

[8]*In re Gordon's Estate*, 8 N.Y.2d 71, 168 N.E.2d 239, 202 N.Y.S.2d 1 (1960).

[9]*Morone v. Morone*, 50 N.Y.2d 481, 407 N.E.2d 592 (1980).

[10]*Berenan v. Berenan*, 645 P.2d 1155 (Wyo. 1982).

[11]*Kinnison v. Kinnison*, 627 P.2d 594 (Wyo. 1981).

[12]Carol S. Bruch, "Property Rights of De Facto Spouses Including Thoughts on the Value of Homemakers' Services," in *Fathers, Husbands, and Lovers—Legal Rights and Responsibilities*, ed. Sanford N. Katz and Monroe L. Inker (Chicago: American Bar Association, Section of Family Law, 1979), pp. 283–318.

[13]Ibid.

Marriage

A generation ago, in a more romantic and innocent age, a bride and groom automatically pooled their assets and bank accounts and thereafter held everything "joint." Two generations ago, a bride gave up her job. It was considered a reflection on the new husband's ability to support a wife if she continued to work. She disappeared into the house in order to be a proper housewife and, eventually, mother. Young people today may find that impossible to believe. The question today is: "When are you going back to work after having a baby?" In that faraway day, it was: "Are you going to work after getting married?"

THE TRADITIONAL MARRIAGE AND PROPERTY OWNERSHIP

The traditional marriage had an influence and significance that extended far beyond the image conjured up of a bride in a white gown and veil, orange blossoms and bridal attendants, a nervous bridegroom, champagne, and all the rest of the paraphernalia. The traditional marriage carried with it the imprint of ancient and hoary legal doctrines relating to property that affected the attitudes of generations of married couples. Dominion over property brought into the marriage by either party or acquired during the marriage was influenced by concepts that originated centuries ago. The legacy of those days imposed upon the couple a reluctance to overthrow tradition and adopt a modern-day attitude, which would require each of the parties to act as a responsible individual having control over his or her own property. That reluctance still exists today.

We have seen, in Chapter Three, the importance of paying heed to state labels on your property ownership as a married couple, particularly with reference to the label "JTRS." We will be returning to this topic more than once, especially since joint tenancy is still the usual and most prevalent form of ownership for married people. For the time being, and even though it seems out of order, the subject of married property ownership will be viewed from the standpoint of the situation that exists years after the wedding day. "What happens when married people make a will? Is this something young couples have to think about even before they have children? Why can't we own everything jointly?" To answer these questions and to lay the foundation for further inquiry into choices in marital property ownership, it is necessary to start with estate planning, a subject that most marrieds feel they will not tackle until way into their middle years.

"SHOULD EVERYTHING BE JOINT?"

Estate planners will cry loudly, "No, everything should definitely not be joint." Estate planning involves what goes into a will, among other things, and, as we have seen, wills deal only with separately owned property and not with property that passes automatically to the surviving joint owner. A good deal of estate planning is tax planning. The goal is to save as much as possible for the family. It is legal and legitimate to do this, within the parameters of the Tax Code. Even the wealthiest—in fact, especially the wealthiest (who, one would surmise, can afford to share with Uncle Sam)—engage in this kind of planning.

MARITAL DEDUCTION

In 1948 attention was given by Congress to the inequality that existed between the married people living in community property states and the married people living in separate property jurisdictions. In the community property states, because of the unique attributes of marital community property, the estate of the first spouse to die included only one half of the community property (plus separately owned property that was not part of the community). This meant that the surviving spouse was recognized as the owner of one half of the community property without having it diminished by federal estate taxes. Legislation enacted in 1948 provided for a 50 percent marital deduction from estate taxes for property that "passed" to a surviving spouse (see Appendix I). This covered both types of marital property—community and separate. In the community property states, 50 percent was the amount that passed to the surviving spouse. In the non-community property states, property passed if it was held in joint ownership with the decedent spouse, if it was willed to the surviving spouse, or if it passed by reason of the laws of intestacy (no will).

The IRS Code provisions enacted in 1948 remained essentially the same until the Tax Reform Act of 1976. During those 28 years, the deduction in that form became the pivotal point in property planning for married people whose estates were potentially subject to federal estate taxes. There were various changes over the years, but one knew that basically the marital deduction was at least 50 percent of the adjusted gross estate. The adjusted gross estate was and is the value of the estate less certain deductions from the estate for debts and administration-related expenses. In brief, if a married individual provided in his will for the passing of at least 50 percent of his wealth (or $250,000, whichever was greater) to his spouse, that 50 percent would not be taxed on the transfer! (The 50 percent deduction also applied to property passing to the spouse via joint tenancy survivorship.) The same 50 percent applied, with variations, to lifetime transfers to a spouse.

"SAVE THE SECOND TAX" PLANNING

The way in which estate planners utilized the 50 percent marital deduction was to establish, in their (usually male) client's will, a clause providing for the transfer of 50 percent of the estate to a trustee for the client's children, with the *income only* (a life estate) (plus portions of the corpus, as needed) to the surviving spouse for life. This half was taxed at that time, but only that once. The estate planners were fearful that if it had been simply left to the wife, it would be taxed twice, once when she received it and a second time (assuming that she had not used it up) when she died and it became a part of *her* estate, and thus again eligible for estate taxes. By means of this type of planning, the family inheritance could be greatly preserved from diminution by federal estate taxes.

MARITAL TRUST

Sometimes, because of doubt as to the wife's ability to manage property and finances, both portions of the husband's estate were placed in a trust. This was spoken of as the "marital trust." Such a trust had to contain certain language that assured the spouse's power to dispose of the assets in order to "qualify" for the marital deduction. This type of will was sometimes referred to as a "Trust A, Trust B" will. The word *spouse* is used euphemistically here to mean "wife" because there has been very little doubt that in most instances the husband has been the propertied individual and the wealth or largesse flows from him to the wife and not the other way around.

On the subject of the ability of the "spouse" in financial matters, consider the following:

> Tax considerations aside, a trust arrangement can also be advantageous when there is uncertainty about a spouse's ability to handle an outright disposition of property or the estate includes assets that call for expert management.[1]

Or this:

> There is the aspect of professional management, if for any reason someone other than the surviving spouse ought to manage the property. Either (but often both) of the spouses may view the survivor as an unwise choice to manage property due to inexperience, demonstrated inability to handle property, unwillingness to be bothered with doing so or to accept the constant burden and responsibility of management, or a realization that there is a better person or institution available.[2]

The last is a thinly veiled plea for professional or corporate fiduciary management.

Although through the years state laws have mostly abolished the old common law or community property law preference for male management or husband authority over marital property and females have attained a position of equality with their male counterparts both as to ownership of property and as to recognition of their ability as financial managers, nevertheless the traditional attitude toward women and wives has changed very little. That attitude still places the widow on a protective shelf. The image remains that a loving husband's will must make arrangements to protect his wife from squandering the wealth that she might inherit from him, and so a trustee is appointed who will exercise control over the investment, management, and disposition of assets that are rightfully hers and who will dole out income to her on a periodic basis. A member of the New York Bar has this to say:

> A trust, by its very nature, imparts a "father knows best" attitude toward the beneficiary that results in substituting the trustee for ["father"] in making the kind of decisions affecting "his" property and his family that he made for them during his lifetime. . . . Many marital trusts are created out of a distrust of the wife's ability to manage property or to seek the advice of those capable of giving it. These patterns themselves are changing in the direction of greater financial participation and responsibility by the wife—in a sharing of information and decision among married partners, as a result of which the experience and judgment of the surviving spouse is reliable and the intervention of a trust is thereby inappropriate. . . . Marital trusts, usually prepared by male lawyers for their male clients, conventionally are loaded with put-downs of the client's wife. . . . [Among] these is that the property in question belongs to the husband in the first place and is his to dispose of as he sees fit— subject to those arrangements that he and his lawyer can work out in order to minimize estate taxes.[3]

The will that inspired the title of the article just quoted was that of Edward Harkness. The widow was Rebekah Harkness, and Mr. McQuaid paid tribute to her contribution (from her inheritance) to the cultural life of the country through the Harkness Ballet. The author marveled, "When Edward Harkness died, he left one half of his $55,000,000 estate to his wife, Rebekah, outright. Twenty-seven and one-half million dollars outright—no trust, no strings— simply complete confidence in her capacity to handle this vast estate for purposes that were fulfilling to her and, in Mrs. Harkness' case, to society."

It is only fair to say that in many instances wives might prefer to have their inheritance in the hands of a trustee, either because they wish to be free to pursue other interests or because they have never taken an interest in family financial matters. The "Leave it to John" attitude may be a holdover from the childhood remembrances (Father managed the money) of women of a "certain age" or may result from the fact that our laws, as we have seen, have reinforced the image of male omniscience and financial wisdom. Nevertheless, although studying the financial pages or boning up on how corporations work may not be their dish of tea, it is incumbent on today's women to acquire some awareness of such matters. No one wants to learn in desperation or at a time of crisis. If women do not throw off the innocence that belongs to an earlier era, they will merit the continued "protectionism" that affronts their intelligence.

The story of Mrs. Z comes to mind. A wealthy woman with a closet full of designer clothes, furs, diamonds, and a prestige automobile, Mrs. Z was proud of the fact that Mr. Z took care of everything. Even her department store bills were sent to the office, where Mr. Z's secretary wrote the checks for these purchases. Mr. Z's sudden demise left Mrs. Z in the unexpected position of having to borrow some cash from her brother-in-law to cover immediate expenses! Mrs. Z, one of those women who proudly proclaimed that they had never written a check, was a good candidate for a trust. It is safe to say, though, that her ilk is a disappearing species.

The planning to preserve the marital deduction and to minimize estate taxes usually involved trusts or, at the very least, a single trust. Whether the husband believed his wife should be protected from her inadequacies as a manager of assets (or feared misuse by a future second husband) and left both portions of his estate to her in separate trusts ("Trust A and Trust B"), or whether he merely established one trust (known as a "bypass trust") in order to bypass taxes on the assets in that portion twice (taxes paid once on his estate and again on her presumed later estate), at least *one* trust was created in this type of planning. Wives who attended the planning sessions in lawyers' offices frequently viewed such arrangements with opposition and with skepticism as to the taxwise necessity of the arrangements. Consequently, when the Economic Recovery Tax Act of 1981 created a new 100 percent marital deduction and this type of estate planning became virtually obsolete, there was considerable rejoicing.

MARITAL PROPERTY PLANNING BEFORE
THE ECONOMIC RECOVERY TAX ACT OF 1981 (ERTA)

As we have seen, the complicated provisions of the law prior to 1981 and the limit that was placed on tax-free transfers led people with property to engage in very complicated estate planning. Estate planners' advice for such planning went on in this fashion for many years. Almost invariably, if the married couple owned property jointly, they were advised to sever such ownership. Sometimes this involved gift tax consequences. If the eventual estate taxes to be saved were large enough, however, this was a necessary preliminary step. The reason for this transfer of assets to separate ownership is simply that nothing can be left by a will that is not separately owned by the person who is drawing up the will. We have seen that in the popular estate plan the will divided the assets into two portions. The will-maker (testator) willed one portion to his spouse, either outright or in trust. This was the "marital deduction" portion. If that portion was left in trust, in order to "qualify" for the marital deduction this "marital" trust had to contain certain language that assured the wife's power to dispose of the assets. In other words, *she* had the power to name *her* heirs, who might inherit that portion of her wealth.

It is important to note the special requirements of this type of trust because it has a bearing on a different type of trust in which a wife could inherit an income interest and which would likewise "qualify" for the marital deduction, but *without* the requirement that she have the ultimate power of disposition ("qualified terminable interest" property trust). There was a very technical reason for the requirement (in the prior law) that the recipient and beneficiary of income from a marital trust have control over the disposition of the assets in that trust. Such a requirement enforced the recipient's *ownership*. Otherwise, she would have had only a "life estate" (income only). The ownership requirement was necessary so that this portion of the late husband's estate would pass tax-free to the wife and thus take advantage of the marital deduction. The technical explanation boils down to: Save estate taxes! The *marital deduction portion* could be left outright (just as Mr. Harkness did). The *other portion* (the nonmarital portion) was left (by the language of the will) to the children of the couple *in trust*, with income to the wife for life. Although she could inherit the marital portion outright (and with no trust), the "children's" portion had to be in trust, because legal ownership had to be transferred by the husband's will to a new legal owner (the trustee), thus triggering an estate tax on that portion. The widow's ownership was merely a "beneficial" ownership. The practical effect of this arrangement was that the widow received the *income only* (life estate) from this nonmarital portion of her inheritance.

Clients were assured that the object of these complicated maneuverings was to take advantage of the maximum (or optimal) tax-free marital transfer amount allowed by law. For estates of approximately $500,000 or over, this type of planning was usually recommended. It was not only recommended, but in situations where the client declined to follow the recommendation and insisted on leaving his entire fortune to his wife with no strings, the lawyer would have to protect himself with appropriate copies of advice letters in his files showing that he had recommended such estate planning to the client. This protection was necessary because failure to follow the recommendation would thwart its tax-saving goal. This type of estate planning could save thousands or hundreds of thousands of dollars for children or other beneficiaries of the will. Upon learning, years later, that their inheritance had been diminished by federal estate taxes assessed against the estate of the late husband and then on the same assets in the estate of the late wife these beneficiaries might desire to sue the lawyer. This real danger of charges of legal malpractice was (and is) behind a good deal of tax-saving advice given to clients.

MARITAL PROPERTY PLANNING AFTER ERTA

ERTA, in effect, eliminated *all federal estate taxes on transfers between husbands and wives*. The technical method that achieved this was repeal of the 50 percent ceiling on the marital deduction from *inter vivos* (lifetime) transfers (gifts) or testamentary transfers (at death) between spouses. The result was a 100 percent deduction. Consequently, the need for complicated "save-the-second-tax" planning seemed to have ended. Why only "seemed"? The answer lies in the use of a "unified credit trust" as a part of the planning for large estates in order to save some taxes when these estates are eventually inherited by the generation after the married couple.

NEW CONCEPTS: UNIFIED CREDIT AND EXEMPTION EQUIVALENT

There is one provision of the law that might save taxes and that everyone should be aware of in planning property dispositions. For many years, everyone had the privilege of giving away at death $60,000 without incurring any federal estate taxes. This was known as the estate tax "exemption." In 1976 Congress recognized for the first time in 30 years that inflation had greatly increased the value of most assets and therefore created a new system of taxing estates by use of a "unified credit" against the federal transfer taxes on estates and lifetime gifts. The effect was to equalize the tax obligation on transfers during life and at death. As noted earlier, it had previously been advantageous for wealthy people to give away large sums during their lives because the gift tax was less than the estate tax. In 1976, gifts during life were, for the first time, taxed at the same rate as gifts at death, and the credit against taxes that was enacted in 1976 created a potential for the same tax obligation for life or death transfers. The amount of this credit increased year by year over a five-year period. For transfers in 1981, the credit had reached the highest amount for the five-year phase-in period and amounted to $47,000. When applied to the value of a gift or estate, this created an exemption amounting to $175,625. That figure was known as the "exemption equivalent." What this meant was that *no* federal estate taxes would be due on an estate of $175,625. This, of course, was a much greater tax-free transfer allowance than the old $60,000.

Thanks to the 1981 tax law (ERTA), the unified credit amount was again increased, the new law having provided that it would increase year by year over a six-year period. This meant that the *exemption equivalent* would also increase year by year until 1987 and thereafter (unless it is changed again by legislation), when it would equal $600,000. This is what the legislators meant when they indicated that the new tax law ("new" as of 1981) would eliminate the burden of federal estate taxes for all but the wealthiest individuals. This might be so, presuming that by 1987 inflation does not make $600,000 seem a puny amount.

EXEMPTION EQUIVALENT TRUST

Suppose that you are a wealthy, loving spouse and that you wish to leave your entire estate to your beloved spouse, with no strings attached. This can be done. However, you might reconsider if you are told that a certain amount of your estate will not be taxed if you leave that amount to your children (or other eventual heirs), because that amount is the "exemption equivalent." If that wording bothers you, just leave off the word *equivalent* and think of it as an amount that is the federal estate tax "exemption." You are advised to establish in your will a trust called by lawyers a "unified credit trust" or an "exemption equivalent trust." By means of this arrangement, the amount of assets that equals the amount that is *exempt* from federal estate taxes will be transferred to a *trustee* for the eventual takers (your children). The lifetime beneficiary of the trust will be the surviving spouse (your wife). She will receive the income (life estate) for life from that portion of your assets. (The trust agreement is established whether or not the children are minors.)

The purpose of the trust is to effectuate an immediate transfer of the principal of the trust (called the "corpus") so that this amount can be transferred *exempt* from federal estate taxes. If the widow is so well off that she does not need the income from the corpus, then the transfer to the next-in-line heirs (the children) can be complete and immediate, and if they are not minors, no trust arrangement is necessary. If you wish to ignore this tax-saving device, your will can state that all assets are to be transferred to the widow outright. If, within a specified time, *she* decides that she does not need all of your fortune, she can *disclaim* the exemption amount, and this would allow that portion to go to the next in line without triggering a gift tax, but she would also have to give up the income.

MAXIMIZING THE FEDERAL ESTATE-TAX-FREE TRANSFER

By virtue of the phase-in schedule enacted in the 1981 legislation, a husband can by the year 1987 transfer free of federal tax any amount to a wife *plus $600,000 to anyone else* who is the object of his bounty. A wealthy widow can also transfer $600,000 estate-tax-free. The following table shows the phase-in of the unified credit and the resulting exemption equivalent amount, including amounts that are past history, since the law began with the phase-in in the year 1982.

Phase-In Table for the Unified Credit

Year	Unified Credit	Exemption Equivalent
1982	$ 62,800	$225,000
1983	79,300	275,000
1984	96,300	325,000
1985	121,000	400,000
1986	155,800	500,000
1987	192,800	600,000

SOURCE: IRC Sec. 2010.

HOW WOULD IT WORK?

Here is a schedule showing the federal gift and estate tax rates in effect in 1984.

1984 Unified Gift and Estate Tax Rates

If Taxable Amount Is—		This—	Plus Percent	Over
Over	But Not Over			
$ 0	$ 10,000	$ 0	18	$ 0
10,000	20,000	1,800	20	10,000
20,000	40,000	3,800	22	20,000
40,000	60,000	8,200	24	40,000
60,000	80,000	13,000	26	60,000
80,000	100,000	18,200	28	80,000
100,000	150,000	23,800	30	100,000
150,000	250,000	38,800	32	150,000
250,000	500,000	70,800	34	250,000
500,000	750,000	155,800	37	500,000
750,000	1,000,000	248,300	39	750,000
1,000,000	1,250,000	345,800	41	1,000,000
1,250,000	1,500,000	448,300	43	1,250,000
1,500,000	2,000,000	555,800	45	1,500,000
2,000,000	2,500,000	780,800	49	2,000,000
2,500,000	3,000,000	1,025,800	53	2,500,000
3,000,000		1,290,800	55	3,000,000

SOURCE: J. K. Lasser, *Your Income Tax, 1985* (New York: Simon & Schuster).
© 1984. J. K. Lasser Tax Institute. Reprinted by permission of Simon & Schuster, Inc.

Note that the Tax Reform Act of 1984 deferred until 1988 the reduction of the tax rate to 50 percent for transfers in excess of $2.5 million, which was previously scheduled to take place in 1985.[4]

Hazarding oversimplification, it is probably safe to say that if you wish to roughly estimate your estate tax, you would list your assets (including jointly owned assets, but only one half if you own the assets jointly with your spouse), deduct an estimated amount (such as 10 percent) for estate administration and expenses, also deduct your debts and liabilities, and then, from the figure you arrive at, find the tax (known as tentative tax) on the tax rate table. From the latter figure, deduct the unified credit amount. The resulting figure would be your payable tax. If you are married, you are really not overly concerned, since there is no tax on property passing from you to your spouse. What you may be interested in at this point is the bite that will be taken out of the inheritance of your (and your spouse's) eventual heirs (your children) in order to pay federal estate taxes on the remaining assets from your and your spouse's combined estates.

Here is how a millionaire can plan to take full advantage of the exemption equivalent. Using the allowable exemption for the year 1987 ($600,000), it is easy to see that by the year 1987 a married person can transfer free of federal tax *any amount to a spouse plus $600,000 to anyone else*. If, for example, the husband dies and his wife becomes the wealthy widow, her estate will then be taxed at her death, but the estate will again have an exemption equivalent to $600,000 (or more if new legislation increases that amount). Consequently, *two* transfers of $600,000 each can be made to heirs of the couple without paying any federal estate tax on the transfer!

That is why advisers are recommending to wealthy clients that the wife (usually less wealthy) *build up her assets* so that she at least owns the exemption equivalent amount. Assume a husband with an estate of $1,200,000. He dies in 1987, having left a will providing for a $600,000 "bypass" trust, the principal to the couple's children and the income to the wife for her life. There is no federal estate tax obligation, because the $600,000 is the *tax-exempt amount* and the $600,000 that went to the wife was eligible for the 100 percent marital deduction. On her later death, the wife leaves $600,000 to her children. Again, there is no tax on the transfer of those assets, because that is the *exempt amount*. If the husband and wife have estates in the millions, there will be a tax, to be sure, but by this "credit shelter" trust planning, at least the tax on $1,200,000 will have been saved.

SEPARATE PROPERTY AS A PLANNING FACTOR

It should now be clear that for this arrangement to work, *each* spouse must own *separate property* at least in the amount of the current exemption equivalent. If a wife has never owned separate property after many years of marriage, establishing her separate property ownership may seem a drastic thing to do while she is still married. Nevertheless, in addition to the *tax reasons* for some separate property ownership by husband and wife, which have been discussed above, there are cogent *nontax reasons*. Consider, for example, the wife who has never dealt on her own with a stockbroker, who has never decided when to buy or sell a security or whether to "roll over" a certificate of deposit or a Treasury bill, or who has never written a check on her own account. That same wife, no doubt, has never read the financial pages, never balanced a checkbook, never established a credit rating. The list could go on. The wife who wishes to develop some financial acumen, who, in the time-honored tradition, is used to relying on her husband as being more knowledgeable in financial matters, may welcome the opportunity to discuss her own investment decisions with him (while he is alive), may gain her own expertise, may even remove herself from the category of the "spouse" whose pitiable lack of expertise has been the subject of countless warnings to the other "spouse," such as:

> What should be done if you believe your spouse cannot manage property? You will not want to give complete and personal control. The law permits you to put the property in certain trust arrangements that are considered equivalent to complete ownership. Your attorney can explain how you can protect your spouse's interest and qualify the trust property for the marital deduction.[5]

Regardless of these admonitions to the property-planning "spouse," we are dealing at this point with the need for the wife to have separate assets in order to establish by her will the same arrangement as that available to the husband for saving a tax on the exemption equivalent amount allowed by the federal tax. Whether the husband can tolerate this situation is for the couple to decide. As a matter of fact, if the wife does not have a job, profession, business, or other source of income, the only way in which assets can accumulate on her side of the ledger is by transfer to her sole ownership. This may now be achieved with no gift tax consequences at all, since this privilege for tax-free transfers between spouses was one of the major accomplishments of the 1981 tax law. Once transferred, income from the separate property owned by the wife should be maintained separately in a savings account, money fund, or the like and reserved for future investment. Income from a wife's earned outside sources should likewise be saved separately for her separate investment acquisitions. These tactics apply, of course, only in a situation where all of the income earned by the couple is not needed for living expenses. Whatever lifetime property-planning arrangements are made by a married couple, women, especially, have to be alert to advice proposed by professional consultants because of the need to overcome traditional attitudes toward the ownership of property by married women. One major purpose of *separateness*, in fact, would be to establish patterns of behavior. Another purpose of transfer from the propertied spouse to the nonpropertied spouse (or the *less*-propertied spouse) would be to take advantage of the lower prospective rate of estate taxation on the amounts so transferred.

Perhaps the first time a wife would actually own anything of value on her own would be when she inherits from a parent or grandparent. That would be a starter. This very thing happened to my married daughter. She inherited a small sum from a grandparent. My husband and I discussed it. The conversation went like this (I am "M"; he is "H"):

M: What do you think Jeannie should do with this money?

H: I guess they'll talk to their broker and decide.

M: Why shouldn't Jeannie invest it separately?

H: You said it isn't necessary anymore to keep the *source* of funds separate for a husband or wife in order to prove who is the owner.

M: That's right. Since the Tax Act of 1981, there is no transfer tax between husbands and wives and they can freely transfer money or assets and not have to account for the original ownership. But I still think it is wise for a wife to have her own investments.

H: Why?

M: I'm not sure I can answer that. The answer was easy and is still easy for estate planning purposes, but I do not think they are in a high enough wealth category to be concerned about estate planning, so that would not be crucial to their decision. What do *you* think they should do?

H: I think the partner who has the most investment experience should invest the money. If they have a joint account with a broker, let them put her inheritance in the joint account, and if the husband has dealt with the broker in the past, let him continue to do so.

M: That is exactly what I think they should not do. I believe what we are down to now is a pattern of behavior. If he thinks as you do and it is going to be a bone of contention in the marriage, the wife will be smart enough to assess her priorities and realize that the marriage is more important. However, what I would hope is that the husband will understand the value of separateness and the value of the wife's ability to stand on her own feet as an adult, mature and trustworthy and capable of making her own investment decisions. [Note: That was exactly the option selected by our daughter and her husband.]

"SHOULD ANYTHING BE JOINT?"

Yes, of course. The family home, especially, should be held by the couple in joint ownership. We have already noted the advantage of joint ownership by spouses as a means of protection against creditors or litigants in states that recognize tenancies by the entireties. It has been indicated, however, that the same protection can be gained by separate ownership, provided that the spouse being sued is not the owner (an unknown factor).

There is an income tax consequence of joint ownership that should be weighed by couples when deciding on "joint" or "separate." This has to do with the *basis* that the surviving spouse is handed along with the property that passes to the spouse who owned the assets JTRS with the decedent spouse. According to the law in effect at this time, only one half of the value of any property held in a joint tenancy between a husband and wife will be includable in the estate of the first to die. Because of the unlimited marital deduction, this property would pass to the survivor free of any federal estate tax. Why is it of importance, then, that only one half is included in the estate? It is important because this affects the income tax basis of the property that the surviving spouse inherits. As to that portion (one half) of the jointly owned property, the surviving spouse's basis will be the original basis when it was first purchased as joint tenant property. As to the half that the survivor inherits, the basis will be the date-of-death value. The effect is that as to *that* half, when the property is sold by the survivor, there may be a smaller (or no) income tax capital gain tax to pay—presumably because date-of-death values are greater than original purchase values (at least, this would probably apply to real estate). Date-of-death values give the heirs a "stepped-up basis."

Here is a simple example to see how this works out: In 1950 a couple purchased a small rental property for $25,000. There is no mortgage due when the husband dies, in 1986. The property was held in joint tenancy by the husband and wife. When the husband dies, it is worth $200,000. The wife is the JTRS survivor, and so the property passes to her.

As to the one half that she owned as part of the original purchase, her basis is	$ 12,500 (½ of the price)
As to the one half that she inherits, her basis is	100,000 (½ of the estate value)
	$112,500 (her basis if she sells)

If she sells for $112,500, there will be no tax to pay. If she sells for above that amount, the capital gain will be the difference between $112,500 and the sale price less any expenses of the sale, such as commissions.

The big question: Would the widow be better off if her late husband had owned the property separately? In that case, the stepped-up date-of-death value would be $200,000. If she sold at that amount, there would be no capital gains tax to pay. If she had owned one half as in the situation described above, and sold at $200,000, the taxable gain would be $87,500, which would be taxed at capital gains rates (the difference between $112,500 as the basis and $200,000, the sale price). Should husband and wife each own investment property separately? It will take crystal-ball gazing to know who will inherit from whom. At the time of investment in a certain property, one does not usually think of that as a factor. It is, however, a side effect of a possibly changing mode of holding property for spouses, doing it "separately" instead of "jointly." Food for thought.

WHAT IS "ADJUSTED BASIS?"

The oversimplified example above is an example of basis as merely cost price. This basis usually applies in a purchase of personal property, such as securities. If the asset in question is investment real estate, a factor for depreciation must be taken into consideration. Depending on the dollar amount of the depreciation deductions taken over the years that the property was in use as an investment, the basis would have been reduced. This would apply to the one half of the original purchase (as JTRS owners) by the husband and wife that, according to the current tax law, the wife *owns* (and does not inherit when her husband dies). This would change the basis figure for her half, but it *would not change* the basis figure for the half that she receives on her husband's death, which is the stepped-up date-of-death value. The latter value would also apply to the entire property if it had been owned as separate property by the husband. The depreciation deductions do not apply, and the widow who inherits the husband's separate property receives the fair market value for estate tax purposes (the date-of-death value or the alternate six-months-later value) as the basis. This basis, as we have seen, affects her income tax obligation on a later sale of the property. These are complicated concepts, but for one who is interested, depreciation on investment real property, basis, and stepped-up value all provide additional factors to be considered in deciding *how to own* property. Whether or not the property is depreciable may be of importance in reaching a decision.

CONCEPT OF CONSIDERATION FURNISHED OR "CONTRIBUTION" TO JOINT OWNERSHIP ASSETS: PRE- AND POST-ERTA

For spouses, this IRS method of calculating taxation for federal estate tax purposes of jointly owned property, on the death of a joint owner, is immaterial. For anyone other than spouses, it can be very material, and it will be discussed fully in Chapter Nine. It should be mentioned here, however, because for many years the use of this method in Internal Revenue calculations provided a fierce cause of battle, especially by women's groups (the Farm Women's Lobby, to name one). Women called it the "widow's tax." Here is how it worked.

If a husband and wife acquired property during their marriage and labeled it "JTRS" and then the husband died, the value of the property would automatically be included in the estate of the husband. The widow would inherit the property, and she felt it was rightfully hers, but if she had not contributed marketplace funds to the acquisition of these joint assets, *none of the assets would be considered hers* for federal estate tax exclusion purposes. What is meant by "marketplace funds"? The term refers to dollars earned *outside the home*. Housewifely duties, care of children, the thousand-and-one contributions that a wife makes daily to a marriage were ignored and considered of no value. Therefore, a widow who had not earned dollars outside the home could not prove that she had "contributed" or "furnished consideration" to the purchase of the jointly owned assets. If the value of the assets was estate-taxable by the federal government, she found her inheritance partly depleted by estate taxes.

IMPORTANT CHANGES—THE TAX LAW OF 1981

The 1981 tax law finally changed that situation. As we will see when discussing divorce, state courts led the way in recognizing that housewifely duties did have a value and did contribute toward a marriage and therefore were to be given weight in a marital property dissolution. Congress finally joined this bandwagon when it enacted the unlimited marital deduction. Here is how the explanation prepared by the staff of the Joint Committee on Taxation put it:

> Because the maximum estate tax marital deduction generally was limited (under prior law) to one-half of the decedent's adjusted gross estate, the estate of a decedent who bequeathed his or her entire estate to the surviving spouse was often subject to estate taxes even though the property remained within the marital unit. When the surviving spouse later transferred the property (often to the children), the entire amount was subject to transfer taxes. The cumulative effect was to subject their property to tax one and one-half times, i.e., one half upon the death of the first spouse and again fully upon the death of the second spouse. This effect typically occurred in the case of jointly held property. Because this additional tax fell most heavily on widows, it was often referred to as the "widow's tax."
>
> Although the Congress recognized that this additional tax could be minimized through proper estate planning, it believed that an individual generally should be free to pass his or her entire estate to a surviving spouse without the imposition of any estate tax. For similar reasons, the Congress believed it appropriate generally to permit unlimited lifetime transfers between spouses without the imposition of any gift taxes.

In addition, the Congress determined that substantial simplification of the estate and gift taxes would be achieved by allowing an unlimited deduction for transfers between spouses. Under prior law, it was often extremely difficult to determine the ownership of property held within the marital unit and to determine whose funds were used to acquire that property. These problems generally will not arise with an unlimited marital deduction.

As to jointly held property:

The Congress believed that rules governing the taxation of jointly held property between spouses were unnecessarily complex. In particular, the Congress recognized that it is often difficult, as between spouses, to determine the amount of consideration that each spouse provided for the acquisition and improvement of their jointly held property. Further, because few taxpayers understand the gift tax consequences of joint ownership [true!], there was widespread noncompliance [telling it like it is!].

. . . Congress believed it appropriate to adopt an easily administered rule under which each spouse is considered to own one half of jointly held property, regardless of which spouse furnished the original consideration. (Bracketed comments added.)[6]

The bottom line is that women are now freed from the burden of proving that their contribution toward the acquisition of jointly held marital assets derived from activities other than being a housewife.

CONSIDERATIONS OTHER THAN ESTATE PLANNING

Of course, how a married couple plans to hand over assets to the survivor is not everything! For some marrieds, it is far, far from their minds. Before leaving the subject, however, a reminder is in order. State laws must be consulted. Some states have no state inheritance taxes at all. Some states do not tax property passing from one spouse to a survivor via joint tenancy. Others do not tax interspousal transfers at all. Most states have a type of small-estate administration as part of their probate laws. This type of administration is pegged to the dollar amount of the estate—$7,500, $10,000, or some similar amount. If the estate is within that amount, there is a simplified procedure for transferring the assets. A lawyer's services are not necessary. The documents are usually handled by a clerk of the probate court, and the cost is very small. Some advisers who recognize the wishes of a married couple to retain everything in joint ownership, after reviewing the pros and cons of separate ownership, recommend that the couple *just* maintain individual ownership of assets whose dollar value will fit within the state's small-estate procedure and retain joint ownership of all else. In fact, these advisers point out, joint ownership aids in the simplicity of transferring assets at the death of one of the joint owners, and that is reason enough for the JTRS label.

FAMILY FINANCIAL PLANNING

Is there a middle ground? After having reviewed the various considerations as to type of ownership and factored in the special situations in any marriage, a couple might decide to compromise. Maintain separate investment acquisitions; retain separate earnings that are available for investment; funnel separate earnings into a joint checking account for household expenses on a day-to-day basis and for larger household acquisitions (furniture, appliances, etc.)—without the burdensome recordkeeping as to who contributed how much. If one spouse has a high-risk potential for lawsuits, comments already made with regard to that special situation might be useful. Saving to put children through college is certainly a joint spousal effort, and since the money is going to be used up, those dollars will not go toward property acquisitions. There is, however, one technique for providing college funds in which property ownership is significant. That is the Clifford Trust. This form of tax-sheltered saving for college has been mentioned, but further explanation is in order.

SAVING FOR COLLEGE EXPENSES—THE CLIFFORD TRUST

A Clifford Trust is a short-term trust in which you transfer property to a trustee for a period of more than 10 years (after which time it reverts back to you) to pay the income during that period to beneficiaries you name. When the Clifford Trust is used as a saving-for-college device, you would name your children as beneficiaries. If you name yourself as trustee (which you may do), it is advisable to also name a (supposedly) disinterested cotrustee who has the power to direct payment of the income from the trust property. Most advisers recommend that the parent *not* be the trustee inasmuch as if it is deemed that he/she is in control of the property, the purpose of the trust (diversion of income to the children) might be thwarted. If it is found that the parent was in control, the income from the trust could be taxable to the parent. Another way in which you can destroy all of this careful trust planning is to use the income from the trust for expenditures on items that you are legally required to supply as part of your duty to support your child.

The definition of "support" is a state-directed definition. It may even include college tuition, the very item that you do not want to be included among your support obligations. During the period that the trust is in operation, the income must be distributed to the beneficiary or beneficiaries at least annually. This has to do with the fact that if you do not want to incur a gift tax obligation, the gift must be of a "present" interest (as opposed to a "future" interest). That is because the $10,000 current gift tax exclusion applies only to the gift of a "present" interest. Of course, the child is not presently spending these dollars, but they are building up in the child's bank account over the years. At the age of majority in your state, the child becomes the legal owner of those funds. If you do not trust your child at age 18 (or whatever the age of majority is in your state) to use the funds for college tuition, books, room and board, or any other college-related purpose, and you fear that instead he/she will go backpacking around the world and scatter the college funds to the four winds— if that is a hazard, find another way to produce the funds to pay college tuition! Also, watch developments in Congress—tax reform proposals may attack the Clifford Trust.

There are several planning aspects that you should know about: The trust property reverts back to your ownership at the termination of the trust. If you should die during the term of the trust, the value of the reversion would be included in your estate. That is why it is preferable that this be a parent-arranged device rather than a grandparent-arranged one. The transfer of income to the beneficiary during the time of the trust is a gift. The value of the gift, as established in the Code, is 61.446 percent of the value of the trust property on the date of transfer to the trust.

Assuming that a married couple wanted to transfer property to a trustee in an irrevocable trust ("irrevocable" for 10 years and a day) for the purpose of accumulating college funds for a child and that their intention was to avoid utilizing gift funds that would tap the unified credit, here is how it could work: When a husband and wife agree to treat gifts to a third person (the trust for the child, in this case) as being made one half by each, they double the number of annual exclusions available, provided that the gifts are of *present* interests. Translated, this means that the couple can put $20,000 into the trust for one beneficiary ($40,000 for two beneficiaries). The $20,000 exclusion for one child will cover an amount of $32,548 as the value of the trust property on the date of transfer to the trust.

This amount invested, or property already invested having this value, can build up quite an after-tax nest egg in 10 years, especially in the child's bracket. The earnings must go into a custodial account each year in order to preserve the *present* nature of the gift. As in the case of any custodial account for a minor, the child has access to the funds on reaching the age of majority (18 in most states). There are still more caveats. As mentioned above, if state law provides that the parent's duty of support *includes college*, you, the parents, might be taxed on the income anyway because the funds were used to fulfill your duty of support.

Some advisers recommend limiting the child's trust to a shorter period and tacking on a "marital remainder trust" transferring the value of the remainder interest to a spouse outright. Since there is no tax for a gift to a spouse, this would be a tax-free transfer. The word of caution here is: Since the trust corpus (principal) will be paid over to the spouse when the child's trust terminates, the spousal remainder trust should not be used where there is a possibility of marital discord.[7]

There is, however, a "but" in all of this: But during the term of the trust, there are expenses. In addition to the expense of having the trust document drawn up in the first place, there are annual fiduciary income tax returns to be filed, and income tax returns for the child. At the outset, if you are considering this type of saving-for-college technique, you (or your lawyer) should know your state's attitude toward a parent's duty of support.

OUTRIGHT GIFTS

A simpler form of saving for college is to give a sum outright to your child each year (or as long as you are able to) in a form of custodian gift: "John Jones, Custodian for Johnny Jones, a Minor, under X State Uniform Gifts to Minors Act." The gift may be in the form of a money fund account, securities through a custodian account at the brokers, or any other form of investment. Again, when the child reaches the age of majority in your state, the assets are *his or hers*. Also, you should be careful that your annual gift is not over $10,000 (or $20,000 if you are married). Even though a gift greater in value than the annual exclusion amount would not incur a gift tax because of the unified credit, careful planners usually do not want to encroach on that tidy "credit." Why not? What is the hazard?

WHY NOT TAP THE UNIFIED CREDIT?

Estates and gifts incur the same tax, if taxable. If one gives a gift in excess of the $10,000 annual tax-free amount, he intrudes on the unified credit that is (someday) going to be applied against his estate. Here is how it would work:

> If one died in 1985, there was a unified credit available of $121,800. This amount applied to a taxable estate translates into a sum of $400,000 going to heirs *federal estate-tax-free*.

> If one dies in 1986, there is a unified credit available of $155,800. This amount applied to a taxable estate translates into a sum of $500,000 going to heirs *federal estate-tax-free*.

> If one dies in 1987, there is a unified credit available of $192,800. This amount applied to a taxable estate translates into a sum of $600,000 going to heirs *federal estate-tax-free*.

Since your answer is "none of the above" when it comes to dying, why should you be concerned? Here is the tie-in: If you reduce your unified credit by using up some or all of it with a lifetime gift, you are, in a way, prepaying estate taxes; or, looked at differently, you are cheating your heirs a bit because you are reducing the credit available against your eventual estate. "Reducing the credit" is another way of saying "increasing the estate tax," which is another way of saying, "Sorry, kids, your inheritance is reduced." This is all because Congress decided that lifetime gifts should be taxed at the same rate as inherited gifts. They did not want all those wealthy people to give away their wealth and avoid estate taxes. (See Appendix I.) Consequently, most gift-giving is planned to stay within the $10,000 per year exclusion (or $20,000 for a married couple). If you are wealthy and so inclined, each year you can give away $10,000 to an *unlimited* number of donees, with no federal tax whatsoever. Remember, unless made to a charitable donee, the gift is *not* deductible on your income tax return. Also, your donee does not report the gift as income but, after receiving it, reports its *earnings* as income.

Further explanation regarding gifts: As every individual may give away $10,000 every year to each of any number of donees and as a married couple (by consenting to gifts of the other spouse) may together give away $20,000 every year to each of any number of donees with no requirement for payment of gift tax at all (although the "split gift" of a married couple requires filing a return to document the gift), wealthy people can give away quite a lot! If the nature of the circumstances or the gift indicates a transfer beyond the $10,000/$20,000 is advisable, such a transfer can also be made—without incurring a transfer tax—by using up a portion of the unified credit. In this case, a gift tax return would have to be filed and the tax calculated, but until gifts equal in amount to the current exemption equivalent are made, the tentative tax would be nullified by application of the credit. Would making such gifts be useful? Yes, in certain circumstances, for example, if the gifted asset were likely to increase in value if held until the death of the donor. The *appreciation* of such an asset would escape taxation in the donor's estate. Furthermore, subsequent to the date of the gift the gifted asset would become the asset of the donee and future income from that asset would be taxed to the donee (who is presumably in a lower tax bracket). This type of planning is obviously for the wealthy client, and that individual's lawyer will gladly work out the details of such high-powered gift-giving in his mahogany-paneled office.

GENERATION-SKIPPING TRUST

One other technique for passing on wealth is available to those who desire to use it. This is the ability to bypass the next in line (who are also wealthy and do not need all your money) and give directly to the grandchildren. To avoid too much of this sort of thing, the 1976 Tax Reform Act contained a provision for something known as "the generation-skipping transfer tax." The provision is complex and fraught with difficulties of application and administration—so much so that tax specialists have been campaigning for its repeal. Beneficiaries in generations younger than the donor's are called "younger generation beneficiaries." A trust that has two or more generations of younger generation beneficiaries is a generation-skipping trust for purposes of the generation-skipping transfer tax. There is a $250,000 exemption from the tax on this privilege of transfer of wealth, but the $250,000 exemption is per "deemed transferor" via a generation-skipping trust. If interested, see your lawyer.

INTERSPOUSAL TRANSFERS—ONE MORE LOOK

The above discussion regarding the federal estate-tax-free amount is of concern to married people only insofar as it affects their planning to save dollars from the tax collector when passing on their wealth to the next generation. Before we leave this subject, mention should be made of some of the advice now being handed out to very wealthy married people. It goes like this: Since estate tax rates are based on the value of the estate, it may be that the wealthier of the two spouses should not take advantage of the unlimited marital deduction but instead should leave his/her spouse less than 100 percent of his/her estate (after arranging to have the unified credit amount go to the children directly or in trust with income to the surviving spouse for his/her life), because estate taxes that would eventually be due (on the surviving spouse's estate) might be saved by handing some of that money to Uncle Sam in advance, so that the second estate (having less funds) would incur a lower estate tax! In other words, do not consider the "life" needs or aspirations of your surviving spouse. Consider only the game of saving "death" taxes! This approach is outweighed in ghoulishness only by the trust form of gift to the surviving spouse. For example, "where the surviving spouse is perceived as not having sufficient competence in the area of property management, a power of appointment trust in accordance with Sec. 2056(b)(5) is indicated. Under this provision, the surviving spouse must have an income interest for life and a general power of appointment over the property."[8] The latter means that she gets to say who gets the property after her. There is another degrading type of trust (QTIP) that does not even give her the right to say who gets the property after her. This will be discussed further in Chapter Eight, "Second Marriages."

We leave the topic of marrieds, spouses and surviving spouses, hoping that at least some of the marrieds and spouses at various stages of their married lives will carefully examine all options as to ownership of marital property. If it appears that too much attention has been paid in this chapter to *wealthy* marrieds, an explanation is in order. Marital property planning has traditionally been involved with tax planning because of the historically unequal property-attaining ability of *both* spouses. Changes in American family life, among them the increasing ability of each spouse to acquire property of his or her own, may change the property-planning picture—may even lessen the aggravations in a marriage caused by unequal asset ownership, a factor that sometimes leads to divorce.

NOTES

[1]RIA Recommendations, May 22, 1981.

[2]Peter E. Lippett, *Estate Planning* (Reston, Va.: Reston Publishing, 1979), p. 237.

[3]John G. McQuaid, "Would You Leave Your Wife $27,000,000 Outright?" *Trusts and Estates*, June 1973, p. 426.

[4]Code, Sec. 2001.

[5]"A Guide to Estate Taxes and Planning," in *The Professional Edition of Your Income Tax*, prepared by the J. K. Lasser Tax Institute; ed. Bernard Greisman (New York: Simon & Schuster, 1984), p. 299 in P. 38.10.

[6]*General Explanation of the Economic Recovery Tax Act of 1981*, prepared by the staff of the Joint Committee on Taxation, December 31, 1981 (Washington, D.C., U.S. Government Printing Office, 1981), pp. 233–34.

[7]E. M. Abramson, "Marital Remainder Trusts Are a Good Way to Build College Funds," *Washington Post*, January 14, 1985, Business Section, p. 54; also, *The Wall Street Journal*, September 10, 1984, p. 33.

[8]Don W. Llewellyn, "Estate Planning for the Married Couple," *Villanova Law Review* 28, nos. 3–4 (May 1983), pp. 491–553.

CHAPTER SEVEN

Divorce

In 1982 there were 1.18 million divorces in the United States. One in 200 Americans were divorced in that year alone. Everyone is aware that there are a lot of divorces today and that more marriages probably end in divorce than in the time-honored "till death do us part." No doubt, the quoted phrase is as archaic as the old promise "Love, honor, and obey." Whether we deplore or applaud this situation, it is sobering to remember that a few years ago we deplored (or, at least, parents deplored) young people leaving home and setting up apartments of their own, young people of different sexes living together unmarried, coed dorms, unmarried mothers, working mothers, divorced working mothers, divorced fathers having custody, and children stuck in nurseries for 10-hour days. Whether society has accepted the whole ball of wax or not, one thing is certain: our mores have changed, and they will probably change again in the next generation. If that is the case, perhaps those who want to turn back the clock will *not* like the idea of a baggage of separate assets for each of the two loving people who have entered into marriage; but there may be just as many who think the time has come to adopt this new attitude toward marital property *as a way of life*, and not because of the specter of a possible split-up. Having stated that, it is necessary to reiterate that separation of the couple's assets is not the norm. We still like to think of marriage as a loving partnership, amorous and economic—until the split. *Then* we might wish we had not pooled everything!

PREMARITAL THOUGHTS

At one time, it would have been unthinkable for parties contemplating marriage to simultaneously contemplate the possible end of that marriage in anything other than death. Courts have for some time given credence to premarital agreements providing for the disposition of assets in case of the *death* of one of the parties (such agreements are fairly common in second-marriage situations), but they have been opposed to premarital agreements providing for the disposition of assets in case of the *lifetime* dissolution of the marriage. The latter type of agreement has been considered not conducive to good marital relations and therefore against public policy. However, times are changing, and today most states will enforce at least some forms of premarital agreements in the absence of fraud or coercion, if there has been sufficient disclosure of assets and, in some states, if the division of property is not unconscionable.

Nevertheless, agreement or no agreement, it is now no longer *un*thinkable for prospective marital partners to *think* about the ownership of their assets before entering the marriage. For a starry-eyed bride and groom entering their first marriage, the common tendency has been (and probably still is) to place everything in joint names. Even assets owned individually (perhaps just a bank account) are frequently transferred to joint ownership. Marital acquisitions are likewise mostly "joint." Unless one of the parties has been "wised up" because of an earlier divorce, rarely is thought given to the fact that a different set of rules may apply to division of joint property in a marital split-up than would apply to division of separately owned property. How marital property is titled and how property was owned before the marriage, however, are not the only factors that divorce courts consider in presiding over marital split-ups and the distribution of marital property.

In the discussion that follows, frequent references will be made to tax considerations. As in many transactions affecting property, divorce property transfers may incur tax consequences that should be known to the participants, so that, if possible, their planning can include tax considerations. One further comment is in order. No mention is made of child support, custody, visitation, and so forth. These are entirely different subjects, and the reader will have to look elsewhere for information on them, since this book is concerned primarily with *property*. Payments for child support involve a parent's obligation of support, usually on an ongoing basis. There may be more than one technique for guaranteeing such payments, and there may be tax and nontax considerations here, to be sure, but those matters are not included. Furthermore, only a few brief comments will be made as to grounds for divorce, since those, too, are not what this book is about.

NO-FAULT DIVORCE

In a "no-fault" divorce, the parties merely have to convince a court that the marriage has failed and that statutory requirements have been met. The "fault" of a party is not considered in determining whether or not a divorce (and sometimes even alimony) will be granted. In granting a "no-fault" divorce, each state has certain requirements (time period, residence, criteria for "living apart," etc.), and once having ascertained that those requirements have been satisfied, the court can then look to the division of property or, in increasingly rare instances, the granting of alimony. In an ideal situation, the divorcing parties establish their own agreement for dividing the marital property. If that has been done, the court may accept the agreement and incorporate it into the divorce decree. Otherwise, the court will step in and do the dividing up for them.

Today, there is an increasing recognition by state courts of the monetary and nonmonetary contributions that a spouse makes to the marriage as a homemaker, as a parent, and in support of the other spouse's career potential. The rules of the game have changed. Courts are more and more inclined to consider each spouse's contribution to the marriage in distributing property at the split-up of a marriage, regardless of whose dollars purchased the marital property and regardless of how such property is titled. This has special significance when dealing with jointly owned property that was originally acquired by the investment of one spouse's money.

ATTITUDES TOWARD ALIMONY

The English ecclesiastical courts and the U.S. courts a century ago considered marriage a sacrament and indissoluble. However, a legal separation could be granted, in which the husband had a continuing obligation to support his wife. Remember that at the moment of marriage the husband automatically gained control of his wife's property and income from that property. He retained this control after separation, and with it the corresponding responsibility for his wife's economic support. Employment opportunities for the separated wife were practically nonexistent in those days, and so alimony provided her only resource for financial survival. The first rationale for traditional alimony was that it enforced the husband's obligation to continue to support his wife. Guilt and innocence considerations also entered the picture. (If the wife was found guilty of marital misdeeds, she could not receive support, and if the husband was the guilty party, his punishment was the requirement to pay alimony.) Over the years, authorities have differed as to whether alimony was also paid to compensate the wife for her work during the marriage, and numerous studies have been undertaken in an effort to ascribe a dollar amount to the annual services of a housewife. All of the published results have fallen dismally short of a satisfactory guideline.

The most widely accepted view today is that alimony is necessary in situations where the divorced wife cannot support herself. Here are some often-cited examples: The housewife is too old or is disabled; the housewife is the mother of young children; the wife needs transitional support so that she can go back to school to be retrained for a job; the wife gave up the opportunity to pursue her own career in deference to furthering her husband's career. As a practical matter, the courts often expect that most divorced women, even those with young children, will find a way to work.

The awarding of alimony is within the discretion of the court at a divorce trial. Usually, the statutes of the various states direct or authorize the divorce courts to consider factors that relate both to support and to property division. Many factors enter into the decision and (hopefully) serve as a guide to the courts. In states providing for equitable division, it is not necessary to have alimony paid periodically to be called "alimony." Even if only "property" is divided, the property division statutes contemplate that a major consideration in its division is the "support" of one spouse by the other. The modern way of looking at alimony is that it is necessary to provide for periodic cash payments only when the property available for distribution (including cash) is insufficient for support. Some state laws specify this explicitly. Others imply it.

INCOME TAX CONSIDERATIONS

The income tax aspects of property distribution and *labeling* are an extremely important element of planning both in a divorce and in a marriage predicated on the possibility of divorce (because one never knows!). Here are some things you would want to know about the income tax aspects of alimony: The general rule is that alimony payments made pursuant to a decree of divorce or maintenance payments made under a written separation agreement are taxable as income to the payee ex-spouse and are deductible by the payor ex-spouse. A new wrinkle has been added by the Tax Reform Act of 1984. For divorce instruments executed after December 31, 1984, the parties to a divorce may designate by written agreement that there shall be *no income tax effects* insofar as Internal Revenue is concerned. "Alimony" payments no longer have to be periodic, and they no longer have to satisfy a duty of "support," as established by state law. Certain conditions must be met, one of which is that the payments must be made for at least six years (if in excess of $10,000 for any calendar year). State laws may have more flexibility (suppose the payor gets sick or is out of work during those six years). A speaker at a seminar on the Tax Reform Act of 1984 commented that the parties to the divorce action were not likely to know state law! (A lack that this book, hopefully, will help remedy.) The tax aspects of property distribution in a divorce will be discussed more completely further on in this chapter.

CHANGING ATTITUDES TOWARD MARITAL PROPERTY AND ITS DISTRIBUTION IN DIVORCE

State courts have led the way in recognizing that homemaking services of a spouse constitute a substantial contribution to marital property, regardless of how it was titled, and this contribution may equal the other spouse's monetary contribution in determining rights to marital property. These attitudinal changes developed gradually as the range of "property" interests available for distribution grew and grew. Today the list of those interests might include such items as the value of property rights in business depreciation deductions or the value of business investment tax credits listed on joint personal income tax returns (there was a tax "benefit," was there not?). The item that seems to hurt or shock most is the possibility of distribution of the value of retirement benefits from a job or the value of a professional degree, with their concurrent monetary rewards. These matters will be discussed fully, with a view to understanding how an awareness of changes in court and legislative attitudes can help in planning property ownership.

CONTRIBUTION TO THE MARRIAGE

Historically, the Internal Revenue Service attitude toward the "contribution" of a spouse had to do with contribution in an economic sense. As pointed out in Chapter Six, until the law was changed by the Economic Recovery Tax Act of 1981, a wife's contribution to the acquisition of jointly owned marital assets had to be in the form of dollars earned in the marketplace or from investments or inheritances—or in any way that was *outside the home*. Contribution in the form of housekeeping activities and child care did not count in a widow's plea to avoid estate taxes on assets of her late husband that had been acquired during the marriage with *his* funds (after all, he earned the money *outside the home*). These assets he had lovingly labeled "joint." Of course, she got them by right of survivorship, but not until their value had run the gauntlet of federal estate taxability, with possible resultant diminution. However, before the passage of the Tax Act of 1981, while the Treasury and Congress were still viewing marital joint property as something that spouses acquired in accordance with their dollar or *economic* contribution (an economic contribution was one that had an equivalent value in dollars), states were beginning to recognize that even if they began to equate house-keeping services with *economic* value, the estimated values would be ridiculously low. The equation "Wife's contribution as house-wife = Wife's share of joint property" would lead to a skewed and inequitable result.

States began to view a spouse's nonmonetary contribution as contribution to the *marriage* and not merely to the assets. Under this approach, insofar as JTRS assets and Internal Revenue were concerned, it appeared that a wife would be better off *divorcing* a husband than merely *surviving* him. In the former situation, some states gave her credit for contribution, whether it was in dollars or not; in the latter, IRS rejected her contention that because of her housewifely contribution some of the marital jointly held assets belonged to her *as a wife*, regardless of lack of economic contribution. Eventually, both types of noneconomic contribution—contribution to the marriage and contribution to the joint property (which IRS called "consideration furnished")—were melded into one and Congress adopted the state view. Here is a statement in which the staff of the Joint Committee on Taxation of the U.S. Congress explained the significance of the unlimited marital deduction:

> Under prior law, it was often extremely difficult to determine the ownership of property held within the marital unit and to determine whose funds were used to acquire that property. These problems generally will not arise with an unlimited marital deduction.

As to jointly held property, the staff's "Explanation" states:

> The Congress believed that rules governing the taxation of jointly held property between spouses were unnecessarily complex. In particular, the Congress recognized that it is often difficult, as between spouses, to determine the amount of consideration that each spouse provided for the acquisition and improvement of their jointly held property.[1]

The enlightenment of Congress and its ultimate discovery (as stated above) of facts known to every husband and wife came after an evolutionary process that began where people live—in the states.

As we have seen, in both the common law states and the community property states, wives were viewed as protected, dependent, child-bearing adjuncts of the marital committee—not as full-fledged members. The present-day assertion by wives of ownership rights in marital property began in the states, not as a protest against federal estate taxing policies, but as a demand for—simply stated—*fairness*. Here is an example of the usual thinking: Some northwestern states applauded and followed *Murdoch v. Murdoch*, a Canadian case. The facts were that for 15 years Mrs. Murdoch had spent her full time in helping her husband operate a ranch, title to which was held in his name alone. On divorce, she claimed a one-half interest in the ranch. Denied. The court found that all she had done "was the work done by any ranch wife."[2] In the early cases in this country, the goal of those trying to advance the cause of wives was to consciously espouse the partnership concept. An important support for the partnership principle came from the federal government; a 1963 Committee on Civil and Political Rights of the President's Commission on the Status of Women adopted this policy recommendation:

> Marriage is a partnership to which each spouse makes a different but equally important contribution. This fact has become increasingly recognized in the realities of American family living. While the laws of other countries have reflected this trend, family laws in the United States have lagged behind. Accordingly, the Committee concludes that during marriage each spouse should have a legally defined and substantial right in the earnings of the other spouse and in the real and personal property acquired as a result of such earnings, as well as in the management of such earnings and property. Such right should survive the marriage and be legally recognized in the event of its termination by annulment, divorce, or death. This policy should be appropriately implemented by legislation which would safeguard either spouse against improper alienation of property by the other.[3]

A summary of what some states have been doing in this area will show just how far attitudes have changed from viewing a wife's acts as the normal and expected tasks performed by a ranch wife or a farm wife, and *not* as a contribution to the marital wealth nor in the nature of acts of a business partner, to demanding recognition of almost anything a wife did to enhance the marriage in determining her rightful share when splitting marital property.

SOME CHANGING STATE MARITAL PROPERTY ATTITUDES ILLUSTRATED

In 1978 the Code of Maryland was revised. Here is what the preamble to that revision states with regard to domestic relations laws:

> The General Assembly declares that it is the policy of this State that marriage is a union between a man and a woman having equal rights under the law. Both spouses owe a duty to contribute his or her best efforts to the marriage, and both, by entering into the marriage, undertake to benefit both spouses and any children they may have.

The General Assembly declares further that it is the policy of this state that when a marriage is dissolved the property interests of the spouses should be adjusted fairly and equitably, with careful consideration being given to both monetary and nonmonetary contributions made by the respective spouses to the well-being of the family.

In the District of Columbia Code, a specific provision—Sec. 16-910(b)(1981)—states:

The court shall... consider each party's contribution to the acquisition, preservation, appreciation, dissipation or depreciation in value of the assets subject to distribution under this subsection, and each party's contribution as a homemaker or to the family unit.

Iowa has enacted a statute that defines "marital property" and directs the court in a divorce proceeding to consider the factor of a spouse's "homemaker" contribution in determining maintenance and property distribution. Some states permit only property acquired during the marriage to be distributed; other states include premarital separate property or the increase in the value of separate property. Some states will include separate property if marital property assets are considered insufficient. In Arkansas, for example, marital property is divided equally, but if the court determines that this will lead to an inequitable result, other property can be tapped under special criteria spelled out in the statute. In Wisconsin, there is a presumption of a 50–50 split of marital property. This, however, can be rebutted by either party, and the property split can be arranged in accord with special criteria.

EQUITABLE DISTRIBUTION "PROPERTY" GUIDELINES

Here are some of the types of "criteria" in states having equitable distribution guidelines in their statutes (to assist the courts in their difficult task): The length of the marriage; the age, health, and position in life of the parties; the occupations of the parties; the amount and sources of income; vocational skills; employability; the estate, liabilities, and needs of each party and the opportunity of each to acquire further capital assets and income; the contribution of each party (including services as a homemaker) in acquiring and preserving marital property and assisting in its appreciation or dissipation; loss of inheritance or pension rights; and the possibility of support in addition to property distribution or property distribution in lieu of support.

Here are some other state statutes. In Minnesota, the equitable division statute creates a presumption that each spouse has made a substantial contribution to the acquisition of income and property while the spouses have been living together as husband and wife. Furthermore, the statute provides that furniture and household possessions may be equitably divided without regard to time of acquisition. In New York and North Carolina, there are specific provisions for a monetary award in situations where it would be impractical or infeasible to divide the property in kind (for example, interests in a closely held business or an interest in a professional practice). North Carolina provides that pension rights (vested or not yet vested) are not divisible per se but that their value may be considered in reaching an equitable division. Several states have specific provisions regarding the marital home; usually, the award either of title or use and possession is in the direction of the ex-spouse having custody of the children. Some but not all state courts can order title changes. Those that cannot can consider the value and balance the equities by making a monetary award to the nontitled party. Nebraska provides that in the absence of an approved property agreement, the divorce court shall view pension plans as subject to division. An Oklahoma court verbalized its reasoning with regard to pension benefits as follows:

> [It is not significant] . . . whether the pension is "vested" in the sense that it is now due and owing [since] it is a valuable right, purchased through joint efforts of the spouses to the extent that it was enhanced during the marriage; and as such, it should be regarded as having been jointly acquired during the marriage. The pension should be divided between the parties "as may appear just and reasonable," by a division of the property in kind, or by setting the same apart to one of the parties and requiring the other . . . to pay such sum as may be just and proper to effect a fair and just division thereof.[4]

The expansion of "property" subject to equitable division in a divorce to include retirement benefits has been a phenomenon of the last 10 years. The attachment of the "property interest" label to pension benefits that may be payable in a remote period of time but are available *now* in a marital dissolution has raised a multitude of questions, not the least of which are: If the state law says make an apportionment *now*, how is this done? What is the value of the pension benefits? What are the tax consequences of the apportionment?

PENSIONS

Whether you accrue retirement benefits through employment with a private employer, government, or the military or as the employee-owner of your own small business, those benefits are "property" that is available for divorce distribution. In 1982 Congress enacted, and the President signed into law, the Uniformed Services Former Spouses' Protection Act, which provides that military pensions are no longer insulated from state distributions of marital property.[5] Previously, military ex-wives were out in the cold with respect to sharing in their ex-husbands' pensions (*McCarty v. McCarty*). [6] A state decision that relied on *McCarty* was *Smith v. Smith*[7], but this and other state decisions prior to the enactment of the military pension law have been made ineffective because cases have given the statute retroactive application. Thus, if retired military personnel lived in a state that did not touch military pensions, a divorce would at least leave this portion of their wealth intact. The newest federal legislation on the subject, the Retirement Equity Act of 1984, provides, effective January 1, 1985, a uniform national procedure for implementation of state court orders distributing private retirement benefits in general in connection with divorce and marital separation.

One method by which state divorce courts reach an employee's interest in a retirement plan is to award to the employee spouse all of his or her benefits and to award the nonemployee spouse *other* property equal in value to her or his share of the present value of the benefits awarded to the employee, or the courts may award a percentage to be paid when the pension is collected.

ECONOMIC REALITIES: "HIS/HER"

In *Explanation of Divorce Provisions, Tax Reform Act of 1984* (Chicago: Commerce Clearing House, 1984), from which the above information was gleaned, "*his or her* benefits" and "*his or her* share" are carefully stated. Although many women are now garnering their own retirement benefits, most of the state case law, statutes, courts, and *litigants* in a divorce would accept the reality that at present the larger pension benefit is generally the result of the husband's work. The purely societal reason for this is that, as things now stand, even if the wife worked during the marriage, in most cases *he* had the opportunity to be the major earner and therefore the major piler-up of a future retirement income. This would be especially true if the wife took time out to have children. (Of course, in any divorce proceeding where *each* spouse had retirement benefits building up in that spouse's "property owner-ship" inventory, *both* potential pensions will generally be placed on the scale).

Similarly, if a state court orders the appropriation of pension benefits to satisfy obligations of alimony and child support that are fastened on the plan participant (meaning the one who earned the money from working and thus became a "plan participant" in his company's pension plan), usually it is the husband's pension that will be attached. In only the rarest instance is *she* required to pay *him* alimony. Inasmuch as the Internal Revenue Code pro-vides that, in order to qualify for income tax exemption, an employer's pension plan must provide for certain distributions protecting the interest of the employee's *spouse* (not just the employee), *spouses' interests* are very much on the minds of legislators. This legislative concern has now been extended to the interests of *ex-spouses*. In actual practice, benefits in most cases inure to the female ex-spouse (or spouse). Widows, wives, and ex-wives must be protected and provided for.

As we have seen, Congress has sought to preserve the interest of non-employee spouses in the pensions being built up as part of the employee spouses' employment benefits. For a retirement plan of a corporate business or a noncorporate business (Keogh) plan to retain its tax-exempt status, the provisions of the plan regarding distribution of benefits must require a joint-and-survivor annuity payout to a *married* participant unless the *married* participant *and spouse* elect *in writing* not to take a joint and survivor annuity. Such written waiver by the participant and participant's spouse must be executed in the presence of a notary or plan representative.

IRAs

What about IRAs? An Individual Retirement Account (IRA) can be transferable property. Is nothing sacred? As the law is at present, in addition to the retirement plan maintained by your employer, you may have your own. You may make deductible contributions to an IRA of up to $2,000 a year of earned income. A working husband and wife may contribute up to $4,000. If you have a nonworking spouse, you may contribute and deduct up to $2,250 and this applies whether or not you live in a community property state. (Even though under community property laws, a *non*working spouse is still considered to have earned half your salary, the deductibility of contributions to an IRA on her behalf is limited to $250.) Suppose you contributed to an account on behalf of your nonworking spouse and then you get divorced later in that year. You have made an excess contribution, and you will want to withdraw it before a penalty tax is slapped on it. Suppose you decide (since you have used tax-deferred dollars to contribute to the IRA in the first place) to let your ex-spouse have that as part of the divorce distribution settlement. A thought strikes you. Maybe it would then be taxable? No, you are lucky. To set your mind at rest, here is the provision covering that situation:

> *Transfer of Account Incident to Divorce.*—The transfer of an individual's interest in an individual retirement account or an individual annuity to his former spouse under a divorce decree or under a written instrument incident to such divorce is not to be considered a taxable transfer made by such individual notwithstanding any other provision of this subtitle, and such interest at the time of the transfer is to be treated as an individual retirement account of such spouse, and not of such individual. Thereafter such account or annuity for purposes of this subtitle is to be treated as maintained for the benefit of such spouse.[8]

Suppose your ex-spouse then wants to continue the IRA? There are very restrictive rules as to the amount of deduction allowed for contributions to an IRA established by a former spouse. The best thing for the new owner of the IRA account to do is to add the allowed contribution per year based on earnings.

EFFECT OF RECENT TAX LEGISLATION

We have spoken freely of the widening list of property and property interests that make up the inventory of property owned by one or both of the divorcing parties. We know that until the tax law changes of 1981, certain limits were set on tax-free transfers between married people (50 percent marital deduction limit, etc.). The tax law of 1981 provided for future tax-free transfers between spouses, during life or as part of an estate. What about transfers between ex-spouses?

HISTORY AGAIN—THE DAVIS CASE

Everyone who went through a divorce and property distribution prior to the Tax Reform Act of 1984 had at least a passing familiarity with the theory and law regarding the taxation of property transferred to satisfy (pay off?) a divorcing wife's claims against her about-to-be ex-husband. If you were one of the unfortunate husbands, you may have emitted cries of rage. Here is why: A lump-sum property settlement incident to separation or divorce had significant tax consequences. If you transferred your own separate property in exchange for the release of your divorcing wife's "marital rights," such as the right to support (remember, state law often requires support of a wife), and the property transferred was worth more on the date of transfer than you had paid for it, you had an income-taxable capital gain!

For example, in 1970 you separately bought 200 shares of ABC Corporation stock. It cost you $20,000. In 1983 you transferred the stock to your divorcing wife, Betty, and thought you had a bargain because the stock was worth $100,000 on the date of transfer. This is similar to what happened in the now-famous *Davis* case, which reached the Supreme Court on appeal and established the law on this issue for many years, much to the exasperation of male clients and their lawyers. *Davis* held that a transfer of property from one divorcing spouse to another, which transfer was part of the divorce property settlement, triggered a tax owed by the spouse who did the transferring. The theory was that the release of marital rights by the wife was the "consideration" for the property transferred to her, *as though it were a sale.* Had the husband received $100,000 for the stock in an actual sale, he would have owed a capital gains tax on the difference between $20,000 and $100,000. So far, one cannot argue with this rationale. Here's the stinger: In an actual sale, the seller would have an $80,000 profit out of which to pay the tax on the gain. By transferring the securities as part of a divorce settlement, the poor transferor (the husband) gets no money out of the deal with which to pay the tax![9] How did the transfer affect the wife? She picked up a new *basis*, the value of the stock on the date of transfer to her. If she sold it on that day, she would have had no tax to pay.

In order to avoid the adverse consequences of this harsh result (for the divorcing husband), lawyers went to a great deal of trouble to try and prove that the divorcing wife (the transferee) actually had a predivorce ownership share in the very property being transferred. This was easy enough to prove if the marital property of the divorcing couple was held in some form of co-ownership (including community property) in such a way that each party got back (in a division) only what that party already owned. If that could be shown, then a transfer of property containing elements of co-ownership could be a nontaxable transfer. You cannot *transfer* to someone what that person already owns. For property held as JTRS owners or as tenants by the entireties (in states recognizing that form of husband-and-wife co-ownership), there was usually no problem. A Massachusetts court, however, held that a wife had nothing more than an "expectancy" and not *present* co-owner-ship. Most state courts would not so rigidly follow the traditional common law interpretation.

In the *Davis* case, the husband tried to argue (through his lawyer) that the wife was only getting back what she already partially owned. The Court said that the rights of the wife under Delaware law did "not even remotely reach the dignity of a co-ownership." The Court held that the wife's potential claim against her husband's property placed a burden on it not very different from the burden caused by his duty of support. Her right to ultimately own some of it did not give her an equal present co-ownership. Therefore, he was transferring something of value to her that she did not already own. Result: Internal Revenue had a right to tax the transfer. This has now been changed. As we saw in Chapter Three, the Tax Reform Act of 1984 overruled the dependence of Internal Revenue on state interpretations—in this case, to the advantage of divorcing husbands.

EFFECT OF TAX REFORM ACT OF 1984

The Tax Reform Act of 1984 in effect overruled the *Davis* case and the line of reasoning that followed that landmark case of 1962. The 1984 act treats transfers in connection with a divorce in much the same manner as gifts between spouses are treated. This means that the divorcing spouse who is the transferor of property on which there was a gain (the husband in practically all cases) no longer has to report that gain on his income tax return as though he had sold the asset; instead, the transferee (the wife) will have a gain if and when she sells the asset and, just as in gifts, will have to use as her basis the original cost (to the husband). If the property was investment real estate or business property, the basis might be "adjusted." IRS regulations should be consulted.

Certain conditions must be met. The transfer of property must be in accordance with a written agreement between the ex-spouses, and divorce must occur within a specified time. If the agreement provides for alimony payments instead of property transfer, the parties may also agree that the alimony payments will be excluded from reportable income by the payee and not deductible by the payor. This is a change from the usual and previous rule that alimony and separate maintenance payments under a court decree are income to the payee and deductible by the payor. The theory now is that the parties may, by their acts, clothe "alimony" (formerly fulfilling a marriage-derived obligation of support) with some of the appearance of lump-sum payments or property transfers. The payments, however, must be in cash, must end on the death of the payee-spouse, and must be made for at least six years (if in excess of $10,000 in any calendar year). There are more complex parts of this new rule, so that even without the further congressional changes or add-ons that may occur, the interpreting and planning it requires can be expected to keep the divorce bar and divorce litigants busy for some time.

PROPERTY TRANSFER OR ALIMONY—WHAT DIFFERENCE DOES IT MAKE?

The intent of the state equitable distribution statutes is to put a cap on the stringing out of divorce controversies. If the philosophy of equitable distribution is applied to a no-fault divorce, the divorcing couple's property is divided "equitably," taking numerous factors into consideration. The factors generally boil down to what is "fair." If the divorcing couple can divide up their property themselves and agree, the divorce court judge will pat them on the heads and smile as the judge puts the stamp of court approval on their property distribution agreement. It might seem unrealistic to expect two people whose lives have reached the point where they cannot stand the sight of each other to sit down and work out "what he gets and what she gets." This does, however, happen. As a matter of fact, many cases are settled, and usually it is with the services of the attorneys for each of the parties that agreements are worked out.

Essentially, the Tax Act of 1984 says: If you divide up your property (or if the court does it for you) and your agreement is made a part of the divorce decree, there will be no immediate tax effect. If one party transfers property to the other, either real property or personal property (a house or securities, for example), regardless of what was paid for that property, it will be given a value as of the date of transfer for purposes of satisfying the requirements of the divorce decree designating distribution of property. Furthermore, such a transfer will have the tax effect of a transfer between spouses—which we know is zero.

Here is an example: You transfer (give) to your loving wife a block of securities for which you paid $5,000. You (as a careful person) kept the brokerage confirmation slip: ABC stock, 100 shares at $50 a share years before the marriage. You tell your broker to reregister the stock in the separate name of your wife and in her separate account (maybe your lawyer told you she should have separate assets for estate-planning purposes). The stock is now worth $70 a share, or $7,000. Later, the stock goes up to $90 a share. She says, "Honey, I think I will sell." She has a capital gain of $4,000 (the difference between the basis of $5,000 and the $9,000 sales price), which you report on your joint income tax return, of course. If the same transfer is made to your ex-spouse incident to a divorce property settlement, you get credit for $7,000 toward the total property settlement and she walks away with your 100 shares of ABC stock. Later, maybe years after the divorce, she sells the stock for $9,000. She has a capital gain of $4,000 (the difference between *your* basis of $5,000 and *her* selling price of $9,000). She alone reports the capital gain on her next income tax return. (For comments on transfer of shares in a family owned business, see Chapter 10.)

Suppose the transfer was real estate instead of securities. Investment real estate would have been depreciated, and the basis would have been "adjusted" to reflect the depreciation deduction taken each year since the property was purchased. Spouses and ex-spouses who have investment real property transferred to them incur the same tax obligation. On a sale, the depreciation taken reduces the basis (cost), and the difference between that figure and the sales price is the capital gain, recognizing that accelerated depreciation deductions might trigger recapture at ordinary income tax rates on a sale. The ex-wife and the wife are on the same footing with regard to reporting income on a sale (just as you would be if you had sold at that time). If the real estate transferred to your ex-spouse is the family home, no depreciation would have been taken. In general, the rules for deferring gain (if another home with cost in excess of the sale proceeds is bought) would apply. If one of the sellers who buys a new home is over 55, the $125,000 capital gain forgiveness would apply.

Aside from the fact that you probably want to call up your accountant to check these things out, how can this information help you in your property planning? Since most people presume that a marriage will last, the best course to follow still seems to be a course providing for ownership of marital property that a happily married couple would take. The family home would usually be jointly owned. Ownership of other assets would follow a thought-out plan.

Whether property in a transfer incident to a divorce is categorized as "alimony" or "maintenance" is important, especially to a high-bracket payor (husband). Remember that although a husband may now transfer appreciated property to a divorcing spouse and achieve credit for the appreciated value, he still purchased the property with after-tax dollars. If, instead, he makes periodic payments of cash and such payments are accepted in the language of the divorce decree as "support" or "alimony," then such payments are deductible from the payor's income and reportable as income by the payee (the ex-wife). Sometimes it is not clear whether the payments are deductible periodic payments of alimony or payments for the release of marital rights by the ex-wife. In the latter case, the payments would not be deductible by the ex-husband or includable by the ex-wife in their future separate income tax returns. If the ex-wife does not wish to be saddled with the income tax obligation of the payments, her goal is to prove that these are payments made for release of her interest in marital property, which interest she had by virtue of the marriage. The Tax Act of 1984 provides specific criteria for determining which is which and, furthermore, permits the parties to designate by written agreement that payments that might otherwise be considered alimony should be excluded as income by the ex-wife and not deducted by the ex-husband—in other words, should appear to be in the nature of a nontaxable transfer. Time will tell whether these new rules will smooth or fuel divorce property distribution disputes.

RETIREMENT BENEFITS AS PROPERTY AVAILABLE FOR DIVORCE DISTRIBUTION—INTERPLAY BETWEEN FEDERAL AND STATE LAW

We have seen in the "Pensions" section that states have not considered the equity building up in pension plans as having the status of remote property unreachable for divorce distribution—but, instead, have de-insulated such property interests. A law signed by the president on August 23, 1984, reaffirmed the states' view. The Retirement Equity Act of 1984 quickly became known as "the women's bill." Its purpose was to provide greater pension equity for women. Pension plans are now required to provide survivor benefits, which cannot be waived except by a written election by the spouse of a plan participant (see page 95). Various other provisions change the important previous legislation of 1974 (Employees Retirement Income Security Act, or ERISA) in ways that stress changing work patterns and the "new" status of marriage as an economic partnership. Likewise, the breakup of a marriage is not to be considered a signal that the protective attitude toward a spouse's rights in the other spouse's retirement plan is to be relaxed. A wife's protected interest extends beyond marriage and protects the ex-wife.

This represents a major reversal of prior policy and law. Previously, a provision in the Internal Revenue Code described acts that would disqualify an employer's pension plan (for tax-deferred status). One of those acts was to allow a plan participant to "assign" or "alienate" his (potential) benefits. The aim was to protect these assets against creditors' claims. This was called the "spendthrift" provision. The employee-participant could not look to his potential wealth and use it as a future down payment on a Jaguar or otherwise as a pledge for debts. If a state law permitted such an assignment or alienation, the federal law prevailed and overrode the state law. The Retirement Equity Act has reversed this and created an "exception" by stating that a right to any benefit payable with respect to a participant pursuant to a qualified domestic relations order is not the kind of assignment or alienation that the law previously prohibited. If you follow these twists and turns, you can see that what *was prohibited* (for your best interests) is *now permitted* (for hers). Here is what the Senate Finance Committee Report stated:

> Under the bill, if a domestic relations order requires the distribution of all or a part of a participant's benefits under a qualified plan to an alternate payee, then the creation, recognition, or assignment of the alternate payee's right to the benefits is not considered an assignment or alienation of benefits under the plan if and only if the order is a qualified domestic relations order. Because rights created, recognized, or assigned by a qualified domestic relations order, and benefit payments pursuant to such an order, are specifically permitted under the bill, State law providing for these rights and payments under a qualified domestic relations order will continue to be exempt from Federal preemption under ERISA.[10]

Definitions: "Participant" is, of course, the one whose retirement benefits are being slashed to share with an "alternate payee." The latter character in the plot is the ex-wife. A "qualified domestic relations order" is a divorce order following a certain prescribed form. As to tax status, the "alternate payee" is treated as a distributee and taxed accordingly.

WHO PAYS WHAT TAXES?

As we have seen, transfers of property incident to divorce are now nontaxable, just as transfers of property between spouses are nontaxable. Therefore, it would appear that transfers of retirement benefits under qualified domestic relations orders are nontaxable. This would only apply, however, where the transfer is in a form recognizable as a presently transferable amount. For example, in cases where an employee has a portion of his retirement plan account in his own contributions or has a vested portion then the value of those contributions or that vested portion could be apportioned (if ordered by a state divorce court) between the employee (called "participant" above) and the nonemployee spouse (called "alternate payee" above). In such a situation, the transfer would be similar to a transfer between spouses and there would be no income tax consequences to the nonemployee divorcing spouse. If, however, the nonemployee spouse receives benefits in the form of an annuity or a portion of the employee's annuity, such benefits would be taxed as ordinary income in the hands of the nonemployee spouse. (The employee's portion could be taken as a lump-sum distribution if desired and as such would be eligible for favorable lump-sum 10-year averaging distribution tax rules according to present law.)

FUTURE PROPERTY INTERESTS

State divorce courts have the almost impossible task of determining how to divide up a future property interest, one that has not matured and may never mature. What if the potential future retiree dies before the retirement date? The ex-spouse might have had in hand *her* share of his pension, but he never lived to enjoy *his* share. On the other hand, suppose the court decides that the nonemployee spouse must wait until the pension payout date for her share and the employee not only decides to pass up the opportunity for early retirement but also opts instead for late retirement. How long should she have to wait? Could the employee be coerced into early retirement? Suppose the court decides to place a value on the future pension and to use that value to balance out the division of property. Suppose it gives the nonemployee spouse a greater percentage of the currently available assets, in exchange for a hands-off agreement as to the pension, and the employee spouse (who aspires to the pension someday) a smaller percentage. Suppose the pension is the major asset and there are no other items to balance against the future pension.

Suppose, suppose. The possibilities are seemingly endless, and all of them produce some potential for unfairness. In most states the portion of the employee's interest in his future pension that is subject to division upon divorce would not include any amounts added to his pension rights *after the divorce*, and in some states it would not include amounts acquired *before the marriage*. Once a *policy* regarding the division of pension benefits has been established, the state courts have to decide on methods of distribution, evaluation, current or deferred division, the shares to be awarded each spouse, and so on. Even if a state, for example, makes a distinction between property acquired *before marriage* (which would exclude the proportionate share of pension benefits that accrued prior to the date of marriage) and property acquired *during the marriage*, a decision would still have to be made as to whether or not to include within marital property an *increase* in the *value* of premarital pension funds that accrued *during* the marriage. It is easy to see that the state's attitude toward appreciation of premarital pension funds could make a dent in the nest egg that the employee thought would be his alone.

If the divorce is now ancient history and the divorce court never even considered or had presented to it the matter of pension benefits, in community property states it has been held that the nonemployee spouse might bring a subsequent action for partition of those benefits, unless barred from doing so by a statute of limitations. In most common law states, however, the property interest of the nonemployee spouse is viewed as one that exists as a result of the divorce proceedings, and a later action to divide the benefits would generally be barred by the failure of the court to consider such property at the time of divorce. Additionally, the employee ex-spouse could successfully deny the interest of the nonemployee ex-spouse.[11] The summarizations of state laws in Appendix II may provide some guidelines as to the law in your state or some insights as to the *evolving* new laws on this subject. The important thing to remember is that an understanding of property interests *available* to the courts for distribution in case of divorce is useful in many ways. It could even be critical in states where, by failure to state your claim to a share of a property (for example, pension rights) at the time of the divorce hearing, you may have waived and therefore lost those rights forever.

INSURANCE

If a divorce decree provides that, after the payor's death, alimony payments are to continue by means of life insurance proceeds that would replace the alimony payments made by the payor during life, the proceeds are includable in the income of the recipient spouse as alimony. If in a divorce one spouse assigns an annuity contract for the benefit of the other spouse in accordance with a court decree, each annuity payment is taxable to the payee spouse if the payments are "periodic" and for "support." Under the new provisions of the Tax Reform Act of 1984, assigning the contract itself is nontaxable (it is treated just like a spousal gift) because it is "incident to a divorce."[12] As part of the benefits of the transfer, the transferee spouse will be eligible to recover the "investment in the contract" made by its original buyer.[13] Should this seem unclear, review the insurance item with your attorney if it is a part of your divorce considerations.

SPOUSAL INTERESTS IN PROFESSIONAL DEGREES AND LICENSES

This is a category of property interests in which law is just beginning to be established at the state level. In California, a community property state, a case was heard that achieved national notoriety, *In re Sullivan*. A divorcing wife had put her husband through medical school. The trial court held that the marital community should be paid back the amount of any "community" funds that were used to acquire the education, degree, and license. That court likened the value of the separate property that the professional education represented with the separate value of a business. If an increase in the value of separate property is attributable to the ability or activities of either spouse, that "increase in value is considered to be the property of the community." An appeals court, however, stated: "Medical education is not property and cannot be divided upon divorce."[14] The *Sullivan* case was appealed to the California Supreme Court, and that court returned the case to the trial court because a new law had been enacted (effective January 1, 1985) specifying certain reimbursement if one spouse's work had substantially enhanced the earning capacity of the other spouse.

Here is a summary of the status of professional education as "property":

One of the skirmishes in the running battle for economic justice upon divorce involves the recognition of spousal contributions to the career (and/or career potential) of the other party. The classic case is that of the housewife who puts her medical student husband through school, only to be handed a divorce summons when the diploma is handed to her husband. In the trade, this phenomenon came to be known as the "medical student syndrome."

The symptoms and attendant problems no longer are an occupational disease solely related to medical education; the contagion has spread to other professions and occupations. Indeed, it may now be the husband who puts a student-wife through graduate school. Understandably, the spouse who put the other through school likes to get a portion of the enhanced earning power of the graduate while the other resists such a mortgage on his or her future.

Various theories have been utilized by the contributing spouse— from equitable distribution of "property," to quasi-contractual remedies—to preclude the unjust enrichment of the student.

It has been held that a professional degree is—and is not— "property" subject to equitable distribution and that a professional license is—or is not—marital property. Some decisions hold that such contributions should only be reflected in the amount and duration of alimony or maintenance. Some decisions give what, in effect, is an "out-of-pocket" measure of damages. Other cases, in some measure, look at the "loss-of-the-bargain."[15]

States have varied in dealing with this problem. This area of developing property rights has a "tip-of-the-iceberg" aura. It bears watching. Here, for example, is how another writer put it:

> Current settlements in no-fault marital dissolutions do not ade-quately protect wives who have experienced depreciation of their human capital through periods of nonmarket labor. Fairness dictates that wives be compensated at dissolution for the difference between their decreased lifetime earning potential and their husband's enhanced earning power resulting from the couple's allocation of their human capital to market and nonmarket labor. Attorneys representing college-educated, middle and upper class wives can clearly demonstrate the economic value of foregone investment in the wife's career and the husband's enhanced earning capacity to obtain a more equitable settlement for their clients. Consideration of appreciation and depreciation of human capital at dissolution would give wives and husbands a greater sense of surety and could enhance the quality of intact marriages. Commitment to traditional or non-traditional roles could occur with confidence that equal protection exists for both marital partners. With legal recognition of human capital concepts, either spouse could confidently choose to invest themselves in their home and family instead of a career.[16]

WHAT ABOUT TANGIBLE PROPERTY DISTRIBUTION?

Suppose you have something tangible: The family heirloom diamond your wife's grandmother gave her on the marriage, the valuable coin collection your father gave you, urging you to cherish and value it. The rules are different in most of the states. Some states permit only property that was accumulated *during* the marriage to be divided. Others consider separate property reachable if marital property assets are insufficient to provide equitable distribution. In drawing up separation agreements, lawyers must be especially careful to *except* certain cherished items belonging to one or the other of the parties. Some states specifically exclude gifts and inheritances made to one or the other of the spouses from availability for distribution in a split-up. Consider: Wife has wealthy relatives. Doting affluent widowed aunt gives prospective bride valuable securities as an engagement present. Bride retains securities as her separate property after marriage. Years later, divorce occurs. Is ex-bride's property reachable for distribution? Most states would say no.

In community property states, property is divided along equal lines, as to value, but special circumstances are considered. Although we are emphasizing no-fault dissolutions, a word is in order regarding the attention given to "fault," particularly in community property states. In some community property states, evidence may be presented as to marital misconduct that would decrease or eliminate the guilty party's share of the community property. Although judges may still, humanly, be influenced by evidence of blatant fault in awarding alimony or property, in the states in general there is a trend to minimize the importance of marital misconduct.

In the common law property states (all states but the eight community property ones), courts have no general power to distribute property on divorce except for jointly held property. As to nonjoint property, title is significant and is given weight. The engagement gift to the bride, to which she holds title, would probably be immune from a claim by the nontitleholder spouse in a split-up. This would also hold true for the coin collection given to the husband prior to the marriage. However, the "appreciation of premarital property," if such appreciation is the product of contribution from one or the other of the spouses *during the marriage*, is a factor to be considered in the split-up distribution. Some authorities argue that since the present philosophy is that marriage is a shared enterprise, the contributions of both parties to the acquisition and preservation of assets, and not title, should be the crucial factor.[17] It is, however a practice in certain states to allow courts presiding over a divorce to change title to properties.

MARITAL PROPERTY—SOME NEW CONCEPTS

Hopefully, a trend will develop toward minimizing battles over property division in a divorce, if the trend toward divorce itself does not begin to curve downward. A proposed uniform law that is currently making its way around state legislatures is the Uniform Marital Property Act. The intention of the proposed legislation is not merely to lay the foundation for a less combative situation in divorce but to provide an atmosphere of fairness and to apply uniformly among the states present-day concepts of property ownership for married people. Almost all of the states now have a form of law providing for equitable distribution on marriage dissolution, but there is not much agreement as to what is *equitable*. Should the property available for equitable distribution just include property acquired during the marriage? Should it include all of the property owned by either of the divorcing spouses? Should it look to the title of the individual partners as to which spouse owned which property and leave the property alone if it is so titled? While the Uniform Act would not answer all of these questions, it might alleviate some of the sore spots in property division conflicts as well as in other situations where property devolution has heretofore not reflected the true marital proprietorship.

Here are some of the things the act would do: It would refer to property as "marital property" or "individual property." As noted in Chapter Three, traditionally property has been viewed as "community" in the community property states and as "separate" in the common law states. If states adopted the Uniform Act, property acquired during the marriage would be marital property and each spouse would have a present 50 percent interest in that property. Individual property would be everything else— property owned by either party before marriage, property acquired either before or during marriage by gift or inheritance, increases in the value of individual property that did not result from the personal efforts of the other spouse, and so forth.

WHAT ABOUT TITLE?

Under the Uniform Act, title could be in the name of either spouse or both spouses, and control would follow accordingly. Refer to the definition of property in Chapter One. Remember, *control* is the key factor in ownership of property. Any outside individual, business, or entity that deals with the title-holder (whether the husband or the wife) would be protected in that reliance. This is a far cry from the situation that existed when the dower rights of a wife in real estate held in her husband's name necessitated that a prospective buyer secure her signature on the deed of conveyance, in order to extinguish her inchoate dower rights. You can now see the significance of a state's abolition of dower. Reference to the state summaries in Appendix II will indicate whether this holdover concept from the common law still prevails in your state. The Alabama Supreme Court, in a 1977 decision, had this to say in declaring unconstitutional (on both the state and federal levels) a state law that denied a wife the right to mortgage her real property without her husband's concurrence:

> Although the purpose of this legislation was to protect the wife, and "not limit her power of alienation," ... the issue is reduced to whether it is constitutionally permissible when its effect is to treat married women, in dealing with their separate property, different from all other adult persons. Single women, divorced women, widowed women, and all men are free to transact business, contract, and alienate property, free of all legislative restraints. Only married women are perceived to require restrictions on one of such rights, i.e., alienation of their property, theoretically to protect them against their own actions.[18]

Decisions of this kind led the way in many states to erosion of the old common law principles (often derisively called "notions") that "protected" the wife in ways that restricted the husband in dealing with property (the wife's right of dower) while clothing the husband with superior authority in handling her, his, and their property. Many states have abolished the estates of dower and curtesy. Likewise, in some states the concept of tenancy by the entireties for husband and wife has been reduced to a simple joint tenancy with survivorship, as the latter form of ownership applies in cases of joint owners who are not spouses. What is the difference? Remember that in a tenancy by the entireties one tenant (spouse) acting alone cannot destroy the joint tenancy. The survivorship is built in so long as the parties are married. Consequently, as we saw in Chapter Three, a creditor of one of the spouses would have to wait until the other spouse died before the debtor spouse's interest in jointly held assets could be attached to pay the debt, assuming the debtor spouse survived. Not all of the states have done away with these common law concepts, although the trend is in that direction for the simple reason that property dealings today require the attribution of responsibility and freedom to *control* one's property, regardless of marital status.

HOW WOULD THE UNIFORM MARITAL PROPERTY ACT CHANGE THINGS?

Mary Moers Wenig, a professor at the University of Bridgeport School of Law, states:

> Claims of third persons arising during an obligee's marriage can be satisfied from the obligee's individual property and from marital property; claims which antedate the marriage can be satisfied from the obligee's individual property or from his or her earnings during marriage. Broad scope is granted to husbands and wives to enter into marital property agreements which may vary the effect of the act. Marital property can be held in survivorship form or transferred to trust without losing its marital property characteristics if this is what the spouses want.
>
> The act is a property act, not a divorce act. Therefore, to use Reporter Cantwell's metaphor [Cantwell is a member of the Drafting Committee for the act], in the event of divorce, the act takes the couple up to the steps of the courthouse, each with his or her undivided one-half interest in marital property in hand, and leaves them there. The divorce law, and whatever power of equitable distribution the state has given to the court, then takes over. Because the act is a property act, at death of either spouse, that spouse has power of testamentary disposition over his or her undivided one-half interest in the couple's marital property.[19]

William Cantwell, chairman of the Bar Committee on the Uniform Marital Property Act, had this to say in an interview with financial columnist Jane Bryant Quinn:

> Under equitable distribution, it shouldn't matter which spouse formally owns the property. In practice it matters very much. "It's the psychology of it," says William Cantwell, Denver attorney and author of the UMPA. "If the husband has the investments in his name and a court tells him to give half to his wife, he'll think he's been taken to the cleaners. He resents being divested of his property,

and may make it hard for his wife to collect. But if the couple knows right from the start of the marriage that half of the property belongs to each, they're more comfortable about making a fair distribution."[20]

A STATE OF FLUX

Up for grabs! This expression may be just the way to summarize divorce property distribution. State legislatures and courts have come a long way from the common law precepts and mores of our early colonial days. There is, in fact, a longing look cast more and more at the marital property system that prevails in the community property states. The Uniform Marital Property Act is a model for states to adopt or build upon in revising their statutes to bring the common law and community property systems more in line with each other, while at the same time eliminating the antiquated gender-based distortions in each of these systems. However, courts today are still referring to arguments for and against passage of the Married Women's Property Acts, arguments that were being presented more than 100 years ago! So don't look for immediate alignment of all state legislatures behind the uniform marital property legislation. Besides, even if unanimity in the attitudes of states toward marital property does develop, there will still be a wide divergence in the solutions to marital property division in marital dissolution. A lot of property might still be "up for grabs."

NOTES

[1]Both statements from *General Explanation of the Economic Recovery Tax Act of 1981*, prepared by the staff of the Joint Committee on Taxation, December 31, 1981 (Washington, D.C.: U.S. Government Printing Office, 1981).

[2]41 D.L.R.3d at 376, 13 R.F.L. at 194. Cited in Carol S. Bruch, "Property Rights of De Facto Spouses Including Thoughts on the Value of Homemakers' Services," in *Fathers, Husbands, and Lovers—Legal Rights and Responsibilities* (Chicago: American Bar Association, Section of Family Law, 1979).

[3]Committee on Civil and Political Rights, *Report to the President's Commission on the Status of Women* (1963, Washington, D.C.: U.S. Government Printing Office), p. 15.

[4]*Carpenter v. Carpenter*, 657 P.2d 646 (Okla. 1983).

[5]Pub. L. No. 97-252, 96 Stat. 718, 730-35 (1982).

[6]*McCarty v. McCarty*, 453 U.S. 210 (1981).

[7]*Smith v. Smith*, 458 A.2d 711 (1983), 9 *Fam. L. Rep.* 2371 (Del. Fam. Ct., March 14, 1983).

[8]IRC Sec. 408(d) (6).

[9]Davis—T.C. Davis, 62-2 USTCP9509, 370 U.S. 65, 82 S. Ct. 1190, 1962.

[10]Senate Finance Committee Report, as reported in *Retirement Equity Act of 1984—Law and Explanation* (Chicago: Commerce Clearing House, 1984).

[11]*Cousins v. Cousins* (Tex. App.), 595 S.W.2d 172 (1980) (Oklahoma law); *Triebelhorn v. Turzanski* (Sup. Ct. Colo.), 379 P.2d 757 (1962). Referred to in *Retirement Benefits and Divorce* (Chicago: Commerce Clearing House, 1984), p. 23.

[12]IRC Sec. 1041.

[13]"Explanation of Divorce Provisions," in *Tax Reform Act of 1984* (Chicago: Commerce Clearing House, 1984), p. 16.

[14]In *re Sullivan*, 134 Cal. App. 3d 634, 184 *Cal. Rptr.* 796 (1982) *Family Law Quarterly* 17, no. 4 (Winter 1984), p. 389.

[15]*Family Law Quarterly* 17, no. 4 (Winter 1984), pp. 388-89.

[16]*Family Law Quarterly* 16, no. 3 (Fall, 1982), Elizabeth Smith Beninger and Jeanne Wielage Smith, "Career Opportunity Cost: A Factor in Spousal Support Determination," p. 201.

[17]*Birkel v. Birkel*, 9 FLR 1049 (Pa. 1982). Mentioned in Gary N. Skoloff, "Contribution Is Key to Establishing an Interest in Premarital Assets," *National Law Journal*, June 6, 1983 pp. 22-23.

[18]*Peddy v. Montgomery*, 345 So. 2d 631.

[19]Mary Moers Wenig, "The Marital Property Act," *Probate and Property* 12, no. 1 (Summer 1983), p. 9. Reprinted with permission of the American Bar Association from *Probate and Property Newsletter*, a publication of the Real Property, Probate and Trust Law Section.

[20]"Shared Property Ownership Should Be Part of Marriage Laws," *Washington Post*, August 22, 1983, Business Section, p. 50.

CHAPTER EIGHT

Second Marriages

TRADITIONAL MARRIAGE

The traditional first marriage is the one with the bride in a long white dress, the bridegroom and ushers in dark blue, white, gray, light blue, or you-name-it formal outfits, the bridesmaids in pastels, a flower girl sprinkling petals as she goes down the aisle, a catered reception, a fancy dinner, music, dancing, and so forth (or at least some version of this)—all paid for by the father of the bride. The "traditional" thing about the marriage is that it really is the first—for both parties.

The traditional second marriage occurs years later. The scenario is more subdued. Perhaps the bride is in a beige long-sleeved, daytime-length afternoon dress, the bridegroom in a dark business suit. Adult children of both parties attend the wedding. After champagne and tiny sandwiches, the couple drives away in his Cadillac Seville. He paid the bills.

In the "traditional" second marriage, the parties have each lost a first spouse to death. After all, marriage traditionally ended that way, did it not? There are, of course, many variations of the pre-second-marital life situation of the participants. Maybe one was never married or had been divorced. Maybe one has young children by a deceased spouse and the new spouse adopts those children as his or her own. The age of the spouses is a significant factor. However, we will focus our discussion on the *really* traditional situation, in which *property* is an important part of the pre-second-wedding plans, both prospective spouses are widowed and have children, and each prospective spouse has property that he or she wishes to leave to his or her own children. The property was accumulated during the prior marriage, and the original partner, who was the father or mother of the children, certainly hoped that his or her children would inherit it.

THE EFFECT OF STATE ELECTIVE SHARE LAWS

Since laws, as drafted, cannot cover all of the possible exceptions that might make them fairer or more realistic, individuals covered by a particular law sometimes take actions to create, through agreement, their own exceptions. If these agreements tend to provide satisfactory solutions to potential controversies and are not illegal, they will usually be given weight by state courts. For example, some states provide that a surviving spouse has a "right of election to take an elective share of the estate" of the decedent spouse (approximately one third or some other specifically spelled-out proportion). Why an election? As we saw in Chapter Three, according to the laws of most states, it is impossible to disinherit a spouse. If a will is drawn up and *no share* is left to the surviving spouse, in every state that "left-out" spouse may "elect" to take a statutory share. The statutory share is usually the share that the statute books designate as the surviving spouse's share in case the decedent spouse died "intestate." Dying intestate means dying without leaving a will. In that case, various portions are left to a surviving spouse, children, parents, and so forth. Do you wish to disinherit your son? You may do so in most states by leaving him out of your will. (Of course, he may sue your lawyers or someone else whom he might blame for influencing you to disinherit him, but he will usually find no statutory right to a share of your estate unless you die without a will.) On the other hand, your spouse has a statutory right to a share. What, then, is the "exception" to the law that people create by their own agreements? The exception provides for the avoidance of the statutory forced share by an antenuptial agreement whereby one or both parties to the agreement promise not to exercise the election to take against the will.

ANTENUPTIAL AGREEMENT

An antenuptial agreement is a contract between a man and a woman entered into before marriage, in contemplation of the marriage and in consideration of the marriage, whereby the property rights of the prospective spouses are determined or whereby property is earmarked for one or both of them or their children. An antenuptial agreement has been held valid if it is fair and if it has been fairly made by individuals legally competent to contract. In an antenuptial agreement, the parties may vary or rearrange or relinquish rights and interests that they would otherwise acquire in each other's property and estate by reason of the marriage. Most important, they may agree to forgo their respective rights to election to take against each other's estate.

Courts have generally approved of antenuptial agreements, if properly made, because such agreements promote marital tranquillity and avoid disputes concerning property. There are certain requirements: there should be full disclosure of each party's financial worth; there must be evidence of good faith, candor, and sincerity in matters related to the agreement; there must be no coercion. Suppose he is a wealthy, propertied oilman and she is his secretary, beautiful but possessing only her clothes? Courts have held that if the provision for the wife in an antenuptial agreement is disproportionate to the extent and value of the husband's estate, the presumption arises that he intended to minimize or conceal his wealth. Suppose they are married for 10 years, living lavishly, and then he dies and she regrets signing the antenuptial agreement, which provided her with $500 a month for a few years after his death—and nothing more. What then? Is she locked into a bad bargain? Not necessarily. Courts have sometimes held that the proper measure of fairness in an agreement of this type is whether the provision made for the wife will enable her to live comfortably, if she survives her husband, in substantially the same way that she lived with him during their marriage. Bear in mind, though, that courts vary widely in interpreting these agreements.

IS A WRITTEN AGREEMENT NECESSARY?

Consider a situation in which the parties to a prospective second marriage hold each other in the highest degree of love and esteem but, perhaps because of total reliance on their very compatibility, fail to formalize their verbal promises to each other to respect the wishes of the other in the matter of leaving the property owned by each partner to the children of the original spouse's late husband or wife. Certain acts can be performed during a marriage from which a court could find an intention to behave as though a written antenuptial agreement had been entered into. Certain acts (gifts of property, registering securities in joint names with right of survivorship, etc.) could be found to constitute consideration for the marriage and for the surviving spouse's forbearance from exercising the statutory right of any such surviving spouse who has been disinherited in a will to take against the will. Evidence of actions supporting an *oral* antenuptial agreement between the parties might be put forth, for example, by adult children opposing the widow's (or widower's) reaching for a statutory share. This, of course, is in the realm of family squabbles that no one wants to see materialize. Written agreements might avoid such unpleasant situations. A written agreement, in fact, might negate any inference that an implied, unwritten agreement existed. As we saw in Chapter Five, in the case of a nonmarital arrangement a written contract eliminates doubt that the partners *contracted* regarding their *property* prior to the nonmarital event, and the same reason might exist for entering into a written contract prior to a second marriage.

For example, Bill, a widower, meets charming widow, Mary. After an appropriate sedate courtship, these two mature people decide to get married. Bill is more affluent than Mary. Each has grown (and married) children and some grandchildren. Mary's lawyer drafts an antenuptial agreement somewhat in this form (from the author's files):

SAMPLE OF ANTENUPTIAL AGREEMENT

WHEREAS MARY _____ and BILL _____ intend to be married within a short time, and

WHEREAS BILL and MARY have disclosed to each other the nature and extent of their various property interests, sources of income, and general financial condition, and

WHEREAS BILL desires to make a reasonable and sufficient provision for MARY in release of and in full satisfaction of all rights which after their marriage MARY might or could have, by reason of the marriage, in the property which BILL now has or may hereafter acquire, or in his estate upon his death, and

WHEREAS MARY desires to accept this provision in lieu of all rights which she would otherwise acquire, by reason of the marriage, in the property or estate of BILL,

IT IS THEREFORE AGREED:

(1) RELEASE OF MARITAL RIGHTS. MARY hereby waives and releases all rights including, but not limited to, dower, statutory allowance in lieu of dower, distributive share, right of election against a will, widow's allowances, or otherwise, which she may acquire by reason of her marriage to BILL in any property owned by him at any time or by his estate upon his death. This release is executed in consideration of the payment expressed in (2) below.

(2) PAYMENT FROM ESTATE. If MARY survives BILL as his lawful widow, there shall be paid to her from the estate of BILL outright, free of any estate or inheritance taxes, the greater of $_____
or_____ percent of the "net estate" of BILL. Such sum shall be paid to MARY as soon as may be practicable. Until so paid, such sum shall constitute a charge upon the sum in lieu of all other claims, statutory or otherwise, that she may have against the estate of BILL by reason of their marriage. For the purpose of this agreement, "net estate" shall mean the residue remaining in the estate after the deduction of all valid other debts and funeral and administration expenses, but not any liability for estate or inheritance taxes.

(3) NECESSARY DOCUMENTS. Each party shall execute and deliver whatever additional instruments may be required in order to carry out the intention of this agreement, and shall execute and deliver any deeds or other documents in order that good title to any property can be conveyed by BILL free from any claim of MARY acquired by reason of this marriage. BILL shall execute a will, or a codicil to an existing will, embodying the obligations contained in this agreement.

(4) TRANSFERS BETWEEN THE PARTIES. Notwithstanding the provisions of this agreement, any other rights acquired by MARY by virtue of any transfer or conveyance of property by BILL to her during his lifetime, or by will upon his death, shall not be limited or restricted in any way.

(5) SEPARATE PROPERTY. Except as herein provided, each party shall have complete control of his or her separate property, and may enjoy and dispose of such property in the same manner as if the marriage had not taken place. This provision shall apply to all property now owned by either of the parties and to all property which either of them may hereafter acquire in an individual capacity; provided that BILL shall not, in the absence of a written consent by MARY, transfer any property for less than full consideration in money or money's worth if at the time

of such transfer, or imminent thereto, his net worth is less than $_____.

(6) RELEASE OF PROPERTY RIGHTS BY HUSBAND. BILL releases all rights in the property or estate of MARY which he might have by reason of their marriage, whether by way of curtesy, statutory allowance, intestate share, or election to take against her will, under the laws of any jurisdiction that may be applicable.

(7) DISCLOSURE OF FACTS. BILL acknowledges that he has disclosed his full net worth to MARY and that such net worth is in excess of $_____. BILL acknowledges that the present approximate net worth of MARY has been disclosed to him and that such net worth is in the approximate amount of $_____. MARY and BILL acknowledge that they have had the advice of independent counsel and that they are entering into this agreement freely and with a full understanding of its provisions.

(8) EFFECTIVE PERIOD. This agreement shall become effective upon the marriage of the parties and shall bind the parties and their respective heirs, executors, and administrators, unless the marriage is legally dissolved. For the purpose of this agreement, in the event of a common disaster MARY shall be presumed to have predeceased BILL.

(9) ENTIRE UNDERSTANDING. This agreement contains the entire understanding of the parties, no representations or promises having been made except those set forth herein.

IN WITNESS WHEREOF, the parties have signed, sealed, and acknowledged this agreement on the day and year first above written.

_____
BILL   (SEAL)

_____
MARY   (SEAL)

Please note: This document contains provisions protecting Mary. Bill's lawyer will draft clauses to protect his interests.

Unfortunately, in the case of Bill and Mary the agreement was never negotiated. Years later, Bill died. Sadly, a family squabble ensued. The adult children proposed to deal "fairly" with the new widow as they had had a comfortable relationship with her during the years of the marriage to their father. However, everyone had a different concept of what was "fair." During the eight years of her marriage to Bill, Mary had provided him with love and companionship and had extended her affection and attention to an enlarged family circle that included his sons and their wives and several grandchildren. Mary ministered to Bill's needs during illness and thus relieved family members of these chores. The family had recognized these facts and had expressed appreciation to Mary on several occasions. Alas, it seems that Mary's contribution of her physical and emotional strength was rewarded with just that—appreciation.

It appears that after having failed to enter into a written agreement prior to his marriage to Mary, Bill had denuded himself of his wealth by lifetime gifts to his children and grandchildren during the time that he and Mary were married. Of course, although no share was left to her in Bill's will, Mary could have availed herself of the privilege of taking a statutory share of her late husband's estate (by taking "against the will" in which no share was left to her), but it soon became apparent that this once wealthy gentleman had died almost a pauper.

A clause like Paragraph (5) of the sample agreement might have prevented this result. Bill had made gifts to his children that reduced his net worth to an insignificant amount. An ill person might, in panic or by clearheaded design, do just that. The wife in this scenario had no agreement to protect her and was therefore left out in the cold. Electing to take a statutory share of a minimal estate would have gained her nothing, and the will provided her with the same zero. The adult children proposed to compensate her in a totally inadequate manner. She contemplated a suit for fraud but realized that there was little to be gained. She had no written agreement to protect her, so she accepted the unfair hand that she had been dealt. What if she had refused to go through with the marriage unless the husband entered into a written agreement? Probably, no marriage. In retrospect, she views the whole experience with distaste.

This is only one example of a possible way in which these two people of past middle age might have handled their premarital property planning in order to avoid later unpleasantness with adult children. The facts might be entirely different. The classic case is that of the rich widow who, due to inexperience in financial matters, turns her inherited fortune over to her new husband, who then "invests" (squanders, loses?) it. In such a case, her children are at peril that their potential inheritance from their father will never reach their hands. Therefore, they will want to encourage a premarital agreement reserving assets, including even a trust arrangement.

A DIFFERENT ARRANGEMENT

The discussion above has not touched on federal estate taxes. However, taxes on transfers between spouses were very much on the minds of Congress when it enacted the Economic Recovery Tax Act of 1981. That was the act, remember, that eliminated transfer taxes between spouses. The 100 percent marital deduction! Regardless of whether the spouse was first, second, or third, as was mentioned in Chapter Six, a new type of trust came into existence simultaneously with the 100 percent marital deduction. A review of the typical estate-planning advice for a married couple is in order at this point. Before the Economic Recovery Tax Act of 1981, people of even a modest amount of wealth usually sought the advice of tax lawyers in drawing up wills. Everyone had an idea that there was a certain way to do things so that federal estate taxes could be minimized; and responsible people felt morally obligated to listen to their estate-planning advisers in order to see that family accumulations went to the next generation and not to Uncle Sam. The goal of these advisers was to "save the second tax." (The "second tax," of course, was the possible tax on the assets that were not used up by the surviving spouse and so became a part of that spouse's estate and therefore might be taxed again before the next generation got its hands on it.) This was accomplished by means of a trust giving the "principal" to a trustee for the next in line (presumably the children), with the income from that principal being periodically paid to the spouse (the widow in most planning scenarios) for life. If the principal was of an amount large enough to incur a federal estate tax, the tax on the transfer of the principal would be paid out but would occur only once.

It was complicated planning. As explained in Chapter Six, assets that "qualified" for the marital deduction might also be (and frequently were) placed in a trust, with income only to the widow, but there was a catch. *She* had to have control and be able to designate her beneficiaries. The goal of the drafters of estate tax legislation is to pinpoint *ownership* so that the *owner's estate* will be taxed. Normally, in a transfer of this sort it was completely untenable for a gift to a spouse to "qualify" for the marital deduction if that gift provided for "ownership" in the hands of a trustee, with the spouse receiving *income only for life (a life estate)*. Whether the marital deduction was the old 50 percent or the new 100 percent, unless the surviving spouse *actually* or constructively *owned* the property, the value of that property did not "qualify." This is what is meant by "qualifying." In tax terms, "qualify" means "be eligible for."

QUALIFIED TERMINABLE INTEREST PROPERTY TRUST

The Tax Act of 1981 changed all that. Congress included in the law provisions that overturned estate tax and property philosophies that had been long in place. To state it simply: As a result of this legislation, a spouse (read "husband") can now give or will a surviving spouse (wife) an *income-only interest for life and not the property itself* and the whole thing will "qualify" for the 100 percent marital deduction, so such a transfer *will incur no federal tax*. The spouse who does the giving (by visiting his lawyer's office while the lawyer spells all of this out for him and then drafts the will accordingly) may now designate *his* heirs as the recipients of the *principal* when the spouse receiving the *income* dies and her life-income interest is thus terminated.

The mechanics are complicated, but, simply stated, such a transfer is accomplished by means of a trust. The nomenclature is "qualified terminable interest property trust." Broken down, it states that property transferred by such a means is "qualified" (eligible) for the 100 percent marital deduction (no federal estate tax on transfer to a spouse) even though the property being transferred is an *interest only* (remember the distinction between an interest and total ownership pointed out in Chapter 1) and the "interest" ends with the end of the life of the holder of such an interest. The legal title to the property *principal* is in the trustee, who will dole out the income from the property for the life of the holder of the *income-only interest*.

Remember when you were a child and your Aunt Alice gave you $50 for a birthday present and your father said he would hold the $50 and let you have the interest for spending money? He opened a bank account with his name as trustee for you, as beneficiary, and he let you see the interest as the numbers were recorded on the passbook. Perhaps you were given the pennies to spend—or were allowed to watch the miracle of compound interest. (One day you probably received the $50, which you now know was principal.) The spouse having an income-only interest is in a similar position vis-à-vis the principal—although it will never be hers because her total interest ends with her death.

There are some who believe that the unique concept of "qualified terminable interest property" was enacted as part of the Tax Act of 1981 because there are a number of divorced congressmen, just as there are a lot of divorced constituents. The opinion has been expressed that these divorced congressmen might have decided on their own behalf or on behalf of their divorced constituents to do something about the unfettered control that was about to be allowed spouses who inherited wealth from their deceased spouses and therefore scotched that freedom by allowing terminable interests (lifetime interests only) to *qualify* for the marital deduction. One can see that in the case of a second marriage a husband might be torn between wanting to leave *something* for the second wife and yet wishing to preserve the bulk of his assets for *his* children.

It should be noted that the privilege of establishing a qualified terminable interest property trust (dubbed "QTIP" by lawyers and others dealing with this technique for property transfer) may be used for *part* or *all* of an estate. For example, depending on circumstances, each participant in a second marriage could transfer to the other a portion of assets on an income-only basis, while designating that the principal of that portion plus all other assets are to be transferred to each spouse's own children. Second marriages have always provided work for tax and estate-planning lawyers. Although the (new) QTIP trust might serve a useful, but limited, purpose in certain special situations, the (old) ante-nuptial agreement entered into before a second marriage is a time-tested common device for assuring that inheritances go to each partner's own children. The two techniques are not the same. A lawyer would help you determine which might be preferable for your purposes.

SEE YOUR LAWYER

Any prospective participants in a second marriage where there is a potential conflict over the ways in which to accomplish the desire of either or both future marriage partners to preserve pre-second-marriage property for pre-second-marriage children should see a lawyer. The above discussion has only scratched the surface of the

QTIP technique, which is essentially only one method of accomplishing this purpose. It is an extremely complicated provision of the tax law. The law provided that by doing things "thus and so," one could *seem* to transfer largesse to a surviving spouse while preserving the tax-free interspousal tax privilege. Of course, this works both ways. Let us say that *she* is the wealthy one. In that case, *she* would be the donor of the income-only interest to *him*. (Will he docilely accept a "no control of principal" admonition?) Thus far, however, in most cases there has been a fear lest *his* fortune find its way into *her* hands.

It might seem that a widow would welcome a trust giving a surviving spouse (wife) an income-only interest in certain property for life and then transferring the property that produced the income to the late husband's own children. Perhaps. The difficulty with this seemingly attractive inheritance is with the "income-only" aspect. The words are loaded with hazards. People have a childlike faith in anything labeled a "trust" and think that a "trust" providing "income only" to a beneficiary certainly must be a money tree that one only has to shake occasionally (monthly, annually, etc., according to the terms of the document) in order to provide a constant shower of "income." If that were the case, we could all turn our property over to trustees with directions as to where to send the income.

Remember that the grieving widow who is the beneficiary of an "income-only" interest in property may receive *nothing* if the property is mismanaged, if the market changes, if the income dries up, and so forth. Court dockets occasionally contain lawsuits against trustees for mismanagement of trust property. If one adheres to the doctrine of having *control* over one's own property, it could be frustrating to find that the inheritor of QTIP assets cannot control his or her investment, cannot will the assets, and cannot even *give* those assets away without triggering a gift tax. A surviving spouse who is in this exact spot would have no recourse; the law states that once established by direction in a will, such an arrangement is irrevocable. For some, it might be preferable to have a *smaller* gift of property outright than a *larger* principal providing "income only" (or to elect a statutory share against the will). Additionally, it should be remembered that "trusts" spell "fees." There are trustees' fees, accountants' fees for annual fiduciary tax returns, and the like.

It is very possible that QTIP trust provisions are cropping up more and more in the newly drafted or revised wills of affluent husbands who are contemplating marriage with charming (and less affluent) widows. This seems like a made-to-order technique for enabling the second husband to appear generous while in actuality preserving the very thing that the second marriage might have hazarded—an eventual gift of his property to his children. It might also be desirable to spell out the understanding of the parties in an antenuptial agreement. Both parties should understand what the technical language in the will means if there is a QTIP clause—and *how it would work*. The following words might be helpful:

> The possible effects of a QTIP transfer should be explained to a client interested in this type of transfer for a gift or bequest to a spouse, . . . the lawyer should have the client's spouse present at a three-way conference (consisting of lawyer, client, and client's spouse), a record should be on file showing the information imparted to the client and to the spouse who might be the income beneficiary of a qualified terminable interest, together with evidence of acquiescence. Informing ultimate beneficiaries might not be practical, although it would be helpful.[1]

Do not forget that the children are waiting in the wings for the property to finally become theirs when the income-only holder dies and that transfer taxes will then have to be paid, if owed, thus diminishing their ultimate inheritance.

OTHER USES OF QTIP TRUSTS

In certain situations, QTIP trusts might simplify estate administration. For example, an elderly husband and wife might be suitable clients for QTIP trust planning if their ultimate beneficiaries are the same and the surviving spouse might not wish to manage the property. Provision for a QTIP trust in a will might eliminate or simplify administration of the second estate while preserving the estate tax advantage of the 100 percent marital deduction. As in the case of an outright bequest to the surviving spouse, there would be no federal estate tax until the second death. Just now being proposed—and, indeed, being written into wills—are some new and complicated provisions utilizing such a trust combined with other bequests following the life estate of the surviving spouse (such as a gift to a charitable organization). Remember, however, that provision for a *trust* to handle property bequeathed to a surviving spouse is not necessary or (in most cases) desirable in order to avoid the federal estate tax on the death of the first spouse. Congress took care of that in enacting the 100 percent marital deduction. Remember also that in today's world the surviving wife is just as likely to be a capable money and investment handler as her late husband.

Some of the technically convoluted wills utilizing the QTIP trust contain language that is almost incapable of being understood by even the most experienced corporate executor. Future surviving spouses may be the ones to find out that they've been "had." If there is anything in the way of income, it will first have to be shared with the trustees administering the trust property. Disgruntled future heirs might be waiting for the income beneficiary to die until *they* inherit. If the surviving spouse decides that such antagonism is too much to live with and decides to give away the life income estate, there could be a gift tax obligation. The amount of tax paid could be recovered from those who received the gift—but it might take a lawsuit to do it!

WHY DISCUSS THIS COMPLICATED DEVICE? LET THE LAWYERS HANDLE IT!

Precisely why this topic is being discussed here. The client or clients who go into the lawyers' mahogany-paneled conference room without the slightest idea that this device exists could be bowled over either because it sounds too technical for ordinary people to understand (therefore, don't worry, the lawyers know what they're doing) or because it sounds like just what they've been looking for before jumping into a second marriage. Mr. Client will explain it all to the attractive Mrs. X. Both Mr. Client and Mrs. X now know enough (hopefully) to at least ask a few questions and demand a few explanations of what to expect after the wedding. A wife who belatedly learns that her inheritance from a husband will be in the form of an income-only trust might take a dim view of the whole arrangement.

NOTE

[1]Margaret B. Schulman, "How and When to Use the New Marital Deduction Qualified Terminable Interest Trust," *Taxation for Lawyers*, January–February 1982, p. 196.

CHAPTER NINE

Property Relationships with Adult Children and Others (Not Spouses)

JUNIOR GROWS UP

Who could believe that that darling tow-headed little boy would grow up to be a physical giant towering over you and a business and financial genius as well! "That son of mine knows everything!" Well, almost. No law or custom decrees that you must defer to the ideas of the next generation, even though it is an adult generation. As we saw in the last chapter, a primary concern of our adult children is that they inherit whatever we have for them to inherit. Presuming that there are a comfortable number of valuable assets to be concerned with and presuming that the future inheritors of your wealth are not independently wealthy beyond your wildest dreams, this is a legitimate family matter.

GIFTS

In Chapter Six, "Marriage," we dealt with some estate-planning concepts and with the tie-in between gifts and estates. Gifts have generally been presumed to relate to *lifetime* transfers of money or property. Such gifts are called "*inter vivos*." Another type of gift occurs when property is *willed* to another. In this case, the gift does not become complete until the death of the donor. Such gifts are called "testamentary." Both types of gifts are also called "transfers." As we have seen, Congress in 1976 equalized the federal taxes on transfers by gifts during life and at death. While wealthy people who wish to do so may still make gifts in order to remove the potential appreciation of an asset from a future estate and the income from that asset from their income tax bracket, many of them usually stay within the $10,000 annual gift tax exclusion ($20,000 for married donors who join in making the gift). There is no law that says you may make a gift of *only* up to $10,000 a year to each of your donees. (Incidentally, you may give $10,000 a year to each of *any number* of donees—everyone in the telephone book if you wish—without incurring a transfer tax.) Furthermore, no actual out-of-pocket tax is paid on the gift to a donee that is valued above the $10,000 exclusion. The tax is computed, to be sure, and a gift tax return is filed, but the tax you would have paid is reduced by the total *credit* for estate and gift taxes that Congress enacted in 1981, which will be fully phased in by 1987 (and remain the same until changed again by law).

Here is how it works: A gift of more than $10,000 to any one individual in a year (or $20,000 for a joint gift by husband and wife) requires reporting and can incur a gift tax. The tax is computed on the basis of the same rate schedule that applies to testamentary transfers (gifts that occur at the death of the donor). The current schedule is listed below:

1984 Unified Gift and Estate Tax Rates

| If the Taxable Amount Is— | | The Tax Is— | | |
Over	But Not Over	This—	Plus Percent	Over
$ 0	$ 10,000	$ 0	18	$ 0
10,000	20,000	1,800	20	10,000
20,000	40,000	3,800	22	20,000
40,000	60,000	8,200	24	40,000
60,000	80,000	13,000	26	60,000
80,000	100,000	18,200	28	80,000
100,000	150,000	23,800	30	100,000
150,000	250,000	38,800	32	150,000
250,000	500,000	70,800	34	250,000
500,000	750,000	155,800	37	500,000
750,000	1,000,000	248,300	39	750,000
1,000,000	1,250,000	345,800	41	1,000,000
1,250,000	1,500,000	448,300	43	1,250,000
1,500,000	2,000,000	555,800	45	1,500,000
2,000,000	2,500,000	780,800	49	2,000,000
2,500,000	3,000,000	1,025,800	53	2,500,000
3,000,000		1,290,800	55	3,000,000

SOURCE: J. K. Lasser, *Your Income Tax, 1985* (New York: Simon & Schuster, 1985), p. 298. © 1984. J. K. Lasser Tax Institute. Reprinted by permission of Simon & Schuster, Inc.

A taxable gift occurs if the value of the gift is over $10,000. A "tentative tax" figure is arrived at by referring to the tax rate table. The unified credit (see Chapter Two) is then applied to this figure (called tentative tax) and if anything remains *after* subtraction of the credit, *that* would be the tax. So you can see, the gift would have to be quite large to incur a tax. However, by making lifetime gifts and dipping into the unified credit, the donor might be handing on to his heirs an estate tax problem that would not have existed if the lifetime gifts had not been made. Both lifetime transfers and transfers made at death are cumulated for estate tax rate purposes. However, those gifts that were *not* in excess of the $10,000–20,000 *annual exclusion* become forgettable items. You never have to account for such gifts.

Why go into these complicated details? Anyone wealthy enough to make sizable and potentially taxable gifts will surely see his or her tax adviser. If you are a less wealthy donor, however, it is useful to know that, for example, if you give your son $10,000 and his wife $10,000 because they are buying a home and they consider you parsimonious because you can really afford to give them $50,000, you can say: "Do you want it now, or wouldn't you rather have the entire credit to apply later, so that perhaps there will be no estate tax to pay?" When your children realize how the system works, they may not grumble over your hoarding the unified credit so that *they* will reap the benefits of having a *full* unified credit to apply to a tentative tax against your ultimate estate. It is difficult for people to understand that saving the unified credit does nothing for the donor. After all, he is not out of pocket anything if a taxable gift increases the potential estate tax by using an amount of the unified credit. Some advisers believe it is estate planning of the most generous sort to work out *lifetime* gifts while preserving the unified credit to decrease the impact of federal taxes on an estate.

TAPPING THE UNIFIED CREDIT

What if you do see an advantage in a taxable lifetime gift? That could occur in an inflationary period when a gift of real estate, for example, may continue to rise in value *after* the gift has been made. The appreciation now belongs to the donee and will never be taxed as part of your estate. If that or some similar situation exists because of the nature of the gift property, remember that a federal gift tax return must be filed. (Also, a state tax return must be filed if the state law requires it and if the state imposes a gift tax. Some do not.) This may be an overlooked item when a parent conveys a personal residence to a child.

The preparation of a federal gift tax return is a detail not to be missed. This return can establish the value of the gift. There is an interesting quirk in the law here. If no gift tax is paid, the statute of limitations will not run against a possible audit (and challenge as to value) by IRS. If the tax is not paid because the tax credit absorbs it, there will be no beginning date for the statute of limitations to run against. This is referred to as "tolling the statute." The statute of limitations *never* runs if a tax return is required to be filed and is never filed. What can happen, then, years later, is that a gift for which no gift tax return was filed will have to be reported on an estate tax return. At that time, the value of the transfer might be questioned. Even if there is a gift tax return on file and no tax was paid at the time of the gift, it is still possible for an auditor to question the stated value. As a consequence, it is necessary to maintain adequate records to document the value of gifts (especially if no gift tax was paid, because the tax is covered by the unified credit).

WHEN A LIFETIME GIFT BECOMES PART OF YOUR ESTATE

As we saw in Chapter Two, a word of caution is in order. Regardless of what *you* think, attention must be paid to IRS rules. If you "give" your house away, even if you report this on a gift tax return, state the fair market value on the date of the gift, and pay a gift tax on the transfer, the Internal Revenue Service may come along as an uninvited participant when your estate is settled and say that the value is included in your estate *because you continued to live there without paying rent* (transfer with retained interest)!

This is a frequent scenario: Widow lives in family home (now having an inflated price), which she wants to give to her daughter. The house is worth $250,000. Her attorney prepares a gift tax return, and a title company prepares a deed conveying the property to the daughter. No gift tax is paid to the federal government, because the tax, which would have been $70,800 in 1985, is balanced against a unified credit amount of $121,800. The widow dies in 1987. Her estate (without including the house) is valued at $600,000. It would appear that no estate taxes are due. However, an estate tax auditor notes that the house conveyed in 1985 was a "transfer with retained interest." It might be that the transaction as a gift is negated for estate tax computation purposes because *after* conveying the house to her daughter, the mother lived in it rent-free until she died. Although the transfer to the daughter in 1985 avoids probate, the house, now valued in 1987, becomes an estate asset. Presume a value for the house of $260,000. When this amount is added to the $600,000 that appeared on the estate tax return, the estate becomes valued by IRS at $860,000. The Transfer Tax Rate Schedule Table designates a tax of $248,300 on $750,000, plus 39 percent on the excess over $750,000. The tax on the excess is $42,900. We now have the following:

Step 1: $248,300
       +42,900
      $291,200 tentative tax

Step 2: $291,200
     −192,800 unified credit
    $ 98,400 tax

This is the kind of thing that can happen when a lifetime gift is thrown back into the estate for estate tax purposes. There are various techniques for avoiding such a tax burden on the estate. It would be desirable to consult a tax attorney when involved in such planning. (Please remember that the example is oversimplified.)

JOINT TENANCIES—A SOLUTION OR AN ADDED PROBLEM?

Suppose the widow had conveyed the house to herself and her daughter as joint tenants with right of survivorship (JTRS). Then the problem might have been halved (assuming that state law permits severance by one joint tenant). The mother would have given away *half* of the house (assuming, of course, that she had owned it *all*) and should have been paying rent for the half of the house that was conveyed to the daughter. However, since for estate tax purposes Internal Revenue Code section 2040(a) applies a "source of the consideration" test to fix value to be reported at the death of a joint tenant, if the mother dies before the daughter, the entire value of the property (not one half) will be included in her estate. And the mother has given up more than just half of the house—she has given up her *control*. If she later wishes to sell the house, she cannot do this without the daughter's concurrence, because the daughter owns half.

Suppose the widowed mother received from her late husband's estate a rental condominium apartment that the couple had maintained as an investment. Insecure about owning this asset alone, the mother, let's call her Jane, has a title company transfer ownership to her and daughter Mary and son Sam. Mary is a divorced schoolteacher with a modest income and receiving no alimony; Sam, an unmarried importer-exporter, is outrageously "comfortable." The rental property that Jane received as an inheritance is yielding a good return. The immediate result of the new joint ownership arrangement is that the income must now be shared. Sam does not need it; Mary would like it but could get along without it; Jane, the mother, needs it all as part of the income she requires for living expenses.

If the joint ownership is JTRS (joint tenancy with right of survivorship), then on Jane's death, Mary and Sam will inherit all of the property and will own it as surviving joint tenants. The new owners are now Mary and Sam, JTRS. Sam could say, "I don't need it, Mary—you take it all," but in that case he would be making a gift and a whole host of new problems would develop. If the joint ownership established by Jane had been as tenants in common, then when Jane died, her one third would presumably have been inherited by Mary and Sam on a 50–50 basis. Thus, they would share ownership as tenants in common of their original one third and now each owns half of Jane's third, making Mary and Sam each 50 percent owners. If Sam gets married or Mary remarries and they wish their shares to go to their respective spouses, there would be no problem. If Jane had retained the property and let Mary and Sam inherit it, they would also have taken as tenants in common, as that is the way most states would interpret a will clause leaving property to heirs.

Suppose Jane had decided to create the joint ownership with her children, Sam and Mary, and then had decided after creating the joint tenancy that it would be better to sell the property. Will all of the profit be hers? No, it will belong partly to the other owners, Sam and Mary. JTRS ownership is not merely a label.

The law attaches a significance to such ownership of property that may not be what the nominal owners have in mind at all. Furthermore, the element of control again is a factor. Jane has given up *control* of her own property.

The list of complicated rules with regard to joint ownership goes on and on. There are possible gift tax consequences, estate tax consequences, actuarial computations to determine the probable number of years of "enjoyment" by each of a number of joint tenants having disparate ages (for purposes of ascertaining value), and tax consequences on the termination of a joint tenancy. The subject has been made the content of an entire book, *Joint Property,* by Alexander A. Bove, Jr.

JTRS WITH GRANDCHILD

The rules dealing with joint tenancies may also vary, depending on the *type* of property held in this fashion. As we saw in Chapter Two, when Grandmother goes to the bank and buys a CD listing herself and Grandson Michael as JTRS owners but keeps the certificate and receives the income from it as well, she has *given* nothing so far as Internal Revenue is concerned. Just as with retaining a home and living there after "giving" it away, Grandmother in buying a CD jointly for herself and someone else *with her money* has made a "transfer with retained interest." The transfer would be a gift only at her death. Anything *given at death* would be an estate asset for estate tax purposes. There is an effect, however, that might be what Grandmother had in mind anyway. The JTRS CD that she held is immediately transferable to Grandson Michael on Grandmother's death. Sometimes the "best-laid plans" go astray. Suppose Michael later acquires a little sister and Grandmother dies thereafter before she has had a chance to extend her largesse to her newest grandchild? Unintentionally, improper designation of assets intended as gifts can either *distort* or *implement* an estate plan. While the *size* of the estate may not present a federal tax problem, the donor of a gift would like to know something about the federal and state rules that might apply, so that in the case of a small gift (at least a gift within the $10,000 exclusion) an attorney need not be consulted.

Here are some guidelines.

"LIFETIME" GIFTS WITH RETAINED INTEREST

As we have seen, when you give property away but retain some rights or control over it, the law requires that the property be included in your estate. The rights or control could include such things as keeping income from property after giving it away, living in real property (this means retaining a "life estate"), retaining the right to revoke the gift, and retaining the right to change the beneficiary of the property (as beneficiary of life insurance even if the policy is given away).

JOINT BANK ACCOUNTS

Either party may withdraw money from a joint bank account. If you have put all of the money in, you may withdraw it at any time. If you have put all of the money in and your joint owner withdraws money, then you have made a gift to the joint owner in the amount withdrawn. This holds true *unless* the account is a "convenience account." In that case, either party may put money in or take money out or write checks, on a joint account, and if no gift is intended, there is no gift when the party who puts *less in* takes *more out*.

U.S. SAVINGS BONDS

To buy a U.S. savings bond for a donee, you must register the bond in the donee's name when the bond is purchased. This makes the bond an immediate gift. If the donee is a minor, then the form is: "_____, Custodian for _____, a Minor, under (State) Uniform Gifts to Minors Act." The delivery to a donee of bonds registered in your name will not transfer them to the donee. You must have the bonds reregistered. You are liable for the tax on interest earned on the bonds while they are registered in your name, and you must report such interest on your income tax return.

SECURITIES

Securities registered in the name of your donee clearly represent a gift. Your donee must establish an account at your brokerage firm (or you will do it for him). If you transfer certificates to your donee, you must endorse the certificates to your broker and the transfer of ownership is complete when the corporation's transfer agent records the transfer on its record books.

SECURITIES IN A "STREET" NAME

A "street" name is used to deal on margin or to facilitate trading. If you establish such an account with your funds but label the account joint for yourself and another person, and the securities are still registered in the name of the broker, you have not made a gift to the other person. The gift will occur when the other person sells a security and withdraws the funds. An account in a street name is like a joint bank account set up by one person.

IMPORTANCE OF BASIS

When you give someone a security, whether by using your funds to purchase the security and labeling it joint or by making the security an outright gift, you should tell the donee your basis, that is, the price you paid for the security. If you purchase the security currently *for* the donee, the basis would be current information. If, however, you purchased 100 shares of XYZ stock a few years ago at $10 a share and the stock is selling at $25 when you give those shares to your nephew on his graduation from college, you should tell the nephew that you paid $1,000 for the shares. The value of the gift on the date of the gift is not a crucial amount for gift tax purposes unless it is over $10,000 and thus more than the gift-tax-free exclusion. However, the dollar amount that *you paid* for the stock is information that your donee must have for income tax reporting. When he sells the stock, his capital gain will be the difference between *your* basis and *his* selling price. He need not hold the stock for six months in order to qualify for long-term capital gain treatment. He may sell immediately, and so long as *your* and your donee's holding period together qualify for long-term capital gain treatment, your donee's will on the sale. (Filing a gift tax return if required or desirable for documentation purposes is the donor's obligation, and, if a taxable gift, gift tax is paid by the donor.)

This type of gift is a part of overall financial planning. Your donee nephew is presumably in a lower tax bracket than you are, and so if he sells and pays a capital gain tax on the sale, it will be at a lower rate than your tax rate would be. This is somewhat like the type of planning that goes into the contribution of an appreciated security to your favorite charity. You get the advantage of a deduction for a charitable donation on your current income tax return at the *higher value* of the security on the date of the gift. Since the charitable organization pays no income tax, any capital gain that might have occurred between the value when you purchased the security and the value when you donated it is not taxed (if you held the security for the time required for long-term capital gain treatment). Of course, the gift to your nephew is *not* deductible.

CARE OF AN ELDERLY PARENT

A time may come when planning for the care of an elderly parent is on your property-planning agenda. For one thing, establishing a short-term trust for a parent might be good planning—in somewhat the same manner as utilizing this device to transfer income to a lower-bracket child. Assume the parent is in a lower tax bracket. If that parent requires the incurrence of extensive medical expenses not covered by insurance (nursing care, for example), income transferred to the parent as taxpayer would be more likely to be eligible for the income tax deduction for medical expenses than your own greater income would (if the parent were your dependent). If property is transferred to a lower-bracket parent, so that the income from the property becomes the income of that parent, it is possible that large medical expenses or expenses for care would be fully deductible (above the 5 percent floor), whereas your own income might be too great to have those expenses make a dent above the 5 percent floor. In addition, you would have to prove that the parent was a dependent in order to claim those expenses as a deduction.

EQUITY SHARING

In Chapter Five, "Cohabitation," we discussed an arrangement for two cohabitants to share ownership of a condominium. In a similar manner, an arrangement being promoted currently for a parent and an adult child or a child and an elderly parent to purchase a residence together is the "Equity sharing" concept.

Successful businessman Tom has a son, Jim, who has just started at the bottom rung of his professional ladder. Jim has found an attractive condominium but cannot swing the down payment. Father and son buy together on a 75–25 percent basis. Tom will pay 75 percent of the down payment and make 75 percent of the mortgage payments, will qualify for the loan, and (probably) will cosign Jim's 25 percent obligation on the mortgage. But, you are saying, what about the discrepancy? That is taken care of by a rental payment from Jim to Tom at the fair market rate (but at only 75 percent of that rate because Jim owns 25 percent). The figures seem to work out. The 75 percent owner has interest payments to deduct and depreciation on the portion he rents to Jim. Jim also deducts his share of the interest on the mortgage, pays a reasonable rent but less than he would have paid if he had rented the condominium, is building up equity, and has a place to live. For ownership of this sort, Tom and Jim would be tenants in common and an agreement spelling out their respective interests should be drawn up, following the outline in Chapter Five.

This type of ownership might also work if the owners are a more affluent son and a lower-income parent. This, in fact, might be a desirable way for the parent to buy a retirement home, with the greater percentage being purchased by the child, who will inherit the property anyway.

These types of properties would have to be strictly investment properties for the more affluent purchaser (who will take the depreciation deduction), and care would have to be taken to avoid having them labeled vacation properties. The rules as to "vacation homes" are strict, and they may become stricter if any new tax legislation is passed by Congress. Nevertheless, equity sharing is a legitimate way to handle a property acquisition and provide family benefits. Further investigation would be necessary if it seems to suit your situation.[1]

NOTE

[1]See Robert Guenther, "All-in-the-Family Mortgages Start to Show Some Promise," *The Wall Street Journal*, May 29, 1985, p. 33.

CHAPTER TEN

Special Situations, Special Types of Property

LIFE INSURANCE

Life insurance has traditionally served to provide an instant estate and to replace the earning power of the family's economic provider should that individual die prematurely. Historically, the father has been the breadwinner and the mother the caretaker of the home and young children. Therefore, the young father has been the one to buy life insurance to cover the eventuality of his death at a time when the mother was still needed at home. The hope was that the policy proceeds would enable her to remain in the home and care for the children. The traditional scenario does not play out well today. The mother might be working outside of the home and supplying a greater portion of the family's income than the father while the children are being cared for in an all-day nursery. It will be up to the family to decide whose loss of earning power would create the greatest loss for the family. It may be that both parents' lives should be insured.

As to the type of policy a young insured should buy, opinions vary. Term insurance (pure insurance) buys the greatest amount of protection per premium dollar and thus releases more dollars for an income-producing investment. At a young age, the premium is relatively low since the insurance company is not at high risk of paying the face amount of the policy. Many other factors should go into the decision, however, as to whether to buy "pure" insurance or "permanent" insurance (sometimes called ordinary life), which builds up a cash value over the years. For example, the cost of term insurance premiums will increase in proportion to your increasing age when renewed for another term; ordinary life has level premium payments. Future insurability may be lost because of health changes. Of course, insurance companies' products cover many projected life changes. Some term policies are convertible to permanent without evidence of insurability. The costs to the insurance company are covered by the additional premiums paid, but this cost passed on to the purchaser reduces the hazard of his/her future noninsurability.

These are just a few of the many factors to consider. Young people who have never felt the need for insurance previously but suddenly face new responsibilities (birth of a child) should "bone up" at the local library *before* exposing themselves to the education received from the insurance salesman. Life insurance is an asset that requires special attention because of the variety of products available.

Another traditional use of life insurance has been to provide liquidity for an estate, thus preventing forced sale of estate assets to provide funds for estate administration and federal and state death taxes, as well as for the family's current cash needs. The need for liquidity for payment of federal estate taxes has been reduced by legislation of recent years that enlarged the dollar value of an estate that can pass to beneficiaries and heirs free of federal estate tax and by the introduction of the unlimited marital deduction for transfers between spouses. In fact, insurance payable to an estate or owned by the decedent can waste dollars by requiring inclusion in the gross estate for federal estate tax purposes. The value of the insurance thus included might make an estate otherwise federally nontaxable (because of the unified credit) taxable.

One way to handle the problem is to transfer the ownership of a policy already owned by the insured to the insured person's beneficiaries or to a trust for the beneficiaries, or to have the insurance actually acquired and owned by a trust or someone other than the insured, provided that person has an insurable interest. Why is it so important to have someone else own the policy? Section 2042 of the Internal Revenue Code specifically includes within a decedent's gross estate the value of life insurance in which the decedent possessed any "incidents of ownership at death." These incidents of ownership include certain elements of control. Since we have learned that control is one of the key aspects of ownership, it is easy to understand that such things as retaining the right to change beneficiaries, the right to borrow against the cash value in a policy, and the right to change the payout options are ownership rights that must be relinquished if the desired goal is to keep the insurance out of the estate. The federal estate tax regulations fully describe other incidents of ownership. Most important, the named owner of the policy must be other than the insured.

Prior to the 1981 tax legislation removing all limits on the marital deduction, it was considered desirable for a less-propertied spouse to own the insurance on the life of the wealthier spouse. Thus, if the wealthier of the two should die first and have a taxable estate, at least the value of the insurance proceeds would not be included in the gross estate of the decedent spouse and the dollars would be available for estate taxes or for the use of the surviving spouse. The ownership of the policy as between spouses is now no longer a key factor as it was in prior planning where the goal was to keep the value out of the larger estate.

If estate taxes are a potential problem, the problem will be magnified when one surviving spouse owns *all* of the assets and there is no marital deduction to soften the blow of estate taxes at that spouse's death. Insurance companies have always proved creative in marketing new products and quickly perceived that life insurance proceeds to provide liquidity for estate taxes will no longer be needed when the death transfer is being made between spouses. Therefore, they have produced a new insurance product covering both spouses' lives but payable on the second death. Anyone interested might look into this new type of insurance.

Planning for transfer of the large estate with a minimum of diminution by estate taxes should only be undertaken with the advice of your tax adviser. Some techniques to consider were described in Chapter Six. If insurance is to be used in your planning, consideration should be given, in some circumstances, to placing ownership in a trust, as stated above, with the trustee designated to receive the proceeds and distribute the same to your beneficiaries in accordance with the terms of the trust. An irrevocable insurance trust avoids probate but might expose the transferor to gift tax liability, particularly if you transfer income-producing property to the trust for use in paying the premiums. There are no income tax savings, inasmuch as Code Section 677 provides that the grantor is taxable on trust income applied to the payment of premiums on policies of insurance on the life of the grantor or his/her spouse. If the trust is unfunded with income-producing property, then the insured may annually transfer the cash necessary for premium payments and the trustee uses these funds for paying the premiums. Advisers have different opinions as to whether payment of the premiums directly by the insured (although policy ownership is in a trust) would endanger the *nonownership* the insured is trying to achieve. Premiums are paid with after-tax dollars, whether paid by the trust or the insured. The insurance *proceeds*, of course, are not subject to income taxes, whether paid directly to named beneficiaries or to a trust.

For a middle-aged individual with a sizable income, a spouse, and grown children, continuing to pay insurance premiums may be a poor use of the money. Considering the effects of inflation on any fixed dollar amount payable at some future date, assets owned by each spouse during the marriage might provide a better investment option than continuing to build up an insurance estate. With each spouse having management and control over his/her separate assets, there is greater opportunity to invest in property that keeps pace with inflation and to ensure the immediate independence of the surviving spouse on the death of the decedent spouse.

Life insurance, of course, is needed at certain periods in one's life or in connection with certain situations other than estate planning. This is particularly true when insurance is purchased in connection with a business. Some uses of insurance in business planning will be discussed in the following sections of this chapter.

OWNERSHIP OF A BUSINESS

Ownership of one's own business could absorb all of the funds available for investment to the exclusion of availability for any personal investment asset acquisition, but being "boss" of your own business is a typical part of the American dream. Sole proprietorship is the simplest and least expensive form of business organization to operate insofar as the mechanics of organization and day-to-day operations are concerned. There is no need for a charter; no need to comply with statutory requirements as in setting up a corporation; no need to have elaborate minutes of stockholders' meetings prepared or directors' records of actions taken; no need to have your acts clothed in the corporate form. Your decisions may be solely your own.

If your business is profitable enough you will be concerned with retirement planning. With passage of the Tax Equity and Fiscal Responsibility Act of 1982 (TEFRA), differences have been largely eliminated with regard to contributions made by a corporation to a tax-exempt pension plan and contributions made by a noncorporate business. Formerly, there was a limitation on allowable contributions to plans of a self-employed unincorporated business owner or self-employed professional (or those individuals operating in the partnership form). However, this disparity has been removed and, assuming the prosperity of the business, this could prove to be the biggest boon to the business owner, thus eliminating the need to look further afield for a tax shelter. Contribution to pension plans is the tax deferral method looked on with favor by Congress. There are, of course, strict rules to follow with regard to coverage of rank-and-file employees, since Congress' concern is chiefly pension plans for *employees*, who, in most instances, are not affluent business owners.

There is one big advantage that exists when business is conducted in the corporate form (or partnership having limited partners), and that is that legal responsibility for liabilities of the business rests entirely with the entity itself. The corporate owners are not personally liable, whereas the sole proprietor *is* personally liable. There is another form of hazard that a sole proprietor must face—the risk of disability. This is particularly important in a service business that depends on the unique talents of the sole owner or sole professional. Disability insurance would provide some protection, and some form of overhead insurance should be purchased. At an early stage in life, the business owner might not be well endowed with investments outside of the business to cushion a temporary period of incapacity. These very concerns are among the reasons why a sole proprietor might want to team up with a partner or partners.

PARTNERSHIP

A partnership is an arrangement between two or more people to carry on a business. Generally, there is less formality in a partnership than in the operation of a corporation. There are certain other advantages. The possibility of a "double tax" (on corporate income and then again on dividends when received by shareholders) is avoided in a partnership. Also, statutory regulations make operation of a corporation much more complex. However, if you are looking beyond sole proprietorship into other forms of business organization, you should know that in a partnership each partner can legally bind and obligate the others. This means that actions taken by one of the partners can make you personally responsible.

As between sole proprietorship and partnership, there is almost no income tax advantage in the latter. Partnerships file information income tax returns, but they do not pay income taxes. The income earned, after accounting for deductible expenses and capital gains and losses sustained, is passed through to the partners, and the latter report the income in the same form that the partnership information return reported it but in proportion to the partner's share of the business.

Certain partners' responsibility for liabilities can be limited if the form of partnership agreement so states and statutory requirements are met. If the partnership has limited partners, only the general partners are personally responsible for liabilities, while the limited partners' share of responsibility for debts is limited to their capital contribution. However, in this case, the general partners make all the decisions. This form of organization is a favorite one for joint ventures in real estate (or certain other essentially "passive" forms of investment). Of course, this is getting beyond the small business type of entity. In the large limited partnership in which participation is offered to the public, SEC rules must be observed. If you have ever bought a limited partnership share, you learned that you had no voice in the management of the business. You may also have discovered that your limited partnership interest was a very illiquid investment and a type of ownership over which you had very little control. In addition to federal laws covering public offerings of limited partnership shares, partnerships in general are covered by state statutes, which must be observed. Knowing something about tax consequences is also helpful whether the partnership is large or small.

For example, if you decide to part company with your other partners, you must do so carefully. One possibility is to sell your share in the partnership, resulting in the possibility of capital gain or loss treatment. You can't just walk away. You may feel you will be leaving behind responsibility for any subsequent taxes on partnership income, but you will not be able to turn your back on reporting the income because the partnership continues to exist for tax purposes, even if it is made up of only two partners and one of them no longer has anything to do with the business. The way in which a withdrawing partner might be paid for that partner's interest also might have important tax consequences for the remaining partners. The message is: Don't make a move without consulting your tax adviser. Of course, this applies at all times to anyone operating a business in any form.

THE CLOSELY-HELD BUSINESS CORPORATION

The plea just made—never stray far from your tax adviser in business planning—is particularly important in incorporating and operating a business as a corporation. One of the major reasons for incorporating is to have the business earnings taxed at the corporate rate: The first $25,000 of a corporation's taxable income is taxed at 15 percent, the next $25,000 is taxed at 18 percent, the next $25,000 is taxed at 30 percent, the next $25,000 at 40 percent and all taxable income over $100,000 at 46 percent. A different rule applies once the corporation's income exceeds $1 million. These figures are effective up to the end of 1985, but increases or decreases in corporate income taxes are possible in any overhaul of the tax code.

Corporations are treated as taxpaying entities separate from their shareholders for federal income tax purposes, and the income of the corporation is not taxable to its shareholders until actually distributed to them in the form of dividends. This is one of the key planning factors in operating the closely-held corporation. There is a potential conflict between the owners of the corporation who work for the business in high-salaried positions and nonemployee shareholders who would like to see corporate profits returned more in the form of dividends. Payment of salaries is a deductible business expense (once having passed the IRS test of "reasonableness"), whereas dividends are paid with after-tax earnings of the corporation and are income in the hands of the shareholder. The possibility of double taxation exists when the salary-earners are also shareholders who hold most of the stock. These individuals, naturally, would like to see more of the corporate profits paid to them as compensation.

As we have seen, a former reason for incorporating has been minimized by the 1982 legislation (TEFRA) which eliminated distinctions in the tax law between qualified pension plans of corporations and those of self-employed individuals or those operating an unincorporated business. Before the change in the law (enacted in 1982 but generally effective in 1984), there was an advantage in *corporate* retirement plans. A defined contribution plan, for example (a plan basing the employer's deductible contribution to the plan on compensation paid), had a limit of $30,000 a year, while a nonincorporated individual in a business or profession could only contribute $15,000 a year to a tax-exempt plan (often known as a Keogh plan, after its congressional originator). The new law decreed parity between the corporate plan and the noncorporate plan. There are, of course, many other planning considerations, but for those who view incorporation as the ultimate tax shelter because of tax-favored employee pension plans, this change in the law indicates a look to other matters.

One important nontax advantage of the corporate form is that liability of the owners of the corporation is limited to the assets of the corporation itself. Privately owned property is insulated from liability for corporate debts. Therefore, your private fortune is safe. Maybe. Sometimes a lender to (or creditor of) an entity operating in the corporate or limited partnership form wishes to have additional security that the loan or debt will be repaid if the business should fail. That lender or creditor might ask that the individuals who are the (wealthy) owners of the corporation guarantee payment. In that case, they will be voluntarily putting their personal fortunes on the line to the extent of that debt.

There are hazards to be wary of while operating within the shelter of the corporation. One of these is to avoid being classified as a "personal holding company" (with an accompanying higher tax), a special IRS characterization in which the corporate entity is perceived to be a device for holding passive investments instead of conducting a business. Special rules and penalties might apply. Tax planning for any business organization is always important. Because of the intricacies and complexities of the Internal Revenue Code, it is particularly important with respect to the closely-held business operating in the corporate form, and business owners will carefully monitor changes enacted by succeeding Congresses or promoted by new administrations.

Shares of Stock as Property

Shares of stock in a closely-held or family-owned business provide great flexibility of planning for the owners and create certain problems. Freedom of transferability of shares enables the owner of a closely-held business to make gifts of shares. The goal may be to transfer ownership of those shares to someone in a lower tax bracket, so that individual will receive dividends taxable at a lower tax. Sometimes, in the interest of estate-planning, an owner makes lifetime gifts of stock to younger members of the family to exclude anticipated future appreciation from the donor's estate. In fact, the death of a key participant in the business often produces problems. Funds may be needed to continue the business, to liquidate the interest of the deceased shareholder-employee (or partner in a partnership), or to meet tax liabilities. The latter may be eased by special provisions of the Internal Revenue Code applicable only in a hardship situation (such as that which arises when a large part of the decedent's gross estate is comprised of a nonliquid business interest). These provisions include Section 6166, permitting extension of time for payment of estate tax, and Section 303, permitting corporate redemption of stock for federal estate tax purposes without ordinary income treatment.

Insurance owned by the corporation on the life of a "key man" may supply the needed funds for business purposes; indeed, one of the purposes may be to supply the corporation with instant funds for redemption of stock on the death of a key employee-owner. There are many other arrangements for using life insurance to fund a death buy out of a business owner's interest, whether held in corporate or partnership form. In some business arrangements, continuing or surviving shareholders agree to buy the shares of a deceased owner from his estate for an agreed price or a price based on an agreed-on formula computation, and such cross-purchase agreements are usually accompanied by cross-purchase of life insurance. An income tax analysis of any arrangement should be made by your tax adviser. An important document for the corporation is a buy-sell agreement. One who expects to inherit shares of stock in a family-owned or closely-held corporation should exert whatever influence is possible to see that a prospective future property interest will not be jeopardized by an inadequate or nonexistent agreement regarding transfer of shares.

What about transfers in a divorce? Equitable distribution states may vary in the way division of business assets are handled. An ill-considered division might destroy the business. Various formulas have been applied to these divisions. The problem with distribution of ownership shares in a small business on divorce can be similar to the problem arising on the obligation to pay estate taxes. The divorced spouse who does not participate in the business needs income, but the business interest owned, whether corporate shares or partnership interest, produces little except in compensation for the participating spouse's work. A court may order distributions of a share of business profits but is likely to be inhibited in so doing if the interests of other participants are adversely affected. Sometimes spouses own and operate a business together. The first question to be answered is whether the business relation can survive the breakup of the marriage. Thus, in today's world, the contingency of divorce and provision for it may be a natural part of the business documents. An agreement specifying in advance who will retain the business and how the interest of the departing, divorcing shareholder or partner will be paid for may anticipate and solve a potentially difficult set of questions, but enforceability of such a contract must be carefully studied before one relies on it. In some equitable distribution states a spouse's contribution to the success of a family-owned business might be a factor to consider in distributing property on a divorce, and this might apply regardless of which spouse held title to the shares.

PROFESSIONAL SERVICE CORPORATION

A special kind of corporation operating today is the professional service corporation. This kind of corporation is available in most states to certain professions. We have all seen the designation "P.C." or "P.A." (professional corporation or professional association) after one or two or a string of doctors' or lawyers' names on an office door. In these special corporations, the shareholders must all hold the same kind of professional degree. Consequently, if Mrs. Doctor is not also Ms. Doctor, she cannot possibly hold shares in his medical corporation. If the doctor is nearing retirement, there could be a fat pension plan to tap (see Chapter Seven). If the doctor is far from retirement, there is always a divorce claim possibility based on the *Sullivan* case reasoning if the facts are similar (see Chapter Seven).

Professional corporations are a modern phenomenon. Historically, corporate status was believed inconsistent with a professional practice for a variety of reasons, including the fear that incorporation would dilute the individual's liability for professional malpractice. The change came because professionals, who are typically high earners, wanted the privilege of deferring otherwise taxable income by placing a portion of their income in tax-exempt pension funds. This was, and is, the same privilege available to their business counterparts in corporations. The battle began when a few states enacted statutes permitting incorporation of a professional practice; it was won in 1969 when the Internal Revenue Service recognized a professional association as a form of corporation for tax purposes. Thereafter, other states passed enabling acts (which allowed incorporation while preserving individual professional liability for malpractice). The 1982 federal legislation known as TEFRA equalized the permitted ceilings on the amount that can be contributed to a tax-exempt plan whether by a corporation or an unincorporated business or professional. This substantially reduced the incentive for doctors, lawyers and other professionals to incorporate and also makes it easier for those now incorporated to return to operating solo or in partnerships. As a result, some professionals who were incorporated are disincorporating. Dissolution of a corporate practice, if that is the goal, is tricky and must be done carefully to avoid undesirable tax consequences.

FAMILY BUSINESSES

According to an article in *Sylvia Porter's Personal Finance Magazine*, "Family businesses are big business. If you count sole proprietorships, partnerships, family-owned, closely-held corporations . . . and public corporations dominated by a single family, at least 90 percent of all American businesses are family businesses. They account for half the gross national product, employ about half of American workers, and generate the majority of new jobs added to the economy."[1]

"Family" business does not mean "informal." Business formalities must be observed. Historically, a mom and pop business was not automatically classified as a partnership and operated without sophisticated tax or legal advice. As a result, a surviving spouse of a marital business partnership whose status as a partner was not clearly documented very often received no credit on a federal estate tax return for having contributed to the partnership earnings although the couple had filed joint income tax returns and with the earnings had acquired jointly owned property. If the surviving spouse was a widow, almost invariably the business earnings were deemed to have been the property of the decedent spouse and therefore a part of his estate for federal estate tax purposes. As we have seen, Congress in recent years has adopted a more beneficent attitude toward surviving spouses. Nevertheless, it is important to document the form of business entity when spouses or other family members participate. Whether an unincorporated business is a partnership or a sole proprietorship with a family member or members *employed* by the sole owner is an important distinction to make and to clearly establish with appropriate documentation. In some types of planning, it may be more desirable for a family member to be an employee rather than a partner. The pros and cons of the various forms of business organization should be carefully weighed in advance. If later developments suggest that another organizational form would be better, a change can be made.

The comments made in this chapter suggest a few of the considerations raised by ownership of a family business interest. The coverage of topics is certainly not inclusive, and no blueprint has been provided for planning for a particular business organization. That should be left to professional advisers fully informed about the details of both the business and the family objectives.

The topic of the owner's disability and the possibly devastating effect that could have on the business has been mentioned. Various tools are available to give the business person peace of mind. One that has not yet been described in detail is the Revocable Living Trust. The following two sections of this chapter will deal with this topic.

SAMPLE OF A REVOCABLE LIVING TRUST

REVOCABLE TRUST AGREEMENT

THIS TRUST AGREEMENT made this _____ day of _____, 19____, by and between the undersigned Grantor of this Trust, ____JOHN OWNER____ and _____, Bank, a national banking association, and its successor or successors, hereinafter referred to as my "Trustee," WITNESSETH:

ONE: I hereby transfer to the Trustee the property described in Schedule A, attached hereto and made a part hereof, and I may from time to time transfer additional property acceptable to the Trustee.

TWO: My Trustee may receive any other property (provided said property is acceptable to my Trustee), real or personal, transferred, assigned or conveyed to the Trustee by me, my personal representative, or by any other person to constitute a part of the trust principal or trust fund hereby created, to be held, invested, managed and distributed by my Trustee in accordance with the provisions set forth below.

THREE: My Trustee shall pay the net income of the trust (and so much of the principal as I may from time to time in writing direct), at least quarterly, to me or for my benefit during my life. In the event that I should become unable to manage my own affairs (whether or not legally adjudicated an incapacitated or incompetent adult) and be certified to that effect by a physician, my Trustee shall be authorized to continue to pay such income to me or for my benefit and to invade periodically the principal of this trust for the payment of any and all expenses to provide for my comfortable support, maintenance and care, including but not limited to medical and hospitalization expenses and private nursing care. Should I become unable to manage my own affairs, as described above, my Trustee shall also be authorized to pay such portion of the income or principal (or both) of this trust as may be necessary, in the discretion of my Trustee, for the comfortable support, maintenance and care of my wife, JANE OWNER, in her accustomed manner of living, taking into account and considering any other means of support she may have to the knowledge of my Trustee.

FOUR: I hereby reserve the right at any time and from time to time to revoke, alter or amend this trust in whole or in part, in any particular, including but not limited to the power to change or add beneficiaries, by an instrument in writing delivered to my Trustee; except that the duties and compensation of the Trustee shall not be materially changed by any amendment without the Trustee's written approval. Any revocation, alteration or amendment shall take effect upon the delivery of the written instrument to my Trustee. If the trust is revoked in its entirety, my Trustee shall deliver all the trust assets to me as soon thereafter as may be reasonably possible.

FIVE: In the administration of this trust, my Trustee shall advise me of any proposed sales or purchases of investment property, and if I give my Trustee in writing any directions as to such changes in investments, my Trustee shall follow my instructions, in which case my Trustee shall have no liability in respect thereto, as I take full responsibility for any such changes in investments specified by me. If I give my Trustee no written investment directions within a period of time that I will specify from time to time or if I should become unable to manage my own affairs as described in Clause THREE above, then my Trustee may make any such sales or purchases of investments, in its sole discretion, without any written directions from me.

OR (Alternate Clause):

FIVE: In the administration of this trust, my Trustee may make such sales or purchases of investment property as it may deem advisable in its sole discretion; provided, however, that if I give my Trustee in writing any directions as to such sales or purchases of investments, my Trustee shall follow my instructions. If my Trustee follows my written directions, it shall have no liability in respect thereto, as I take full responsibility for any such changes in investments specified by me. In the event I am certified by a physician to be unable to manage my own affairs, as described in Clause THREE above, all investment discretion shall be in my Trustee.

SIX: Upon my death, if my wife survives me, the property in this trust, both principal and undistributed income, shall be transferred to my wife, and the trust continued upon her written instructions, or, on her instructions the trust shall end.

> (OR: Specific provisions may be inserted here, directing the Trustee to distribute the property to certain beneficiaries either outright or in continued trust for a specified period or until a specified event.)

SEVEN: My Trustee (and any successors) shall have the following powers, and any others that may be granted by law, but without necessity of order of any court, all within the terms and conditions as set forth in this trust:

(a) To retain any property or undivided interests in property received from me or from any other source, including residential property, regardless of any lack of diversification, risk, or non-productivity;

(b) To invest and reinvest the trust estate in any property or undivided interests in property, wherever located, including bonds, notes secured or unsecured, stocks of corporations regardless of class, including the stock of the Corporate Trustee [Note: A corporate trustee, as a bank, will certainly want that phrase inserted.], and to keep and maintain funds in savings accounts including the bank or banks of the Corporate Trustee, without being limited by any statute or rule of law concerning investments by trustees;

(c) To sell any trust property, for cash or on credit, at public or private sales; to exchange any trust property for other property; to grant options to purchase or acquire any trust property; and to determine the prices and terms of sales, exchanges, and options;

(d) To improve or repair or lease (as lessor or lessee) any real estate and to grant or receive options to purchase property; including a lease or option that may be made for a term that may extend beyond the period of the trust;

(e) To borrow money for any purpose, either from the banking department of the Trustee, or from others, and to mortgage or pledge any trust property;

(f) To employ real estate brokers, appraisers, attorneys, accountants or other expert assistants and to pay reasonable compensation from trust funds for their services;

(g) To make division or distribution in kind or in money, or partly in kind and partly in money; and if in kind not necessarily pro rata or in fractional shares among beneficiaries;

(h) To vote any stock by itself or by proxy; to enter into any plan or agreement for the sale, merger, consolidation, liquidation, recapitalization or other disposition of any trust property or of any public corporation issuing securities held as part of the trust, and to accept in such transaction any cash, securities or property that the Trustee deems proper.

(i) To determine the allocation of dividends, distributions, profits resulting from the maturity or sale of any asset, and any other receipts and the allocation of payments and expenses as between income and principal; provide (or not provide) reserves from income otherwise distributable for depreciation, obsolescence, or other prospective loss, reduction in value, or casualty; amortize (or not amortize) premiums, and accumulate (or not accumulate) discounts, at which securities or other assets were acquired; provided that all such determinations, allocations and other actions are reasonable;

(j) To exercise any and all options, whether such be options to purchase stock (qualified, nonqualified, restricted or other), or whether such shall be options to purchase other types or kinds of property;

(k) Operate and continue any and all businesses, including proprietorships and partnerships in which I may have an interest or which I may be operating; to liquidate or join in the liquidation of any such businesses, to sell or otherwise dispose of the same as going concerns, to incorporate or cause to be incorporated such businesses, to invest in any such businesses so incorporated as it shall see fit and to retain stock in any such businesses so incorporated without liability for depreciation in value, to become or remain a general or limited partner in any new or continuing partnership and to take such other action (including any election under Subchapter S of the Internal Revenue Code) as it may deem necessary or proper for beginning, continuing or liquidating such business; and to employ agents and advisers as necessary.

EIGHT: To the extent that such requirements can legally be waived, no Trustee or successor Trustee shall ever be required to give any bond as Trustee; to qualify before, be appointed by or account to any court, in the absence of breach of trust; or required to obtain the order or approval of any court in the exercise of any power or discretion hereunder.

NINE: Any Trustee or successor Trustee hereunder shall render semiannually a statement to me and any other income beneficiaries showing the condition of the trust and the receipts and disbursements during the preceding six (6) months.

TEN: As compensation for its services my Trustee shall receive annually those fees set out and published in that fee schedule of my Trustee in respect to this type of trust which is current at the time or times such compensation is payable. If the compensation of my Trustee is not legally and effectively specified by any such fee schedule or by agreement, then my Trustee shall receive the compensation specified in that fee schedule respecting this type trust which is now currently in use and of which I am aware.

The construction of this instrument, the validity of the interests created hereby and the administration of the trust shall be governed by the laws of the State of _____.

IN WITNESS WHEREOF, I have hereunto set my hand and affixed my seal, the day and year first above written.

Witnesses:

_____(Seal)

JOHN OWNER

In token of the acceptance of this trust and to acknowledge receipt of the property described in Schedule A attached hereto, _____ _____ BANK has caused its corporate name to be hereunto signed and its corporate seal to be hereunto affixed by its duly authorized officer, this _____ day of _____, 19____.

BANK   (SEAL)

Witnesses:

By: _____

Trust Officer
TRUSTEE

(Notarization)

[and on next pages: SCHEDULE A]

USING THE REVOCABLE LIVING TRUST

The above material is NOT to be considered an appropriately drafted and complete document. Such a trust document MUST be drafted with your particular concerns in mind. A trust is a very flexible tool of planning, and the types of functions and uses to be accomplished by a trust are innumerable. Trust documents can cover many pages and contain very complex clauses and instructions. The only reason for even setting forth a few of the possible types of clauses to consider is, as stated in the Preface, to give you *a look* at a sample. A complete look at a trust document will be the look you give the instrument drafted by your attorney.

The use of a trust is frequently proposed to the individual actively engaged in business. For some reason these individuals are often targeted for advertisements or mailings exhorting the business person to consider use of a living trust and the bank as a trustee for at least some of his/her assets. For this reason, the "look" described above is included in this chapter, although any person who perceives its usefulness to his/her own needs could benefit from perusal of a trust document and from learning how a trust functions. At the outset, the very act of transferring title or other indicia of ownership of *your* property to the trustee's name (if it means changing Mary Smith to "Mary Smith Trustee") may give you second thoughts.

Perhaps the appeal to the business person is based on the belief that the business person is used to delegating authority. The surprising thing is that not every bank is delighted to receive an interest in a family-owned business, either as part of a trust or an estate to administer, unless there are also other assets. Fiduciary appointments involving family businesses may incur more headaches than profits. Some trust departments prefer not to accept such appointments unless there are sizable nonbusiness assets. If you are the owner of a family business, look into the policy of the bank you might be considering as a possible trustee (or co-trustee) to see how it will assist you with the burden of running the business or transferring the business to those who will run it after you. Additionally, look into the fees charged for bank trust services. Of course, you do not have to use a bank.

Some of the reasons for placing property in a living trust are: You, as grantor of your trust, can place property in the trust, observe its administration, and observe the handling of the property by a trustee or trustees, if you desire; you can control distribution of benefits (including to you); you can relieve yourself of the responsibility for investment decisions (if you wish); you can place the trust in operation by transferring a limited amount of assets; you can revoke the trust altogether if you decide you do not like the arrangement and you have specifically retained that power. You can put your testamentary wishes into the trust, thereby by-passing probate as to assets in the trust. If all of your assets are transferred to trust administration, you eliminate appointing a future personal representative because your trust will take the place of your will. *It will not save estate taxes.* As we have seen, a nonprobatable estate is not necessarily a nontaxable estate. However, if your estate is not distributed by a probate court it is not exposed to public availability and information. If that is a concern, you will be interested in the private manner of distribution that can be achieved by means of a trust.

Evidently a lot of people are interested in a transfer of assets at death other than by court-supervised administration. Norman F. Dacey's book, *How to Avoid Probate,* has had an incredibly popular success. There is, however, one side to the picture that is often overlooked by the potential grantor and minimized in publicity by the potential trustee, and that regards fees. Drafting a trust instrument, administering it, preparing the fiduciary tax returns (which must be filed, in addition to your own return), and innumerable other services all entail fees—so much so, that it has been said that the practicality of a trust is limited to the value of the assets so administered. Is it just for the wealthy, or is it worthwhile even for the person with moderate wealth? Remember, there is no income tax saving achieved by having your property in a trust. It is a pass-through-of-income situation, so the recipient of the income pays the income taxes.

Look again at the advertisements urging us to "take life easy," to devote ourselves to improving our golf game while the Granite Bank and Trust Company handles our financial affairs. There has been a tendency to change the traditional method of conducting trust activities from merely utilizing various investment products to creating a total financial management relationship (with a battery of technological equipment, no doubt). Marketing is an important part of the trust business. Of course, if you really do not want to be bothered with your investments and you really do want to get on with your golf game (and you are willing to pay for the service), perhaps a revocable living trust is just the thing for you.

As mentioned in Chapter Four, another use of a living trust is to handle the affairs of a person who is elderly, disabled, or mentally incompetent and who has no close friend or family member to rely on. Suppose *you* are that person or some day could be. Combined with a durable power of attorney (see Chapter Four), a revocable living trust could work this way: Let's say you established such a trust during your busy working life to meet various investment objectives or merely to test its viability, and let's say that the trust was partially funded. The mechanism would then be in place for *your* agent (previously selected by you personally), who holds the power of attorney from you, to transfer further assets to the trust in order to provide funds for your care, with management by a trustee during your incapacity, thus avoiding any possible need for a court-appointed conservator. One writer carries the planning a bit further and recommends that the exercise of power of attorney be contingent on a well-defined triggering event, such as incapacity, but that such incapacity be certified to by two licensed physicians. If the ultimate power of your agent is to place you (when you are 97 years old) in a nursing home, the certification by physicians helps guard against premature or improper placement in such a facility.

IS THERE ANYTHING ELSE?

Consider this: If you have reached the stage when most of your financial goals and business achievements have been reached, when your investment plots (some good, some bad) have hatched, when you have *lost* money and regained some of your losses, perhaps, now, while you are still in charge, you can place some, most, or all of your investment assets and property in conservative, income-producing, principal-retaining assets. A neat trick, you say. There might be several guidelines to help reach this eventual goal. Utilize specific return investments, such as Treasury bills or notes. Utilize federally insured bank money funds; consider an annuity. Wise heads will immediately cry: "Those investments will not be inflation-oriented. Your dollars will lose value." True. But that might be an acceptable price to pay for "peace of mind" investments. Your goal at this stage of life is to preserve your principal because *you might need it!* Making this type of property your mainstay late in life has one other benefit, often overlooked. Such property requires very little excessive management. This is a goal in itself at a certain stage in life and one that you can arrange for all by yourself by specific planning.

NOTE

[1]Dana Shilling, "All's Well in the Family Business," *Sylvia Porter's Personal Finance Magazine*, February 1985, p. 68.

CHAPTER ELEVEN

Keeping an Eye on Changes

SOME CONCLUSIONS

The first and foremost conclusion is that very little is stable in our changing society. State laws and court decisions interpreting or implementing those laws are constantly changing. So, too, are federal laws that might affect your property ownership plans and tax effects. In fact, one of the complaints frequently heard from ordinary taxpayers and business taxpayers alike is that because of such changes they are unable to *plan*. Planning for change is perhaps the most stable and sensible planning. As this is being written, a complete revision of our federal tax laws is a possibility. A review of those laws up until the time this book is published will be found in Appendix I. The chronology of tax legislation in the U.S. Congress outlined in that appendix focuses on only a few high points regarding matters that would interest a property owner.

The interested owner and investor will be constantly tuned into any pertinent information reported in the daily press or financial publications. New tax legislation is frequently on the congressional agenda late in the summer. Past history shows that major tax legislation sometimes ends its long journey in July, August, or September. It is also no secret that technical mistakes (the revision in Code Section 00000 cannot possibly work with the revision in Code Section 11111) sometimes have to be corrected with a later law known as a "Technical Corrections Act."

TAX LAWS THAT DID NOT WORK (OR MAY NOT)

An entire phase of tax revision may prove unworkable. The Tax Reform Act of 1976, for example, contained a section providing for the application of a "carryover basis" to assets transferred at death. This was hailed as a major improvement at the time. The goal was to eliminate the escape from capital gain taxation that long-term assets had previously enjoyed when they were part of a taxpayer's estate. The old rule (now the new rule) was that at death all of the assets that were owned by the decedent and formed his estate received a "stepped-up" basis. This meant that if these assets had increased in value since they were originally purchased (either by the decedent or by someone else from whom he had acquired them by gift or inheritance), the gain was not taxed, because all of the assets in an estate were valued for estate tax purposes at their date-of-death value (or, depending on the choice made by the executor, the alternate valuation date, six months later, allowed by the Code). The heir or heirs who ultimately received the assets could sell them and not be taxed on the gain for income tax computation purposes. The 1976 law eliminated this seeming windfall.

Some congressmen rejoiced. Here was a way to collect monies for the Treasury. All of those untaxed capital gains would now be taxed. The capital gains tax would be paid by the estate if the assets had to be sold or else by the heirs when they sold. Why did it not work?

Very simply, the provision did not work because no one keeps such records! If your grandfather received a handsome silver tray as a wedding present from *his* grandfather and you inherited that tray, along with countless other valuable heirlooms, from Grandfather's estate and decided to sell those items and use the money for a new automobile that you really needed, *you* had to find out how much the first purchaser had paid. When you sold, you had to pay a capital gains tax on the difference between that original price and the price you received on the sale. There were certain exceptions and complicated computations in the law, but they proved unworkable.

Innumerable seminars were held instructing or trying to instruct tax advisers on how to advise their clients on finding out original basis. All sorts of ridiculous suggestions were made: use old tax records; ask neighbors; look up the cost of silver trays in

1910. A type of recognition of the impossibility of the task was included in the law. If the assets inherited were listed securities, then one did not have to go back to Day 1. Instead, those *listed* securities that had been owned on December 31, 1976, and then became part of someone's estate *after* that date would receive a basis that was the market value on December 31, 1976. Brokers began deluging clients with statements of the values of securities listed on the various stock exchanges on December 31, 1976.

When Congress finally realized that it was impossible to find out the original bases of inherited assets, the law was changed and the rule in effect prior to 1976 was reinstated in 1981. All assets listed on an estate tax return would be handed to heirs with the date-of-death value as the heirs' "basis." This is called "stepped-up basis" (which was just what it had been called before it was abolished). Now stepped-up basis is being touted as a terrific estate-planning device. Think of it. *You*, the owner of properties, may keep them until the day you pass them on to your heirs, all the while knowing that *they* will not have to account for the profit when they sell. The stepped-up basis is not without value. For example, buy a condominium in Wildacre Resorts and rent it out, taking all the allowable deductions for investment rental properties (including depreciation), but it must be held for the production of income. Eventually, when you retire, move into the condominium in Wildacre Resorts. When the kids inherit the property, they get the stepped-up basis, never having to have an accountant tell them that this is the year to "recapture" the depreciation. The reason: That accounting figure is realized in the year of the sale—and you never *sold* during your lifetime. If the heirs sell, they use the date of death value as their basis.

Here is another example of the use of stepped-up basis: Remember, in Chapter Two, when Daughter was given Mother's home, 1900 Vista Lane, and then discovered that because Mother had retained a life interest (in the eyes of IRS) by continuing to live there, the house became an asset of Mother's estate, but Daughter received a stepped-up basis, so that when *she* sold it (because Mother no longer needed it and Daughter had no intention of living there), if she received a price equivalent to the estate evaluation, there was no capital gains tax to pay. Seems good. Will it last? No one knows.

A provision in a more recent enactment, the Tax Reform Act of 1981, "gave" us the QTIP trust concept. Since QTIP trusts are being established mostly by wills and since the makers of those wills are mostly still alive, the working of this technique and the problems inherent in its complicated arrangements have yet to surface. It is too early to tell whether at some far-off date *this* provision will prove unworkable and meet its demise.

Consider another legislative nibble at estate accumulations—the generation-skipping tax. This provision has not been dealt with elsewhere in detail (nor will it be here) because there have been rumblings abroad that the problems and difficulties with its administration may prove insurmountable. In brief, the provision attempts to tax certain usages of life estates to a generation beyond one's immediate children. The goal of the legislators was to enable the Treasury to collect on the corpus being transferred to a future generation. There is a $250,000 exemption, but the provisions are clothed in complicated restrictions and wordiness.

Let us leave this problem. One who must deal with it may well consult with his or her advisers. They will deserve any fee charged. What does the future hold?

WILL "TAX SIMPLIFICATION" WORK?

The tax laws that have been enacted in the recent past have all had a popular title that reflects the wishful thinking of Congress or an administration. For example, it was *hoped* that the Economic Recovery Tax Act of 1981 (ERTA) would be just that. The Tax Reform Act of 1984 and the deficit reduction action that was part of it (or is it the other way around?) *might* reduce the deficit, but no one really believes that these will make the slightest dent in it. The Tax Simplification Act of _____(1986?, 1987?) *might* simplify taxes. Will it? Anyone interested will certainly be watching developments.

Tax simplification and *tax return* simplification are two different things. Most people would be satisfied if the latter could be accomplished.

Since both income and estate taxes are inescapably bound up with investment planning and results, property owners have to maintain diligence in watching routes through Congress. The bill is not a law until it has had the finishing touches applied by the staff of the Joint Committee on Internal Revenue Taxation and has passed both the Senate and the House and been signed by the president. *Then* tax practitioners watch for Treasury regulations telling how the law is to be applied.

It is interesting that, although the purpose of taxation is ostensibly to raise revenue, over the years the power of taxation has been twisted to serve purposes far afield of revenue-raising. From time to time, social purposes have been on the minds of the legislators (tax the rich, don't let families accumulate fortunes and pass them on without paying Uncle Sam for the privilege), or business purposes (give business an "investment" tax credit), or the development of natural resources (the oil depletion deduction) or real estate because this provides jobs (depreciation), or the wiping out of tax measures enacted to implement any and all of the above purposes, because the public is fed up with tax loopholes or with corporate deductions, or adamant about not giving up individual deductions, or ready for anything that would be an improvement over the present system. The continuing legislative process—federal and state, tax and nontax—prevents any of us from adopting a static attitude in acquiring, managing, transferring, preserving, controlling, and just *owning* property.

Chronology of Federal Tax Laws Affecting Property

No guide to ways of owning property would be complete without recognition of the essential input of tax planning. Legislation enacted by Congress and signed by the president is the source of our tax law. The Treasury, through the Internal Revenue Service, promulgates the rules and regulations to enforce and administer the tax laws. It is a common notion, though, that the "Service" is the tax collector and the lawgiver. This is so only because Internal Revenue Service representatives are closest to the taxpayer both in an adversarial capacity and in the capacity of assisting the taxpayer through the maze of tax return filings. Aside from paying a tax on our income, we are sometimes confronted with the obligation of paying a tax on monies that we have not thought of as "income" or of filing a return on transactions that we never thought of as *taxable* transactions. Since taxes affect a great deal of our personal and business or investment planning, it is essential to understand something about tax concepts—past, present, and, possibly, future.

IN THE BEGINNING

The historical theory of taxation was that taxes were imposed as compensation for the protection furnished to the taxpayer by the government. During the pre–Civil War period, the federal government relied almost entirely on customs receipts for its revenues. But following that war, which caused great expansion in federal expenditures, a shift of emphasis occurred. The emphasis began to be focused on ability to pay rather than the benefit supposedly received by the taxpayer. There was a clamor for enactment of an income tax as far back as the 1870s and 1880s. At the same time, there was a movement toward taxing wealth gained by inheritance.

THE INCOME TAX

1913

In 1913 the 16th Amendment to the Constitution was ratified. It states:

> The Congress shall have power to lay and collect taxes on incomes, from whatever source derived, without apportionment among the several States, and without regard to any census or enumeration.

In the same year, Congress passed the first income tax law. That law taxed individuals on net income between $3,000 per year and $20,000 per year. They were to pay a tax of 1 percent on such income.

This is how net income was defined:

> The net income of a taxable person shall include gains, profits, and income derived from salaries, wages, or compensation for personal services of whatever kind and in whatever form paid, or from professions, vocations, businesses, trade, commerce, or sales, or dealings in property, whether real or personal, growing out of the ownership or use of or interest in real or personal property; also from interest, rent, dividends, securities, or the transaction of any lawful business carried on for gain or profit, or gains or profits and income derived from any source whatever.

THE ESTATE TAX

1916

In the Revenue Act of 1916, Congress added an estate tax to our laws. Wealthy people who would be affected by the estate tax then began to transfer their wealth before death. This led to the enactment of a federal tax on lifetime transfers of property in the form of gifts.

THE GIFT TAX

1932

The Revenue Act of 1932 added to our laws a tax on lifetime gifts. A $3,000 annual exclusion was included in this legislation in order to cover such inadvertent violations of the law as might occur because a man gave his wife an expensive gift, such as a fur coat, at Christmas and failed to report it. Therefore, for gifts up to $3,000 no tax was due and no reporting necessary. (The annual exclusion is now $10,000.)

1935

This was the time of the Great Depression of the 30s and Franklin D. Roosevelt in his presidential message of 1935 urged Congress to enact greater taxes on the passage of estates. Congress responded with the Revenue Act of 1935, which contained provisions assessing estate taxes at rates of up to 70 percent.

THE MARITAL DEDUCTION

1948

The next major change in estate and gift tax legislation occurred in 1948, when Congress introduced the marital deduction into the lives of couples planning their estates. This was an attempt to equalize the tax effect of death on married people living in common law states with the tax effect of death on married people living in community property states. Since the enactment of the Revenue Act of 1948, a marital deduction has been available for certain property passing to a spouse. The maximum deduction was 50 percent of a decedent's estate. In community property states, only the share of the estate that had belonged to the decedent separately and the decedent's share of community assets were included in his estate. The surviving spouse's share of community property was not subject to tax. This situation was advantageous to persons residing in community property states and comparatively unfair to married persons residing in non-community property states. Consequently, Congress ended this dual treatment with the passage of the Revenue Act of 1948.

THE WITHHOLDING SYSTEM

The World War II period added the withholding system to our tax legislation. In 1942 Congress legislated that the former Board of Tax Appeals (an early forum for tax controversies) would become the Tax Court of the United States (having judges instead of "members").

MARITAL DEDUCTION REENACTED IN 1954

The marital deduction was reenacted as Sections 2523 and 2056 of the Internal Revenue Code of 1954 and remained in that form until the Tax Reform Act of 1976. During the 28-year period between 1948 and 1976, the marital deduction became the focal point of many estate plans for families. A special team of "estate planners" advised married people, whether their estates were modest or very large, to plan to utilize the marital deduction in passing on their wealth. Some very complicated will structures resulted from such "save-the-second-tax"-by-means-of-a-"marital-deduction-trust" estate planning.

EQUALIZATION OF TAX ON LIFETIME AND TESTAMENTARY GIFTS

1976

The Tax Reform Act of 1976 effected a major overhaul in many areas. For the first time, the tax imposed on transfers at death was equalized with the tax imposed on lifetime gifts. Under prior law, each of these taxes had had a separate schedule, the gift tax rate schedule being three fourths of the estate tax rate schedule for corresponding brackets. Thus, it was advantageous for the wealthy to make gifts during life rather than allow all assets to accumulate and be passed on at death. Equalization was achieved by means of a unification of the estate and gift tax rates. The terms *unified credit* and *exemption equivalent* came into being. The estate tax marital deduction was increased to the greater of $250,000 or one half of the decedent's adjusted gross estate. Other parts of the act also created a need for changes in estate plans, as well as in other types of tax planning. The phase-in period for the unified credit of $47,000 against the estate taxes of a taxable estate (equivalent to an exemption of $175,625) began in 1976; 1981 was the last year of the first five-year phase-in period. The famous "carryover of basis of property" was also a major provision of the 1976 Tax Reform Act. The Tax Reform Acts are now called "TRA—(year)." (Tax laws, by the way, are grafted onto the 1954 Internal Revenue Code, as amendments or new sections added to the Code.)

JOINT INTERESTS OF SPOUSES: FARM OR BUSINESS PROPERTY

1978

In 1978 Congress began to show concern about the basic unfairness of an estate tax that failed to account for a surviving spouse's work in a family business that had been either wholly or partially owned by the decedent spouse. A provision in the Revenue Act of 1978 gave credit for a surviving spouse's "material participation" in the operation or management of such a business. This credit was translated into a specific amount considered to have been contributed to the purchase price of real or tangible personal property held by the decedent and the decedent's spouse in joint tenancy (or tenancy by the entirety) used as a farm or in business. Other complicated provisions provided lots of work for those who interpreted that act and advised with regard to it.

1981—YEAR OF CHANGES

In 1981 Congress recognized that limiting tax-free transfers between spouses had been wrong all along. The Economic Recovery Tax Act of 1981 (ERTA) removed the quantitative limits on the marital deduction for both estate and gift tax purposes, thus allowing unlimited amounts of property to be transferred between spouses without federal estate or gift tax. The act also allowed certain transfers of "qualified terminable interest property" to qualify for this 100 percent marital deduction. Thus, a lifetime income interest only (which previously would not have qualified for the marital deduction) was allowed to qualify for tax-free status of the transfer even though it was a "terminable" interest. This provision of the law remains controversial, but it seems to have been firmly accepted. In addition, the 1981 act increased the amount of the unified credit from $47,000 to $192,800 over a six-year period, so that by 1987 no estate or gift tax would be levied on transfers aggregating $600,000 (or less).

The Economic Recovery Tax Act of 1981 was billed by the Reagan Administration as the largest tax cut in history—almost $750 billion over a six-year period. The act was not considered a revenue-raising measure but strictly tax cut legislation designed to increase savings and spur investment. Among the many benefits intended to provide incentives for business and investors was the new Accelerated Cost Recovery System (ACRS) for property placed in service after 1980. Under this system, a rapid recovery of capital costs was allowed for most tangible depreciable property. The system was, in fact, a bonanza!

As to the controversial "carryover basis" rule for the evaluation of appreciated property in an estate (requiring the decedent's original basis to be passed on to the heir), the Tax Law of 1978 had postponed the effective date until 1980. The provision was then quietly repealed. By 1981 the law had returned to the old-new rule: Property in an estate would receive a stepped-up basis as of the date of death (or, if elected by the executor, the alternate valuation date, six months later. And so the unworkable carryover basis rule passed into history alongside the likes of prohibition as a bad idea.

FISCAL RESPONSIBILITY RETURNS

1982

The 1982 Tax Act, officially titled the Tax Equity and Fiscal Responsibility Act, seemed to do a complete turnabout. It included many changes designed to aid in the collection of existing taxes and to restrict tax breaks. For one, there was a slowdown in the accelerated depreciation schedule. New provisions frowned on personal service corporations and breathed heavily on pension plans mostly favoring owner-stockholders and highly paid employees.

TAX REFORM AND DEFICIT REDUCTION

1984

The Tax Reform Act of 1984 was part of the Deficit Reduction Act of 1984. In that act, the emphasis was changed from *tax* reduction to *deficit* reduction. The extremely complex act contains over 300 detailed sections. Some interesting items: The long-term capital gain holding period has been cut to six months; there is no tax on transfers of property to a spouse during marriage or to a former spouse incident to divorce (*Davis* overturned); interest is to be imputed where interest-free loans are made to family members.

RETIREMENT EQUITY ACT OF 1984

In 1984, that prolific year of tax legislation, a domestic relations act was passed that, though not strictly a tax law, did deal with the tax treatment of benefit payments from a retirement plan that are made to a former spouse in accordance with a qualified domestic relations order. Regulations may clarify the still muddy status of this issue.

ARE WE ANY CLOSER TO SIMPLIFICATION?

A publication entitled *The President's Tax Proposals to the Congress for Fairness, Growth, and Simplicity* (Mt. Kisco, N.Y.: Research Institute of America, 1985) contains 461 closely packed pages. The laws enacted by Congress in 1984 are among the most complex legislation of our tax history. Tax changes are being churned out frenetically. Individuals and businesses alike might benefit from a few years without tax changes so that they can plan on the basis of legislation already on the books.

At this writing, however, there are simultaneous reports that a tax simplification proposal will be on the president's desk "before Christmas 1985" (a house bill, H. R. 3838, was indeed passed on December 18, 1985), that no new legislation will be enacted or even out of committee until well into 1986, that it will be years before tax simplification occurs, and so on.

What to do? The only course of action for a sensible and sophisticated observer is to follow reports of committee action. Nothing is final until the legislative process has been completed. Knowing the present status of the law and some of the background should be helpful. Since new proposals are currently leaning toward rate reductions and the elimination of many tax deductions, advisers are recommending the usual tactics—moving up charitable gifts, paying state tax obligations in advance, and so forth. Insofar as property ownership is concerned, changes based on *possible* tax changes may not be urgent, but remaining alert and informed is always advisable.

Summary of State Laws Affecting Property

INTRODUCTION TO APPENDIX II

The summaries in this appendix are not all-inclusive, inasmuch as a great deal more in the way of state legislation affects property than will be found summarized here. Rather, the summaries cover some of the subject of property as that subject has been dealt with in the preceding text. You may note, for example, that the topic "Marriage" only specifies whether or not the given state recognizes common-law marriages. Other statutory material under "Marriage" would have to do with the legality of certain marriages, the legal age of participants, requirements as to health tests, and so on—none of which is deemed pertinent to readers of this book. Therefore, bear in mind that this appendix is a capsule reference to certain state laws. For more complete coverage, refer to *Martindale-Hubbell Law Directory, Volume VII, Law Digests*, the source of the information listed here. This reference work can be found in some public libraries.

TOPICS COVERED IN THE APPENDIX

The following topics (or topics having some similar name) are covered. Not every state uses the same nomenclature, and for some states you will find subjects that are not on this list. Some version of the following types of subjects, however, will be found for each state.

- Curtesy
- Dower
- Divorce (or dissolution of marriage)
- Husband and wife
- Marriage
- Personal property
- Real property
- Taxation
- Wills (having to do with election or statutory share)

HOW TO USE THIS APPENDIX

The coverage under a particular topic is only intended to give a quick look. Under "Wills," for example, you will not find the *precise amount* of a surviving spouse's statutory share (or elective share against the will), because the information in the statute itself includes references to children of the deceased, children of the deceased from other marriages, surviving parents of the deceased, and so on. The percentage would change depending on the existence of other potential heirs. You will learn, however, whether or not a surviving spouse *may* take an elective share or *may waive* this right in the state in which you are interested.

It is also important to remember that laws undergo frequent changes and that court decisions establish legal precedents further embellishing and interpreting statutory law. The material presented is current up to 1985, but anyone whose planning depends on the up-to-the-minute law should consult an attorney for the latest update on legislation in a particular state or on case law affecting the matter at hand.

You may find that a quick look at this appendix will be very useful in some situations. Here is an example. You have inherited a house in Township X of State Y. You alone have inherited this property from your late grandmother. You do not want it or need it. It is an old building in need of repairs. It is not rentable unless expenditures are made for these repairs. You find, however, that it is salable. The owner of the house next door wants to buy it quickly, because he also has an opportunity, and may choose instead, to buy the house on the other side. You have to make an immediate decision and decide to sell. Your wife, however, is out of the country, and she may be unreachable at the time of settlement. A quick look at the law in State Y indicates that "Dower has been abolished." You may sell the house and convey good title without having your wife's signature on the deed.

Here is another situation in which you might find yourself. Your niece, Betty Smith, is getting married. She is your late brother's child, and you want to give a sizable present. However, the prospective bridegroom, George Gambler, is not to your liking and you have serious doubts that the marriage will last. What if you give the young couple the gift you have in mind and they later get divorced? You quietly go to the summary for your state and find that property owned by either party *prior* to the marriage is not subject to distribution on divorce. Of course, the law of your state (presumably where the marriage will take place) may not be the law followed in the state in which the couple might be living *if* there is a divorce, but a little further search reveals that most states follow that rule. You quickly call your broker and tell him to buy 1,000 shares of Good Corporation Stock in the name of Betty Smith. *Now*. She is getting married next week. P.S.: If Betty has looked into this matter, she might be inclined to retain the stock in her separate ownership.

The material in this appendix is informational only. It would be a mistake to overlook the importance of and necessity for proper legal or other professional advice.

ALABAMA

Divorce

Property acquired before marriage or by *gift or inheritance* may *not* be considered in making allowance for the support of either spouse out of the estate of the other spouse unless such property or income from it has been used during the marriage for the spouses' common benefit. This is also the rule if divorce is granted for misconduct of the other spouse. Misconduct may be considered in determining the amount of allowance to either spouse from the estate of the other spouse, but the excepted property (property acquired before marriage or by gift or inheritance) may not be considered in determining the amount of allowance. This rule is also followed in property distribution. Again, property *used regularly* for the common benefit of the spouses during marriage may be awarded in a property settlement.

Dower and Curtesy

Abolished in Alabama.

Husband and Wife

Alabama is a separate property state. All property acquired by the wife before or after marriage and all earnings received by her from third persons are the wife's separate property.

Marriage

Common-law marriages are recognized.

Personal Property

Tenancy by the entirety does not exist in Alabama.

Real Property

Tenancy by the entirety does not exist in Alabama.

Survivorship as an incident of joint tenancy has been abolished *except* when the document (a deed, for example) uses "with right of survivorship" or other words after "joint tenants." (What this means is that an instrument creating a joint tenancy between two or more parties is construed to mean a tenancy in common unless the survivorship right is included and the instrument shows the intention to create a survivorship right.)

Taxation

There is no inheritance tax in Alabama, but there is an estate tax, equivalent to the amount of the full credit or deduction allowable in computing federal estate taxes under the federal act in effect at the time.

There is no gift tax.

Wills

A surviving spouse has the right to take an elective share, but that right may be waived.

ALASKA

Divorce

In Alaska, courts may divide property obtained during the marriage. Furthermore, courts may, for equitable distribution reasons, divide property obtained by either spouse *prior* to the marriage.

Dower

Dower has been abolished.

Husband and Wife

Each married person may own and manage his or her own property, and these rights are not subject to debts of the other spouse. In other words, Alaska is a separate property state. Either spouse may convey his or her real property as though unmarried.

Note, however, that if real property is conveyed to a husband and wife, the ownership is as tenants by the entirety unless expressly declared otherwise.

While Alaska is not a community property state, there is a statutory provision that if a married person dies holding property that was deemed community property under the laws of another jurisdiction, one half of this property is deemed to belong to the surviving spouse. The other half is the decedent's property.

Marriage

Common-law marriages are not recognized in Alaska.

Personal Property

Joint tenancy may be maintained as to interests in personal property.

Real Property

Joint tenancy has been abolished. All persons having undivided interests in realty are tenants in common. However, joint interests in personalty have not been abolished. Also, tenancy by the entirety is recognized for a husband and wife and may be created by a husband and wife between themselves.

Taxation

The inheritance tax has been repealed. An estate tax is imposed to absorb the federal allowance for state death taxes.

ARIZONA

Curtesy

Abolished.

Deeds

Arizona is a community property state, and a conveyance of community real property is not valid unless that conveyance is executed and acknowledged by both the husband and wife.

Descent and Distribution

The surviving spouse has the right of election to take an intestate share. This right may be waived by contract before or after marriage or by agreement on dissolution of marriage.

Dissolution of Marriage

A court may assign each spouse his or her sole and separate property and divide community, joint tenancy, and other property equitably, without regard to marital misconduct. Property acquired outside Arizona is considered community property if it would have been community property in Arizona at the time of acquisition.

Dower

Abolished.

Husband and Wife

All property, real or personal, owned by either spouse before marriage and any property acquired by gift or inheritance and the profits from such property are the separate property of that spouse. The separate property of a spouse is not liable for the separate debts of the other spouse, and the separate property of a spouse may be conveyed without having the other spouse join in the conveyance.

All property acquired by either the husband or wife during marriage is community property. This applies if the spouses are living in Arizona at the time they acquire the property or if at that time they are residing in a state that has a similar community property law. This does not include property described above as separate property.

A spouse owns his or her separate property and his or her share of community property, and this property passes by testamentary disposition at death or by intestacy if no will was left.

Spouses may create a joint tenancy between themselves by an agreement that shows they agreed that the property would be treated as jointly owned. Any conveyance of community realty requires the joining of both spouses.

Marital rights in property acquired in Arizona during the marriage by persons who were married outside Arizona and then moved into the state are controlled by Arizona law.

Marriage

Common-law marriages are not legal in Arizona but are recognized in Arizona if valid where they were contracted.

Antenuptial agreements are valid if they are not contrary to law or "good morals"; they may affect rights in and to community property.

Personal property

Tenancy by the entireties is not recognized.

Real Property

A conveyance to two or more persons creates a tenancy in common, but joint tenancy with right of survivorship may be created by express words. A grant to a husband and wife is presumed to establish a community tenancy, but it may create a joint tenancy between the husband and wife if the deed of conveyance contains language expressly creating such an estate and the wording is such as to indicate that the husband and wife show knowledge of that provision.

Taxation

There is no inheritance tax. The estate tax is gauged to the allowance for state death taxes in filing a federal return or paying federal estate taxes.

ARKANSAS

Curtesy

Common law curtesy has been abolished, but in its place there is a statutory allowance that is still called curtesy. The allowance is the same as the widow's dower. No conveyance by a spouse without the concurrence of the other spouse can pass title free of curtesy or dower.

Descent and Distribution

The surviving spouse takes a percentage dependent on the existence of other survivors, such as children, and on the length of time that the spouses had been married. There is also a provision with regard to community property of another jurisdiction. If personal property was acquired as community property in a community property state and/or real estate located in Arkansas was acquired with proceeds from or is traceable to community property acquired in another jurisdiction, then one half of such property belongs to the surviving spouse. The other half is the property of the decedent spouse and is not subject to the surviving spouse's right to elect against the will, and no estate of dower or curtesy exists in that half.

Divorce

On a final decree of divorce, each party receives the "undisposed" property that he or she brought into the marriage. One half of marital property is distributed to each party unless the court finds such division inequitable. Marital property is defined as all property acquired by either spouse after marriage. However, it does not include property acquired by either spouse by gift, bequest, devise, or descent; property derived from or exchanged for such property; property acquired after a decree of divorce; property excluded by valid agreement of the parties; and increase in the value of property acquired before the marriage.

Dower

Dower is still a legal estate in Arkansas, and, as was stated under "Curtesy," it applies to both spouses. If a married person dies leaving a surviving spouse and a child or children, the surviving spouse receives (is "vested of") a life interest in one third of all the real property that the decedent spouse owned and fee title in one third of the personal property that the decedent owned. The percentage changes if there are no surviving children. The Arkansas statute mentions creditors; the proportion that the surviving spouse receives "as against creditors" is roughly one third (depending on the nature of the property). There is also a specific provision relating to timber, oil, gas, and mineral property. A married person may release dower or curtesy in real estate by joining in a spouse's deed.

Husband and Wife

A married woman may acquire and hold property of any kind and do business as a "feme sole." Separate property is not liable for a husband's debts. If a married person permits his or her spouse to have control and management of separate property, this raises the presumption that the spouse is acting as agent. But if a wife allows her husband to use her separate property as his own (and thus he contracts debts based on his apparent ownership), she is *estopped* to claim it. The word "estopped" involves the legal doctrine of "estoppel." The statutory provision is mentioned here to alert anyone interested to seek further legal information.

A married person may convey or release rights in homestead, dower, or curtesy through a duly appointed power of attorney. If a husband conveys to himself and his wife, that creates the estate of entirety. Spouses may enter into antenuptial contracts, and the rights mentioned above may be legally released in such an agreement. Neither spouse is liable for debts of the other contracted prior to the marriage nor is a spouse's separate property reachable for debts of the other spouse after marriage.

Personal Property

Tenancy by the entirety exists in personal property, in shares of corporate stock, in bank accounts, and in savings accounts.

Real Property

Joint ownership of husband and wife creates an estate by entirety. Conveyance to a husband and wife creates an estate of entirety with right of survivorship. A conveyance to two or more people (not spouses) creates a tenancy in common unless a joint tenancy (with right of survivorship) is specified.

Taxation

There is no inheritance tax. The estate tax in Arkansas is equal to the credit allowable on the federal estate tax return.

Wills

The surviving spouse may elect between will and any part of property that would have been taken on intestacy (meaning statutory allowances), including dower or curtesy and homestead rights.

CALIFORNIA

Community Property

California is a community property state.

Descent and Distribution

The surviving spouse takes an outright share of the separate property of the deceased spouse. The percentage depends on who the other takers are—surviving children, parents, and so on.

Dissolution of Marriage

California is a community property jurisdiction. The parties may by written agreement divide their property or may stipulate in open court as to property division. Otherwise, the court must, in decreeing legal separation, equally divide community, quasi-community, and homestead property. The court may also award a particular asset to one party to effectuate substantially equal division or may make an additional award where one spouse has been determined to have deliberately misappropriated the community property of the other spouse. A single-family residence acquired during the marriage in joint tenancy is, upon legal separation or dissolution of the marriage, presumed to be community property.

Dower and Curtesy

There is no dower or curtesy right. A surviving spouse of a nonresident decedent has the same right to take a share of noncommunity real property against the decedent's will as though such property were situated in the decedent's domicile.

Husband and Wife

A husband and wife may hold property as joint tenants or tenants in common or as community property. Either a husband or wife (or both) may have separate property. An inventory of the separate personal property of either spouse may be recorded in the office of the county recorder in the county where the parties reside, and such a record is evidence of the title of such property. The separate property of either spouse is not liable for debts secured by community property unless there is a special assent in writing making separate property liable. A conveyance or encumbrance (mortgage) may be made by a married woman in the same manner and has the same effect as if she were unmarried. Joinder of the husband in a wife's conveyance or encumbrance of her separate property is not necessary. A married woman must join with her husband in a deed to release homestead rights or convey or encumber community property.

The *community property* system applies in California. All property owned by either spouse before marriage and acquired by either spouse after marriage by gift or inheritance, together with earnings on that property or enhancement of its value, is the separate property of that spouse and may be conveyed without the consent of the other spouse. All real property situated in California and all personal property wherever situated acquired during marriage by a married person while domiciled in California is community property.

Quasi-community property is all real and personal property wherever situated acquired by either spouse while domiciled elsewhere that would have been community property if the acquiring spouse had been domiciled in California or property that has been received in exchange for such property. [This puts the parties on notice that records should be kept if there is a desire to designate some property as separate.]

Property taken in the names of a husband and wife as joint tenants may be considered joint and not community property if the parties intend it to be joint and this is documented. However, there is a presumption in the law that property acquired by a husband and wife is community property. Unless the husband and wife carefully designate otherwise, a purchaser is protected in his reliance on the community ownership of the husband-and-wife seller.

Management and control of community personal property as to his or her share may be exercised by either spouse. A spouse operating or managing a business or interest in a business that is community property has sole management and control. As to community realty, either spouse has management and control, but both spouses must join in a lease for more than one year or in a conveyance on a sale. On the death of either spouse, one half of the community property belongs to the surviving spouse. If there is no testamentary disposition by the decedent, the decedent's share also goes to the surviving spouse. For those who are domiciled in California, this also applies to personal property, wherever situated, and to real property situated in California even though it may have been acquired while the decedent was domiciled elsewhere if it would have been community property if acquired while the decedent was domiciled in California.

Community property going to a surviving spouse may do so without probate or administration, but in that case the surviving spouse is personally liable for debts of the deceased spouse chargeable against the community property. A surviving spouse may elect that the interest of the decedent spouse in community property be probated, and for that purpose procedures exist for determining what is community property and for apportioning debts.

Marriage

Common-law marriage has not been recognized in California since 1895 but is recognized if it was valid in the state in which it was contracted.

Personal Property

Tenancy by the entirety in personal property is not recognized.

Real Property

Tenancy by the entirety is not recognized. Joint tenancy and tenancy in common are recognized and defined, but a joint tenancy is created only when it is expressly declared as such.

Taxation

The inheritance tax and gift tax were repealed effective June 9, 1982. An estate tax is imposed in California to accord with the maximum allowable state death tax credit under federal estate tax law.

Wills

A surviving spouse has no right of election between a testamentary provision, if any, and a share of the separate property of the decedent (as in the case of intestacy). However, if a spouse attempts in his or her will to make a disposition of more than half of community property, then the surviving spouse must elect whether to take under the will or to take his or her half of the community property. The surviving spouse may take property given that spouse under a will as well as his or her community share.

COLORADO

Curtesy

Tenancy by curtesy does not exist in Colorado.

Dissolution of Marriage

Property is distributed upon dissolution by giving each spouse his or her separate property and then dividing marital property in the proportions that the court deems just. The court is to disregard marital misconduct. The court is to consider these guidelines: Contributions (including contributions as homemaker); the value of the property set aside for each spouse; the increase, decrease, or depletion of property; and the economic circumstances of each party.

Dower

Abolished.

Husband and Wife

A married woman retains the separate real and personal property that she owned at marriage and the income therefrom, and she is not liable for her husband's debts. Nuptial agreements are valid and enforceable provided that full disclosure of assets is made. Neither spouse requires the consent or joinder of the other in order to convey or encumber his or her separate property.

Personal Property

A joint tenancy in personal property may be created by a declaration of joint tenancy in the instrument evidencing ownership.

Real Property

Joint tenancy and tenancy in common are recognized. Tenancy by the entirety is not. Tenancy in common is presumed unless the instrument conveying the property specifies joint tenancy.

Taxation

An inheritance tax did exist, but it does not apply to the estates of decedents dying after December 31, 1979. The gift tax also does not apply to transfers by gift occurring after December 31, 1979. The Colorado estate tax is based on the credit for state death taxes allowable under the federal estate tax.

Wills

A surviving spouse may exercise an election to take possession of up to one half of the decedent's estate by filing a petition for his or her elective share, but property already received by the surviving spouse is charged against the elective share.

CONNECTICUT

Curtesy

Abolished.

Dissolution of Marriage

The court may assign to either the husband or wife all or part of the property of the other. The court may pass title to real property to either party or to a third person, or it may order the sale of such property when in the judgment of the court sale of the property is proper to effectuate the court's decree. In fixing the nature and value of the property to be assigned, if any, the guidelines that the court is to consider are: the length of the marriage; the cause of dissolution; the age, health, station, occupation, amount and sources of income, vocational skills, employability, estate, liabilities, and needs of each party; and the opportunity of each party to effect future acquisitions of capital assets and income. The court is also to consider each party's contribution in the acquisition, preservation, or appreciation in value of the parties' respective estates. The statute gives the court broad discretion in assigning property upon the dissolution of marriage.

Dower

Abolished.

Husband and Wife

Either spouse may dispose of his or her property without having the other spouse join in the conveyance. A wife may convey and receive the conveyance of real and personal property in her own name. A wife's separate earnings are her sole property.

Real Property

A conveyance to more than one person is deemed to create a tenancy in common unless the words "as joint tenants" follows the names (this means joint tenants with right of survivorship). In reverse, a joint tenancy (with right of survivorship) may be converted into a tenancy in common by: Conveyance, mortgage, attachment and execution on a judgment, or dissolution of marriage. Tenancy by the entirety is not recognized in Connecticut.

Taxation

No inheritance tax is named as such, but a transfer tax is in the statute. An estate tax is imposed on the transfer of a decedent's estate that is equal to the amount allowed as a credit against federal estate taxes. There is no gift tax in Connecticut.

Wills

A provision in a will for a surviving spouse is deemed to be in lieu of a statutory share unless a contrary intention appears from the will. The surviving spouse must, in writing, elect to take one third of the estate for life. When a spouse elects to take a statutory share in lieu of the provision for that spouse in a will, general legacies are first taken to satisfy that share before specific legacies are disturbed.

DELAWARE

Curtesy

The estate of curtesy does not exist in Delaware.

Divorce

Marital property is divided as follows: "Upon request of either party in divorce or annulment proceeding, court shall divide equitably all marital property without regard to marital misconduct as it deems just."

Dower

The estate of dower does not exist in Delaware.

Husband and Wife

A married woman holds her property as a separate estate that she may sell, transfer, encumber, and so on. Deeds of real property executed by a married woman are valid "as if she were sole."

Personal Property

Tenancy by the entirety may exist.

Real property

Both joint tenancies and tenancies in common are recognized. There is a statutory presumption in favor of tenancies in common (except with regard to executors and trustees); but a joint tenancy can be created by express statement that the property is to be held in joint tenancy rather than as a tenancy in common. A conveyance to a husband and wife gives them an estate by the entirety "as at common law."

Taxation

There is an inheritance tax. If a gift has been made in contemplation of death, the gift tax is the same as the inheritance tax. There is also a tax on the transfer of real property or tangible personal property situated within the state though owned by nonresidents.

Wills

A surviving spouse has the right to take an elective share of $20,000 or one third of the elective estate, whichever is less, and that amount is reduced by the amount of the transfers that have been made to the surviving spouse by the decedent.

DISTRICT OF COLUMBIA

Curtesy

Abolished. (But see "Descent and Distribution.")

Descent and Distribution

The right to dower applies to the husband or wife. Neither may convey or encumber his or her real property without joinder of the other spouse. No dower attaches to land held in joint tenancy. Dower entitles the surviving spouse to a one third interest for life in real estate owned by the deceased spouse during the marriage. A spouse may release the dower right by joining in the other spouse's deed. The intestate share of the surviving spouse in real estate is in lieu of dower unless he or she files a written election to take dower. In a divorce, the court may retain to the spouse obtaining the divorce his or her right of dower in the other spouse's estate "if it seems appropriate."

Divorce

Upon the final decree of divorce, each party is assigned his or her sole and separate property acquired prior to marriage and his or her sole and separate property acquired during marriage by gift, bequest, devise, or descent. All other property acquired during marriage, regardless of how titled, is distributed in an equitable manner. Among the guidelines are: The duration of the marriage, age, health, occupation, employability, assets, debts, and provisions for the custody of minor children. Fault in breaking up the marriage may or may not be a consideration in property distribution.

Dower

Applies to husband and wife. See "Descent and Distribution."

Marriage

Common-law marriages are recognized.

Personal Property

Tenancy by the entirety exists.

Real Property

Conveyance to a husband and wife as joint tenants (unless otherwise specified) creates a tenancy by the entirety. If not expressly designated as a joint tenancy, a conveyance to two or more persons (including a husband and wife) is a tenancy in common; however, an estate vested in executors or trustees, as such, is a joint tenancy, unless expressly stated to be a tenancy in common.

Taxation

An inheritance tax is imposed by statute. The tax includes real property and personal property, tangible or intangible, having a taxable situs in the District. This applies whether the decedent is a resident or a nonresident and whether the property passes by will or by operation of law. There is no gift tax as such, but the inheritance tax is imposed on gifts made in contemplation of death. Gifts made in contemplation of death (with a presumption that they were so made if they were made within two years prior to death) form a part of the taxable estate. The taxable estate also includes transfers taking effect after the death of the decedent where the decedent retained enjoyment of income or the right to designate beneficiaries. An estate tax is imposed to obtain the credit allowed by federal estate tax laws for state death taxes. Any inheritance tax payable to the District is deducted in determining this tax.

Wills

A surviving spouse who files a written renunciation of the will of the decedent spouse becomes entitled to the share of the decedent's estate to which he or she would have been entitled had the decedent died intestate (with dower if this is elected in lieu of real estate). The intestate share applies if the decedent made no devise or bequest to the surviving spouse or if any estate of the decedent is undisposed of by will. Otherwise, the will of the decedent spouse applies unless the surviving spouse renounces it.

FLORIDA

Curtesy

Abolished in Florida.

Dissolution of Marriage

There is no statute regarding the division of the spouses' property. The court has the power to adjudicate property rights only where these are made an issue by the parties. The terms of any valid property settlement agreed to by the parties generally may not be modified by the court. Where the parties are unable to agree on the disposition of property, then the court has power to determine disposition, based on legal and equitable principles.

Dower

Abolished in Florida.

Elective Share of Surviving Spouse

The surviving spouse of a person who dies domiciled in Florida has the right to an elective share of the estate of the deceased spouse. No elective share exists in the Florida property of a decedent who was not domiciled in Florida. The size of the elective share is spelled out in detail in the statute.

Husband and Wife

Real or personal property may be held in the name of either the husband or wife or in the names of both. A married woman may contract, sell, convey, mortgage, etc., her real and personal property (except homestead property) without joinder of her husband. Both spouses must join in the sale, gift, or mortgage of homestead property. [It is important to consider this provision because you may not think of the Florida condominium as the family "homestead." If you think of buying from a married seller, make sure that the spouse signs the deed, because the condominium might be their homestead.]

Personal Property

Personal (and real) property may be held by a husband and wife as tenants by the entirety.

Real Property

All interests in real estate that were recognized by common law are recognized in Florida. Survivorship as to joint tenancies has been abolished unless the instrument expressly provides for it. Where property is conveyed to a husband and wife, however, they are presumed to take as tenants by the entirety (with resulting survivorship). In case of divorce, former spouses become tenants in common.

Taxation

There is no inheritance or gift tax in Florida. The tax on the estates of resident and nonresident decedents is equal to the amounts allowed as credits or deductions from similar taxes levied by the United States or any state.

Wills

If an election is filed, the remaining assets of the estate after payment of the elective share (as indicated above under the topic "Elective Share of Surviving Spouse") are distributed as though the surviving spouse had predeceased the decedent. The surviving spouse has the right to "dissent" from the will of the deceased spouse.

GEORGIA

Curtesy

No tenancy by curtesy in Georgia.

Divorce

Property acquired by the parties during marriage is subject to equitable division. After separation, no transfer of property by either party (except in payment of preexisting debt) will pass title so as to defeat the vesting of property according to the verdict of the jury or court in a divorce action. Agreements as to property, alimony, etc., made between the parties in contemplation of the divorce are valid.

Dower

The right of dower has been abolished by Georgia laws.

Husband and Wife

The property of the wife at the time of marriage remains her separate property, and any property acquired by her (or earnings, etc.) during marriage remains separate and is not liable for any debt of the husband. When a transaction between a husband and wife is attacked as a fraud on the creditors of either the husband or wife, the burden is on the married person to show that the transaction is fair, and not in a fraudulent act. Either spouse may convey or encumber his or her real estate without joinder or consent of the other. A wife must join in her husband's conveyance of real property to which he obtained title in her right.

Personal Property

Joint tenancy with survivorship as under common law (including tenancy by the entirety) has been abolished. However, rights of survivorship may be created by contract. An instrument of title in favor of two or more is construed to create an interest in common without survivorship unless the instrument expressly refers to the takers as joint tenants or as taking jointly with survivorship.

Real Property

The word "heirs" is unnecessary to create a fee simple estate. Every properly executed conveyance creates a fee simple estate unless a lesser estate is mentioned. Thus, estates for the life of a tenant may be created by an express agreement or by operation of law. Any conveyance to two or more persons is construed to create a tenancy in common unless the instrument contains reference to joint tenants. Tenancy by the entirety is not recognized.

Taxation

There is no inheritance tax in Georgia. The estate tax is equal to the credit allowed on the federal estate tax return, and credit is also allowed for death taxes paid to another state on the transfer of property outside Georgia.

Wills

A married person may by will make provision for a surviving spouse in lieu of a year's support, in which case the surviving spouse must make an election. A legatee having a claim adverse to the will must elect whether to claim under the will or against it (unless that legatee is also a creditor).

HAWAII

Curtesy

Hawaii has adopted the Uniform Probate Code, which has provisions for election by a spouse to take the prescribed share. However, for rights in the property of a married person that accrued prior to July 1, 1977, the husband has a life interest in one third of the lands owned by the wife in fee simple at her death and an absolute right to ownership of one third of her remaining property. During her life, he has no curtesy right, inchoate or otherwise.

Divorce

A court has discretion to divide and distribute any property of the divorcing spouses, real, personal, mixed, and joint or separate.

Dower

Although Hawaii has adopted the Uniform Probate Code, for rights accruing prior to July 1, 1977, a wife has a dower right to one third of the land owned by her husband at any time during the marriage and is also entitled to ownership of one third of his remaining property at his death. After July 1, 1977, Hawaii law allows the wife only one third of lands owned by the husband at any time during the marriage prior to July 1, 1977, that are not included in his net estate; the remaining property is then subject to the spouses' elective share provisions as set forth in the Uniform Probate Code as adopted in Hawaii.

Election

Both spouses have the right to elect the statutory share.

Husband and Wife

A married woman may contract as if sole and may control her property, both real and personal, as if sole. Agreements and deeds between spouses in contemplation of divorce or separation are valid. Agreements for support and maintenance made in contemplation of divorce or separation are valid if approved by the court but are subject to modification if changed circumstances are shown.

A husband may not release the wife's dower right by power of attorney from the wife.

Marriage

Common-law marriages are not recognized in Hawaii.

Personal Property

Tenancy by the entirety exists for shares of corporate stock, automobiles, and so forth. However, a motor vehicle registered in two or more names presumes ownership in joint tenancy.

Real Property

A conveyance or devise to two or more persons is construed to create a tenancy in common unless it appears from the instrument that it was intended to create a joint tenancy or a tenancy by the entirety.

Inheritance Tax

Property and interests subject to the estate and transfer tax are governed by the new act applying to the estates of persons dying after June 30, 1983. This act taxes all property passing by will or inheritance laws from a resident decedent and all property of a nonresident decedent within the state, and any gift of such property that is made in contemplation of death (or that is to take effect in enjoyment or possession after death) is liable to tax. When real or personal property is held in the joint names of two or more persons or there is a bank account in the names of two or more persons payable to the survivor, then Hawaii law imposes an inheritance tax on the entire property on the death of one of those named joint owners. However, survivors may prove original ownership of all or part of such property. This is similar to the federal law. As to property in the joint names of a husband and wife, the tax is imposed on one half only.

There is a provision for reciprocal exemption from tax if the decedent is a resident of a jurisdiction that exempts a Hawaiian nonresident from tax on personalty that has a nontangible situs in the decedent's state of residence.

Dower is not taxable.

As to the estate tax, a new law applies to the property subject to the estate tax of any person who dies after June 30, 1983. Under this law, the estate tax is imposed on estates to equal the federal credit allowed for state taxes paid on the transfer of taxable estates. An additional tax is imposed on the transfer at death of real property situated in Hawaii and of tangible personal property having an actual situs in Hawaii even though owned by a nonresident of Hawaii. Reciprocal enforcement of death taxes is provided for in the case of nonresident decedents.

There is no gift tax (except for a tax on gifts made in contemplation of death).

IDAHO

Community Property

Idaho is a community property state. The specifics are covered under the topic "Husband and Wife."

Curtesy

Abolished. Spouses have a right of election.

Descent and Distribution

Idaho has a provision regarding quasi-community property. This is defined as "all personal property, wherever situated, and all real property situated in Idaho which has heretofore been acquired or is hereafter [after 1972] acquired by the decedent while domiciled elsewhere and which would have been the community property of the decedent and the surviving spouse had the decedent been domiciled in this state at the time of its acquisition plus all personal property, wherever situated, and all real property situated in this state" which was acquired in exchange for property that would have been community property had the decedent been domiciled in Idaho at that time. Specific provisions stipulate that 50 percent of quasi-community property belongs to the surviving spouse, while the other 50 percent is subject to the testamentary disposition of the decedent or goes directly to the surviving spouse if it is not disposed of by the will of the decedent.

An "augmented estate" consists of a restoration of property or its value to a decedent's estate if the decedent "gave" the property to a person other than the surviving spouse without the consent of that spouse. The statute also spells out other ways in which a decedent might have removed property that would otherwise have been part of the community property of an estate. The elective share is based on the "augmented estate." A surviving spouse may renounce or waive the elective share, and this may also be done before or after marriage by a written contract, after fair disclosure. Such a waiver is also allowed as part of the property settlement entered into after or in anticipation of separation or divorce.

Divorce

A court presiding over a divorce divides community property "as may be just." Agreements as to property transfer that may have been made during the marriage to take effect on death are revoked by divorce.

Dower

Dower does not exist.

Husband and Wife

All money or other property owned by either spouse before marriage or received afterward by gift or inheritance and earnings or proceeds from such property are that spouse's separate property. Spouses may by written agreement specifically provide that all or specified property shall be the separate property of one spouse or the other. A community obligation incurred by a husband or wife without the consent in writing of the other spouse will not obligate the separate property of the nonconsenting spouse. One spouse may convey real property to the other spouse, and thereafter it is presumed to be the separate estate of the grantee spouse. The grantor spouse executes and acknowledges the conveyance. All property acquired after marriage is community property. This includes the rents and profits of the separate property of either spouse—unless the instrument by which such property is acquired by one spouse provides that the rents and profits are for that spouse's sole and separate use. A husband and wife have joint management and control of community property. If community real property is placed in a revocable trust, it retains its community property character.

Neither a husband nor a wife may sell, convey, or mortgage community real property unless the other spouse joins in by executing and acknowledging the deed or other instrument of conveyance.

In connection with property succession on the death of a spouse, real property in another state owned by a domiciliary of Idaho would be included as quasi-community property (defined above) *if* the laws of that state permit the descent and distribution of such property to be governed by the laws of Idaho.

Marriage

Common-law marriages are recognized. A common-law marriage exists when the parties consent to be married and mutually assume marital rights, duties, or obligations. When properly executed and recorded, marriage settlements may vary the rights of spouses from those listed in statutes.

Personal Property

The presumption is that all property acquired during marriage is community property. Tenancy by the entirety does not exist.

Real Property

Conveyance to two or more persons creates a tenancy in common unless the document expressly declares that a joint tenancy is being conveyed or unless the property is acquired as partnership or community property.

Taxation

Although there is an inheritance tax, it is not levied on community property transferred to a surviving husband or wife.

There is no gift tax, but the inheritance tax applies to gifts that are made in contemplation of the donor's death or that are to take effect after the donor's death.

There is no estate tax.

Wills

Renunciation of property left by will is permitted. Written waiver of the right to renounce is also permitted.

In settling the estate of a decedent, expenses are not to be charged against the survivor's share of community property. Where the estate consists partly of separate property and partly of community property, community debts are charged to community property and separate debts to separate property. Administration expenses are apportioned and charged against the different kinds of property in proportion to their relative value.

ILLINOIS

Curtesy and Dower

Abolished in Illinois.

Dissolution of Marriage

A marital property distribution system is used in the disposition of property. Marital property is all property acquired by either spouse subsequent to the marriage. Certain property is excepted from this category and considered "nonmarital," regardless of whether title to that property is held individually or in some form of co-ownership. Increase in the value of nonmarital property during the marriage because of the owning spouse's personal effort does not cause the property to become marital. If nonmarital and marital property are commingled into newly acquired property, however, such property will be marital. A right to reimbursement exists, but the spouse's contribution must be traceable by clear and convincing evidence. In a proceeding for the dissolution of marriage, the court assigns each spouse's nonmarital property to that spouse and divides marital property (without regard to marital misconduct) "in just proportions." Here are the relevant factors that the court is to consider:

1. Each party's contribution to the acquisition of the property.
2. The value of the property.
3. The duration of the marriage.
4. The economic circumstances of each spouse.
5. Obligations and rights arising from prior marriages.
6. Any antenuptial agreement.
7. The parties' age, health, occupation, needs, and so on.
8. Custodial provisions for children.
9. Whether apportionment is in lieu of or in addition to maintenance.
10. The reasonable opportunity of each spouse to acquire future assets and income.
11. The tax consequences of the property division.

Marriage

Common-law marriages (after June 30, 1905) are invalid.

A married woman is entitled to her own earnings. She may make contracts and incur liabilities as if she were unmarried.

Personal Property

Tenancy by the entirety does not exist in Illinois. To create a joint tenancy with right to survivorship in personal property, that intent must be expressed in establishing the tenancy.

Real Property

All common law estates are recognized. Tenancy by the entirety has been abolished. Joint tenancy with right of survivorship can be created only by an express declaration that the estate is a joint tenancy and not a tenancy in common. A grantor can create a joint tenancy with right of survivorship even though he is also a grantee.

(This means that someone owning property as a sole owner can convey it to himself and another as JTRS, if desired.)

Taxation

The inheritance tax was repealed for decedents dying after December 31, 1982. An inheritance tax was imposed on the transfer of the estates of decedents who died prior to that date.

An estate tax is imposed that is equal to the state death tax credit for federal estate tax purposes.

Wills

A surviving spouse may renounce the decedent's will and take a statutory share (the size of that share depends on what other descendants remain).

INDIANA

Curtesy and Dower

Common law curtesy and dower have been abolished. A joint deed of a husband and wife is sufficient to convey any interest of either spouse or both spouses in lands held by them. A married person may execute a deed to his or her separate property as if he or she were unmarried, that is, without the spouse's joinder.

Descent and Distribution

Since common law dower and curtesy have been abolished, a surviving spouse has the right to take a statutory share.

Dissolution of Marriage

The system of property distribution is marital. A court must divide the divorcing parties' property in a just and reasonable manner, based on: (1) The contribution of each spouse to its acquisition; (2) the extent to which it was acquired prior to the marriage; (3) the economic circumstances of the spouses; (4) the conduct of the parties during the marriage as related to the disposition of property; and (5) the earnings or earning ability of each party.

As to common-law marriages, a court decision held that claims brought as a common-law spouse under current Indiana law would not be actionable but that recovery could be based on contractual or equitable grounds (410 N.E.2d 1325).

Husband and Wife

All the legal disabilities of married women with regard to the making of contracts were abolished in 1881. A married woman may acquire, convey, and encumber real and personal property in her own name and may retain as her separate property income and profits from her separate property, business, or service.

A married person may sell, mortgage, lease, or execute any instrument of any kind affecting his or her property as if he or she were unmarried.

When a husband and wife take title to real estate jointly, an estate by the entireties is created. Each will own an equal and unseverable interest. Upon the death of either, the survivor holds the entire estate. Real estate purchased by a husband and wife under a written contract is deemed to be held by them as tenants by the entireties.

Personal Property

Estates by the entirety, however, do not exist as to personal property, except when such property is directly derived from real estate held by the entirety (such as crops).

Personal property that is owned by two or more persons is owned by them as tenants in common unless the instrument expressly states that a joint tenancy is being conveyed. However, a survivorship interest is presumed in the case of personalty that is conveyed to a husband and wife jointly (unless a contrary intent is clearly expressed in a written instrument).

Real Property

A conveyance or devise of land or an interest in land is taken to create a tenancy in common and not a joint tenancy, unless a contrary intention is expressed. A conveyance to a husband and wife (or to executors or trustees) is, however, held by them in joint tenancy.

Taxation

An inheritance tax is imposed on transfers by will, by intestacy, or by lifetime transfers made within two years of death (and presumed to have been made in contemplation of death).

The Indiana estate tax equals the federal death tax credit minus the state death taxes paid.

Wills

A surviving spouse may not be deprived by will, *without consent*, of an absolute interest in one third of both the real and personal property of the decedent. In electing against the will, the surviving spouse is deemed to renounce all other interests in the property of the decedent spouse. The surviving spouse may consent to be deprived by the will.

IOWA

Curtesy and Dower

Abolished in Iowa.

Dissolution of Marriage

With regard to division of property of spouses, the ultimate question before the court is whether distribution of property and assets is "equitable" under the specific facts of the case. Where the accumulated property is not the product of the joint efforts of both parties, or where one party brings property into the marriage, there need not necessarily be division of that property. Otherwise, the court may make such order in relation to children, property, parties, and maintenance of parties "as may be just."

Husband and Wife

All disabilities of married women have been removed.

A married woman may own in her own right real and personal property and manage and dispose of it in the same manner as the husband can dispose of property belonging to him. But the *right of either spouse to a distributive share in the realty of the other cannot be affected by a conveyance or mortgage in which he or she does not join.*

Personal Property

Tenancy by the entireties is not permitted.

Real Property

Common law estates are recognized, but tenancy by the entirety is not recognized. A conveyance to two or more is construed as creating a tenancy in common unless the intent to create a joint tenancy is expressed.

Taxation

There is an inheritance tax.

There is no gift tax, but an inheritance tax applies to gifts made in contemplation of death or to take effect after death. (Gifts made within three years of death are presumed made in contemplation.)

There is an estate tax not exceeding the maximum credit allowed by the federal estate tax law.

Wills

Where an intestate decedent leaves children, or where the surviving spouse of the testate decedent elects against the will, the surviving spouse is entitled to one third in value of all legal or equitable estates in real property. A surviving spouse may elect to take or refuse to take under a will (electing a statutory share instead).

KANSAS

Curtesy and Dower

Abolished. The husband has the same interest in his deceased wife's property as a widow has in her deceased husband's property.

A surviving spouse is given the right to receive an undivided one-half interest in all of the real estate in which the deceased spouse *at any time during the marriage* had a legal or equitable interest.

A conveyance by one spouse alone who has title does not defeat the inchoate interest of the nonowning spouse. This inchoate interest is defeated or extinguished only by one of the following:

1. When the nonowning spouse has consented in writing (usually by joining in the conveyance).
2. By an election to take under the grantor's will.
3. When the real estate is taken by a legal proceeding (as a judicial sale on execution of a judgment).
4. If the nonjoining spouse was not a resident of Kansas at the time of the conveyance and was never a resident during the marriage.

Any purchaser from the spouse who has title receives the entire fee simple, but subject to the inchoate right of the nonjoining spouse, which will ripen into an absolute right on the death of the grantor (titled) spouse. [It appears that although dower and curtesy are abolished in Kansas, they are actually preserved in this statutory form.]

Divorce

The court is to divide real and personal property of the parties, regardless of whether acquired separately prior to or during marriage or acquired by joint efforts of the married couple. In making division of the property, the court is to consider: The age of parties; the duration of marriage; the property owned by the parties; their present and future earning capacities; the time, source and manner of acquisition of the property; family ties and obligations; allowance of maintenance or lack thereof; dissipation of assets; and other necessary factors.

Husband and Wife

Married persons retain as sole and separate property any property, real or personal, owned at the time of marriage, or since acquired by descent, devise, bequest, or gift. A married person may carry on any trade or business and perform services for that person's sole and separate account, and such person's earnings and profits are that person's sole and separate property. However, property acquired by either spouse after marriage, whether held individually or in co-ownership, becomes marital property and is considered such at the time an action for divorce commences. Spouses' interests vest at commencement of the action; the extent of the vested interest is determined by the court.

A married person may buy, sell, and contract with respect to that person's separate property.

It is not necessary for husband and wife to join in conveyances by one of them, except to bar the inchoate statutory interest or where the property being conveyed is a homestead.

Marriage

Common-law marriage is recognized.

Personal Property

Tenancy by the entirety does not exist.

Real Property

Common law estates exist. Joint tenancies and estates by entirety were abolished in 1891. Therefore, conveyance to two or more creates a tenancy in common unless the language used makes it clear that a joint tenancy is intended. Joint tenancy may be created by a grant from an owner to himself and another.

Taxation

There is an inheritance tax. Taxable transfers include all passing of property or property interests. Transfers within one year of death are deemed to have been made in contemplation of death. Transfers to or for the benefit of a surviving spouse are exempt from transfer tax.

An estate tax is imposed on the estate of every decedent in an amount that will enable the state to absorb the maximum credit allowed under the Internal Revenue Code.

There is no gift tax.

Wills

A surviving spouse who has not consented to the testator's will in the testator's lifetime may elect whether to take under the will or by law of intestate succession, but is not entitled to both.

KENTUCKY

Curtesy and Dower

A surviving spouse has an estate in fee of one half of surplus real estate owned by a decedent spouse at death if the decedent died intestate. Also, a surviving spouse takes an estate for life in one third of the real estate owned by the decedent during life but not so owned by the decedent at death, unless such interest has been relinquished. The survivor also has an estate in one half of personalty. This right is barred if the surviving spouse had joined in deeds of conveyance, as to land.

Dissolution of Marriage

Factors are set forth in the law for court-ordered declaration of separate property of the parties and division of marital property. Marital misconduct is to be disregarded (but case law holds otherwise). Written agreement between the parties is encouraged and enforced unless the court finds it "unconscionable."

Husband and Wife

A married woman may acquire and hold property, real and personal, in her own name and may sell, encumber, and dispose of her personal property.

Either spouse may sell, convey, or encumber his or her real property, but the other spouse retains the right to curtesy or dower unless he or she joins in the instrument or releases the right by separate instrument. Gifts or assignment of personal property must be recorded to bind third parties.

Marriage

Common-law marriages contracted in Kentucky are not recognized as valid.

Personal Property

Tenancy by the entirety in personal property is recognized.

Real Property

Joint tenancy is recognized, but the common law right of survivorship between joint tenants is abolished. (This means that if survivorship is intended, it must be spelled out in the document "JTRS and not as Tenants in Common.")

The same thing applies to a conveyance to husband and wife. There is no mutual right to the entirety by survivorship between them, but they take as tenants in common—unless tenancy by the entireties with survivorship is expressly provided for in the conveyance or document.

Taxation

There is an inheritance tax on the transfer of property passing by will or by the intestacy laws of the state.

There is no gift tax, but the inheritance tax applies to gifts deemed in contemplation of death or to take effect at or after death.

In addition to the inheritance tax, an estate tax is imposed for the purpose of taking "full advantage of the credit allowed for state succession duties by federal estate tax law."

Wills

A surviving spouse may, within six months after probate, renounce the will of the deceased spouse and take the dower or curtesy share of the estate as if no will had been made. If the decedent held real estate in fee simple at death, the elective share is only one third of such real estate.

LOUISIANA

Curtesy and Dower

These estates are unknown to the law of Louisiana.

Descent and Distribution

When a person dies after December 31, 1981, and leaves no will, property descends to various persons by law, depending on the classification of the property as community or separate property of the deceased. A surviving spouse inherits the community property share undisposed of by the deceased spouse if there are no descendants. If there are descendants, the undisposed share of the community property is inherited by such descendants.

Divorce

After filing a petition for separation or divorce, either spouse may be awarded occupancy of the family home pending partition of their community property. The court considers the relative economic status of the parties and the best interest of the family. The concept of fault exists. The party against whom a separation has been pronounced loses all advantages to which he or she might have been entitled in considering contributions to the marriage. The party who obtains the judgment preserves the consideration given his/her contributions, even if such contributions were reciprocally made.

Husband and Wife

Separate property of a spouse consists of property acquired prior to the establishment of the community property regime, acquired individually by inheritance or gift, or acquired as the result of a voluntary partition of community property during the existence of the community property regime. A separate property regime may be established by agreement or by a judgment of separation. Each spouse may use and dispose of separate property without the concurrence of the other spouse.

A community property system applies to spouses domiciled in Louisiana. Unless modified or terminated by agreement, this system provides that each spouse owns a present undivided one-half interest in the community property. Spouses may, without court approval, voluntarily partition community property in whole or in part during the existence of the community regime. Property acquired by such partition then becomes separate property. Each spouse may manage, control, or dispose of community property unless otherwise provided by law.

Marriage

Common-law marriages are not recognized in Louisiana.

Personal Property

Tenancy by the entirety in personalty is not permitted in Louisiana.

Real Property

Louisiana law is based on the French civil law and not the English common law. Therefore, Louisiana does not recognize any of the common law estates, such as tenancy in common, joint tenancy, tenancy by the entirety, etc. There is, however, a form of ownership (called a "usufruct"), similar to the common law life estate, in which the title is vested in another.

Taxation

An inheritance tax is levied on all inheritances, legacies, and gifts (called "donations") in contemplation of death.

An estate tax equalizes the state inheritance tax and federal estate tax allowance for state death taxes. The difference between the credit and amount of state inheritance tax (if less) must be paid to the state.

There is a gift tax, with certain lifetime and annual exclusions. Above those exclusions a tax is due on all transfers by gift, with varying rates depending on the amount of the gift.

Wills

In Louisiana there are limitations on disposition by will. The law reserves to descendants of a property owner ("forced heirs") a certain portion of the estate (termed "legitime"). These heirs create a limitation on the disposable (by will) portion of the estate according to a particular percentage described in detail in the law.

MAINE

Curtesy and Dower

Abolished.

Descent and Distribution

A surviving spouse takes a distributive share in the estate of a deceased spouse.

Divorce

All property acquired subsequent to marriage and prior to legal separation or divorce is presumed to be marital property unless shown to be otherwise. The court has broad powers over disposition of marital property. A divorce decree filed in the registry of deeds office for the district where the real estate is located will effectively extinguish the claim of a nonowner spouse and establish any rights in real estate acquired by the divorce decree.

Husband and Wife

A married woman has the same rights and liabilities as a married man. All disabilities of marriage have been removed. A married woman may hold any property, real or personal, as her separate property, and her control over her property is as absolute as the control of her husband over his property. A married person may convey separate property, real or personal, without the joinder or consent of his/her spouse, but real estate conveyed from one spouse to the other requires joinder.

Marriage

The law is unclear on *common-law marriages*, but they "probably" would not be not recognized. Out-of-state common law marriages probably would be recognized.

Personal Property

There is no statutory provision for tenancy by the entirety in personalty.

Real Property

Tenancy by the entirety is not recognized. The presumption is that a conveyance to two or more persons creates an estate in common, unless an estate in joint tenancy and the intention to create such an estate is clearly shown by the language of the document. Thus, deeds naming two or more grantees as joint tenants are construed as vesting a fee simple estate in them *with survivorship*.

Taxation

An inheritance tax is imposed. However, it will not apply to estates of persons whose death occurs after June 30, 1986.

In addition to the inheritance tax (which will not apply to testamentary estates occurring after June 30, 1986), an estate tax is imposed to obtain credit on a federal return for state death taxes paid.

There is no gift tax, but the inheritance tax applies to gifts made in contemplation of death or intended to take effect after death.

Wills

The Uniform Probate Code has been adopted with modifications.

MARYLAND

Curtesy and Dower

Abolished.

Divorce

The Maryland divorce court is empowered to make certain disposition of property in cases filed after January 1, 1979, and may exercise this power after a foreign divorce (granted in another state) if one spouse was domiciled in Maryland when the foreign proceeding commenced and the foreign court exercised no jurisdiction over that spouse or property at issue. The Maryland court, when granting either divorce or separation, may order partition or sale of jointly owned personal property but may not transfer title. When granting an absolute divorce, the court has the same powers as to real property. When granting an absolute divorce, the court is to determine the value of marital property (acquired during the marriage other than by inheritance or gift) and may grant a monetary award as an adjustment of the equities of the parties concerning marital property. Some of the factors to be considered in balancing the equities are: monetary and nonmonetary contributions of each spouse; military pensions or retirement benefits; determination of which property is the family home and family use personal property. The court may issue orders as to the use or possession of such property regardless of how it is titled or owned.

Husband and Wife

All disabilities of married women are removed.

Property belonging to a woman at the time of marriage and all property she may acquire or receive after marriage is protected from the debts of her husband. Property of the husband is his own and free from claims of his wife or her creditors.

Husband or wife may convey, transfer, or encumber separate personal or real property without the consent or joinder of the other.

Marriage

Common-law marriage is not permitted but will be recognized in Maryland if valid in the state where it is contracted.

Personal Property

Tenancy by the entirety is recognized. Husband and wife may acquire personal property as tenants by entireties, and conveyance to a husband and wife is presumed to be held as tenants by the entirety unless a contrary ownership is designated. Also, property purchased with entirety money is entirety property. An instrument in writing must expressly provide joint tenancy if such ownership is intended (instead of entirety ownership).

Real Property

All common law estates in real property are recognized. If a document purports to create other than tenancy in common, there must be language indicating that joint tenancy is intended. Any deed or devise to a husband and wife creates a tenancy by the entirety unless otherwise provided. An owner or owners, including husband and/or wife, may convey to themselves or others without using a straw man.

Taxation

There is an inheritance tax imposed on the value of all tangible or intangible property, real or personal, having a taxable situs in Maryland, passing on the death of a resident or nonresident decedent, or by gift made within two years of death (if in contemplation of death). This includes property in which the decedent had an interest as a joint tenant or tenant in common and property over which the decedent had retained dominion during his lifetime (such as insurance in which he still retained incidents of ownership). There is an *exception*. Property held by a husband and wife as tenants by entireties or as joint tenants that passes to the surviving spouse is exempt from inheritance tax.

There is no gift tax, but the inheritance tax applies to gifts in contemplation of death or intended to take effect at or after death.

A tax is imposed on the transfer of a "Maryland estate" equal to the amount, if any, by which the credit under federal estate tax law exceeds the aggregate of state death taxes payable out of the Maryland estate of the decedent.

Wills

Dower and curtesy are abolished. Either surviving spouse may elect to take a statutory share in election against the will.

MASSACHUSETTS

Curtesy

Curtesy has been abolished in Massachusetts. Curtesy and dower rights are merged together and called dower. A surviving husband is given the same dower rights as a surviving wife.

Descent and Distribution

A surviving spouse must file an election of dower in the offices of the probate registry. This situation applies only to real estate not disposed of by the decedent's will.

Divorce

Alimony may be awarded to either party. In determining the amount the following factors are required to be considered (not precluding other factors): Length of marriage; conduct of parties during marriage; age, health, station, occupation, amount and sources of income; vocational skills, employability, estate, liabilities and needs of each of the parties; and opportunity of each party for future acquisition of capital and income. Discretionary factors are: Contribution of each of the parties in the acquisition, preservation or appreciation in value of their respective estates; and contribution of each of the parties as homemaker to the family unit.

Division of property of the spouses may be ordered in addition to or in lieu of alimony, following application of the same factors.

Property is subject to division irrespective of how title is held or how it was acquired.

Dower

The merged-together limited dower and curtesy rights that remain in Massachusetts are obtained by filing a claim in the registry of probate within six months after approval of an administrator's bond. Dower applies only to real estate owned by the decedent spouse at the time of death. Any encumbrances made during life take precedence over dower rights. The probate court may assign dower. A tenant by dower is entitled to possession and profits of an undivided one third of the decedent spouse's real estate until the assignment is made.

Husband and Wife

All disabilities of married women are removed.

Real and personal property owned by any person upon marriage remain that person's separate property. A married person may receive, receipt for, hold, manage, and dispose of property, real or personal, as if such person were sole.

Either spouse may convey individually.

Marriage

Common-law marriages are not recognized.

Personal Property

There is no statutory provision, but case law indicates that tenancy by the entirety exists with reference to personal property (293 Mass. 67, 199 N.E. 383).

Real Property

Common law estates exist in real property. A conveyance or devise to two or more persons (except a mortgage or conveyance or devise in trust) creates a tenancy in common unless the instrument states explicitly (or by inference) that a joint tenancy is intended to be created in the takers. After August 30, 1979, a conveyance or devise to two persons as tenants by the entirety creates a joint tenancy (and not a tenancy in common) if they are not married to each other.

Taxation

An estate tax is imposed to absorb credit for state death taxes allowed by present or future federal revenue laws.

Wills

A surviving spouse may file in the registry of probate a written waiver of the will's provisions and take a statutory share of the decedent spouse's estate. [Example: If a testator leaves children, the surviving spouse is entitled to one third of personal and real property.]

MICHIGAN

Curtesy

Abolished.

Descent and Distribution

The right of a surviving spouse to an intestate share may be waived by written agreement made before or after marriage.

Divorce

The divorce court may award to either party all or part (as it deems just and reasonable) of the real and personal property (or its monetary value) that came to either party by reason of the marriage. If the property awarded to either party is insufficient for suitable support and maintenance of either party and the children, the court may make a further award to either party of the property of either party. The factors to consider are: Ability, character, and situation of the parties and all other circumstances. A husband and wife who own realty as joint tenants or as tenants by the entirety become tenants in common. If a party contributed to the acquisition or improvement of the other spouse's property, the court may award that party all or an equitable portion of such property.

Dower

Dower is recognized. It is the widow's right to the use for life of one third of all the estate of inheritance owned by her husband during the marriage. If a husband attempted to transfer that property during the marriage, the property would still be subject to the widow's dower at the husband's death. The value would be the value at the date of transfer. However, the dower right will not prevail against a purchase money mortgage given by the husband. A nonresident wife is not entitled to dower in lands conveyed by her husband during his life but only in those he owned at his death. A wife may contract with her husband for release of dower. By joining in her husband's deed, a wife relinquishes and bars her dower right in that property. She may also bar dower by conveyance to her husband or by antenuptial agreement for certain property rights in lieu of dower.

A court granting divorce must include in its decree a provision in lieu of the dower right of the wife in the property of the husband to extinguish claims the wife might have in present or future property of husband.

Husband and Wife

Property owned by a husband or wife before or after marriage (unless joint) is his or her separate property, with the right to manage and dispose of it alone. Separate property of either spouse is not liable for the debts of the other. Exception: A husband's real estate is subject to his widow's dower. A married woman may enter into a written contract, jointly or severally, with another person.

Property may be held by the entireties. Unless otherwise expressly provided, real property conveyed to a husband and wife is deemed to be held by entireties. Personal property in the form of stocks, bonds, debentures, notes, mortgages and other evidences of indebtedness payable to a husband and wife is deemed to be held jointly with right of survivorship in the same manner as real estate held by the entireties; but this presumption does not extend to bank deposits, insurance, or other simple contracts.

To convey or encumber property held by the entireties, a husband and wife must join in the same instrument. A husband need not join in a deed of his wife's separate property. A wife's dower is barred by the wife's joining in the husband's conveyance or may be barred by a separate instrument expressing this intention.

A married woman may enter into a contract with respect to her separate property and carry on business for her own account. She may contract directly with her husband, including partnership with him. If a married woman acts as surety for the obligation of another, including her husband, any judgment on the same may be satisfied out of her separate property whether or not the contract of suretyship concerns that separate property. A married woman may enter into a written contract assigning her separate property as security for the debt of another (including her husband). A contract relating to property made by persons in contemplation of marriage remains in force after marriage.

The community property system no longer prevails in Michigan, although it did. The repealing act became effective May 10, 1948.

Marriage

Common-law marriages are not valid if contracted after January 1, 1957. A common-law marriage valid where contracted is valid in Michigan.

Personal Property

Common law estates are recognized. As to tenancy by the entirety, it is unclear whether such tenancy possesses all the elements of tenancy by the entirety in real property (such as immunity from partition). Joint tenancy with rights of survivorship can exist in bank accounts, securities, and contents of safety deposit boxes. However, the intent to create such a tenancy must be clearly shown by agreement of the tenants.

Real Property

All conveyances of lands made to two or more persons (except executors or to husband and wife) are construed to create estates in common and not in joint tenancy unless expressly declared to be in joint tenancy. A joint tenancy between husband and wife is a tenancy by the entirety, and a conveyance to husband and wife creates such a tenancy. One spouse cannot sever a tenancy by the entirety except by conveyance to the other spouse. The right of survivorship cannot be destroyed if expressly declared in the conveyance creating a joint tenancy.

Taxation

There is an inheritance tax. In cases where the inheritance tax does not equal or exceed the maximum credit for death taxes allowable under federal estate tax law, an additional tax is imposed to absorb the full credit.

Wills

A surviving spouse (widow) may elect dower right or to take intestate share or under the will. The election right and the right to inherit may be waived by either spouse by written agreement before or after marriage.

MINNESOTA

Curtesy and Dower

Abolished. Surviving spouses are entitled to the same share as in case of the intestacy of a deceased spouse.

Dissolution of Marriage

The marital property system of distribution generally applies. The court may make such disposition of marital property as is just and equitable without regard to marital misconduct. If the court finds that either spouse's resources or property, including that spouse's share of marital property, are so inadequate as to work an unfair hardship, the court may also distribute to that spouse up to one half of nonmarital property not excluded by a valid antenuptial contract. All property acquired during the marriage is presumed to be marital property, including vested pension benefits. Nonmarital property is any property acquired as gift, bequest, devise, or inheritance made by a third party to one but not both spouses. Nonmarital property also includes: Property acquired before the marriage, property acquired in exchange for, or increase in, nonmarital property; property acquired after a decree of legal separation; or property excluded by a valid antenuptial contract.

Husband and Wife

A married woman retains the same legal existence after marriage as before.

A married woman may hold any property, real or personal, as her separate property.

A married woman may make (and is bound by) any contract she could make if unmarried.

A husband and wife may convey real estate of either by joint deed. Either spouse may, by separate deed, convey any real estate owned by that spouse (except the homestead), subject to the statutory right of the other spouse. (Conveyance of assets does not defeat a spouse's rights at the death of the grantor spouse.) However, either spouse may, by separate instrument, relinquish rights in real estate conveyed by the other spouse.

An antenuptial contract may be entered into prior to the day of marriage provided there is full and fair disclosure of earnings and property of each party and the parties have the opportunity to consult legal counsel of their own choice. The contract must be in writing and may determine the rights of each party in nonmarital property upon dissolution of the marriage, legal separation, or death. A contract affecting rights to real property may be recorded with the county recorder to protect those rights against a subsequent purchaser.

Marriage

Common-law marriages entered into after 1941 are void.

Personal Property

Tenancy by the entirety does not exist.

Real Property

Tenancy by the entirety is not recognized. A grant or devise to two or more persons creates a tenancy in common unless the instrument expressly creates a joint tenancy.

Taxation

An inheritance tax was repealed for estates of decedents after 1979. A gift tax was also repealed for gifts after 1979.

The estate tax is tied in with federal estate taxes. The marital deduction for estates passing to a surviving spouse is 100 percent after 1981. The rates follow rates in the federal law and provide for a tax to absorb federal credit for state death taxes.

Wills

A surviving spouse who elects to take against the will takes the same share he or she would take in case of intestacy—except that if the decedent left no children, the surviving spouse takes only one half, and not all, of the estate. A spouse's rights are preserved against a person to whom property was conveyed by a decedent spouse to defeat marital rights. At the election of the surviving spouse, such a conveyance may be treated as a testamentary disposition, against which the spouse may elect to take as part of statutory share.

MISSISSIPPI

Curtesy and Dower

Abolished.

Divorce

Mississippi is not a community property state. Property is distributed on the basis of title and special equity.

Marriage

Common-law marriages were valid before 1956 but are now presumed to be invalid if contracted after that date. There is no provision for recognition of out-of-state common-law marriages. Certain marriages are deemed void. Persons whose marriage is void can be imprisoned for cohabitation.

Personal Property

Tenancy by the entirety is recognized.

Real Property

Conveyances or devises of land made to two or more persons, or to husband and wife, are construed to create estates in common and not in joint tenancy or entirety, unless it appears from the instrument that it was intended to create an estate in joint tenancy or entirety with right of survivorship. An estate in joint tenancy or entirety (to husband and wife) with right of survivorship may be created by a conveyance from the owners to others or to themselves.

Taxation

There is no gift or inheritance tax. An estate tax is imposed and such tax is not to be less than the credit allowed on a federal estate tax return.

Wills

A surviving spouse cannot be disinherited. If a will does not make "satisfactory" provision, a spouse can renounce and take the intestate share.

MISSOURI

Curtesy

The estate of curtesy is abolished, but a widower is given the same rights of inheritance, allowances, and exemptions as a widow.

Dissolution of Marriage

The court shall distribute to each spouse his/her property and shall divide marital property as the court deems "just." The relevant factors to consider include: (1) The contribution of each spouse to the acquisition of marital property, including contribution as a homemaker; (2) the value of property set apart to each spouse; (3) the economic circumstances of each spouse at the time the division of property is to become effective; and (4) the conduct of the parties during the marriage. The court is to consider the desirability of awarding the family home or the right to live there for reasonable periods to the spouse having custody of any children.

Dower

The estate of dower is abolished. A surviving husband has the same rights in a wife's real estate as a widow has in the husband's real estate, including the right of election. According to case law, however, a wife may defeat such rights as to her separate property by her conveyance without his joinder. She may release her marital rights in real estate by joining in a deed with her husband or by a prenuptial contract.

Husband and Wife

A married woman may hold as her separate property any property, real or personal, owned by her at the time of marriage; thereafter acquired by gift, bequest, devise, or descent, or purchased with her separate money or means; anything due her as wages; any rights of action; and all income, increase, and profits of her separate property. Such property is not liable for the debts of her husband.

A spouse should either join in or give consent in writing (acknowledged) to a conveyance of the other spouse's separate real property. This would not be necessary if marital rights have been released by prenuptial contract. However, failure to join will not prevent loss of marital rights (unless fraud was present). Because of difficulty in establishing the separate character of property, a joinder is deemed advisable for an effective conveyance.

Marriage

Common-law marriages are null and void, but they are recognized if legal where originally contracted.

Personal Property

Tenancies by the entireties are recognized.

Real Property

These tenancies are recognized: Tenancy in severalty, tenancy in common, joint tenancy, tenancy by the entirety, homestead, and life estates. A grant or devise to two or more persons (except executors, trustees, or spouses) is deemed to create a tenancy in common unless the instrument expressly declares the conveyance to be in joint tenancy. Real estate may be conveyed by an owner or owners to himself or themselves or others or a combination, and the conveyance has the same effect as to whether it creates a joint tenancy, tenancy by the entireties, in common, etc., as if it were granted by a stranger who owned the real estate to the persons named as grantees.

Taxation

There is no inheritance tax.

An estate tax is equal to the maximum credit for state death taxes on federal estate tax return. The state also imposes a generation-skipping tax on a generation-skipping transfer equal to the credit allowed by the Internal Revenue Code.

There is no gift tax.

Wills

A surviving spouse can elect to take against the will. In determining the spouse's share when there is an election, all property is considered even if it is not subject to probate, such as trust property, insurance, profit-sharing plans, and joint property.

MONTANA

Curtesy

No right of curtesy.

Dissolution of Marriage

Montana has a special equity type of system. The court shall equitably apportion property without regard to marital misconduct or recorded ownership, and may protect children by setting aside separate funds for their welfare.

Dower

Abolished.

Husband and Wife

Husband and wife shall support each other out of their property and labor, including nonmonetary support provided by a spouse as homemaker. Otherwise, neither has any interest in the property of the other.

Property of a married person owned before or acquired after marriage is his/her separate property. Earnings after marriage are his/her own. Neither husband nor wife is liable for debts of the other, but property of both is liable for necessaries for family expenses and children's educational expenses.

A wife may convey or encumber her separate property without the consent of the husband. He may do the same with his property. However, both must join in any conveyance or encumbrance of the homestead.

Marriage

Common-law marriages are recognized.

Personal Property

Tenancy by entirety ownership is not permitted with regard to personal property.

Real Property

Ownership of real property by more than one person may be either as: (1) Joint interests, (2) partnership interests, or (3) interests in common. Every interest in favor of several persons, including husband and wife, is an interest in common, unless expressly acquired in partnership for partnership purposes or declared in its creation to be a joint interest.

Taxation

There is an inheritance tax.

An estate tax is imposed to provide the state with the full benefit of the maximum tax credit allowable against the federal estate tax.

Wills

There is a right of election to take against a will.

NEBRASKA

Curtesy and Dower

Abolished.

Divorce

Nebraska follows the marital property system of property division. The court may include inherited property and retirement plans in the marital estate. When dissolution or separation is decreed, the parties can enter into a written property settlement regarding support, maintenance, and property as to themselves and any minor children. The agreement (except with regard to support and custody of minor children) is binding on the court unless the court finds the agreement to be unconscionable. Unless the agreement provides to the contrary, it becomes part of the decree. Terms of the agreement can be enforced by all available remedies. Alimony may be ordered in addition to a property settlement. If parties do not so agree, the court may award alimony and/or property using similar criteria, but the two serve different purposes and are to be considered separately. Except for terms regarding minor children, a decree may preclude or limit modification of its terms.

Husband and Wife

Property that a woman owns at the time of marriage and any increase in value of such property, as well as property she receives by inheritance or gift from another (not her husband), and property she acquires by purchase, is her sole and separate property and is not liable for her husband's debts.

A married woman may sell and convey her real and personal property and enter into any contract concerning the same as freely as a married man. Her contract must explicitly state the intention to bind only her separate property. She may carry on any trade or business and perform any service on her own account; her earnings are her sole and separate property, to be used and invested by her in her own name. Parties may enter into an antenuptial contract barring the right of inheritance.

Both husband and wife, if residents of Nebraska, must each join in a conveyance of the real estate of the other in order to cut off his or her statutory rights therein. A married woman who joins in the conveyance of her husband's property for the sole purpose of relinquishing her statutory rights therein is not bound by covenants in the deed.

Marriage

Common-law marriages cannot be contracted in Nebraska (since 1923). Common-law marriage valid in another state is recognized in Nebraska.

Personal Property

Tenancy by the entirety does not exist.

Real Property

Tenancy by the entirety is not recognized. Tenancy in common and joint tenancy are recognized. There is a conclusive presumption of co-tenancy when interest in real estate is conveyed to more than one person.

Taxation

There is an inheritance tax on all property, including life insurance payable to an executor or administrator, passing by will or intestate laws or by transfer in contemplation of death when such property is part of an estate. Interests passing to a surviving spouse by will are not subject to tax. If joint property was acquired by gift from a third person only the fractional part owned by the deceased is included in that person's estate. The value of assets is determined as of the date of death.

In addition to the inheritance tax, an estate tax is levied on the estate of every resident decedent based on the state tax credit allowed by the federal estate tax.

NEVADA

Community property

Nevada has a community property system.

Curtesy and Dower

Abolished.

Divorce

The residence requirement is six weeks prior to the commencement of the action. There must be actual physical presence within the state of Nevada for the required time (corroborated by credible local witness).

Nevada is a community property jurisdiction. Property rights are determined by the court. It may make such disposition of community property as appears equitable. The court may also set apart such portion of the husband's property for the wife's support, or the wife's property for the husband's support (if he is disabled or unable to provide for himself), or the property of either spouse for the support of their children, as shall be deemed just and equitable. Agreements settling property rights are looked on favorably and are usually approved. A property settlement agreement made when divorce is pending or immediately contemplated is not invalidated by a provision therein that it shall become effective only in the event of divorce. It may be merged in the divorce decree unless the decree specifically provides that the agreement not be merged.

Husband and Wife

The unity of husband and wife and the rule that the residence of the husband is that of the wife unless, having ground for divorce, she establishes a separate residence, are recognized by Nevada courts.

Real or personal property may be held by husband and wife in joint tenancy, tenancy in common, or as community property.

All property of each spouse owned before marriage, and all acquired afterward by gift or inheritance, and profits therefrom, is the separate property of that spouse.

Either spouse may, without the consent of the other spouse, convey, encumber, or in any manner dispose of his/her separate property.

Community property is all property acquired after marriage by either husband or wife, except that acquired by gift or inheritance (or as an award for personal injury damages), together with profits of such property. Other exceptions from community property are property arrangements set forth in a written agreement between spouses, effective only as between them; by a decree of separate maintenance; or by written authorization from one spouse to the other for separate earnings to be appropriated to his/her own use. Either spouse, acting alone, may control community property, with a power of disposition such as the acting spouse has over his/her separate property. Neither spouse, however, may devise or bequeath by will more than one half of the couple's community property. Neither spouse may give away community property without the other spouse's consent. Some other requirements are as follows: Community real property can be conveyed or encumbered only by an instrument executed and acknowledged by both spouses; a contract to purchase community real property must be joined in by both spouses; both spouses must join in a contract of sale; neither spouse may acquire, sell, convey, or encumber assets of a business (including real property and goodwill) where both spouses participate in management without the consent of the other. However, a husband or wife may give a written power of attorney to the other to sell or convey any property held as community property.

On the death of either husband or wife, an undivided one-half interest in community property is the property of the surviving spouse and that person's sole separate property. The remaining interest is the decedent's property and is subject to the testamentary disposition of the decedent. In the absence of testamentary disposition that portion goes to the surviving spouse and is the only portion that is administered by the probate court.

Marriage

Common-law marriages are prohibited. There is no statutory provision as to local recognition of out-of-state common-law marriages.

Personal Property

Tenancy by the entirety does not exist.

Real Property

Tenancy by the entirety is not mentioned in statute but appears to be abolished by implication. Real estate may be held in joint tenancy, tenancy in common, as community property of husband and wife, and/or in condominium. A grant or devise to two or more persons (other than executors and trustees) creates a tenancy in common, unless the instrument expressly declares the estate granted or devised to be a joint tenancy. Joint tenancy may be created without the intervention of a straw man.

Taxation

There is no inheritance tax, estate tax, or gift tax.

Wills

In Nevada the surviving spouse has no right of election to take under intestacy law and against the will. (See "Community Property," above.)

The divorce or annulment of the marriage of a testator (the one who made a will) revokes every interest given to the testator's former spouse by a will executed before the divorce decree unless a separate property agreement or former will was approved by the court in divorce proceedings.

NEW HAMPSHIRE

Curtesy and Dower

Abolished.

Divorce

Upon a decree of divorce, the court may restore to the wife all or any part of her estate, and may assign to her such part of the estate of her husband as may be deemed just.

Husband and Wife

A married woman holds for her own use, free from the interference or control of her husband, all property at any time earned, acquired, or inherited by or given to her either before or after marriage. Every married woman has the same rights and remedies, and is subject to the same liabilities in relation to her property, as if she were unmarried, and she may convey, make contracts, etc., as if she were unmarried.

Real estate may be conveyed directly by a husband to his wife, or a wife to her husband, without the intervention of a third person. A married woman may convey her real estate. A married man or woman who is "justifiably" living apart from his or her spouse because such spouse has been guilty of conduct that constitutes cause for divorce may apply by petition to the judge of probate for the county in which real estate owned by that person is situated for a license to convey the same in such manner as to bar all rights of homestead to the "guilty" party.

If a woman has resided in New Hampshire for six months and is the wife of a man residing in another state, assuming she is residing in New Hampshire separate from her husband, she may convey all real and personal property held by her in New Hampshire, the same as if she were sole and unmarried.

Common-law marriages are not recognized.

Personal Property

Tenancy by entirety in personal property is not recognized.

Real Property

Tenancy by entirety in real property is not recognized. A deed that names grantees to be tenants by the entirety creates a joint tenancy. Conveyances and devises of real estate to two or more persons are construed to create an estate in common and not in joint tenancy unless joint tenancy is expressly provided in the instrument. A conveyance to a husband and wife as tenants by the entirety creates a joint tenancy.

Taxation

An inheritance tax is imposed on all property within the jurisdiction of New Hampshire, real or personal, belonging to domiciliaries of the state and on all real estate within the state belonging to a nonresident decedent, that is transferred by will, by intestate succession, or by gift made in contemplation of death. The transfer to the survivor of jointly held property is deemed a taxable transfer as though the whole property had been owned by the joint owners as tenants in common and had been devised or bequeathed to the survivor.

In addition to the inheritance tax, an estate tax is imposed on the transfer of all estates subject to an estate tax under the provisions of the federal Internal Revenue Code to equal the credit allowed for state death taxes.

Wills

Any devise or bequest to a surviving spouse is held to be in lieu of all his or her rights in the estate of the deceased spouse unless it appears by the will that such was not the intention. A surviving spouse may, instead, file a waiver of testamentary provision for that spouse, and in lieu of that provision receive a distributive share of the estate.

NEW JERSEY

Curtesy

On the death of his wife, a widower takes a life estate in one half of the real property she owned at any time during marriage prior to May 28, 1980, whether children were born or not, unless he has released his right of curtesy by joining in a deed or by conveyance directly to his spouse. An absolute divorce terminates the right of curtesy.

Effective May 28, 1980, all rights of dower and curtesy are abolished with respect to real property acquired subsequent to that date. As to such property occupied jointly with a spouse, every married person has a right of joint possession during marriage. This right of possession may not be released, extinguished, or alienated without the consent of both spouses or the judgment of a court.

Divorce

Pending suit for divorce, brought in New Jersey or elsewhere, or after judgment for divorce, wherever obtained, the court has the power to make orders awarding alimony and to revise the same from time to time. The court may award alimony to either party; in doing so the court shall consider the need and ability to pay of the parties and the duration of the marriage. In addition to alimony and maintenance, the court may effectuate an equitable distribution of certain real and personal property acquired by either party during the marriage.

Dower

On the death of her husband a widow takes a life estate in one half of the real property he owned during the marriage at any time prior to May 28, 1980, unless she had released her right of dower. There is no dower in an estate by joint tenancy except in favor of the wife of a surviving joint tenant.

A widow's right of dower may be released by a deed executed and acknowledged in the manner prescribed by law. Conveyance by a married person directly to a spouse releases inchoate or possible future curtesy or dower in lands conveyed if the conveyance so provides. Absolute divorce terminates the right of dower.

Effective May 28, 1980, all rights of dower and curtesy are abolished with respect to real property acquired subsequent to that date. As to such property occupied jointly with a spouse as their principal matrimonial residence, every married person has a right of joint possession during marriage. This right of possession may not be released without the consent of both spouses or judgment of a court.

Husband and Wife

A married woman's real and personal property owned at the time of marriage or acquired after marriage is her separate property as though she were unmarried. A wife is entitled to earnings of her separate employment and investments. A wife's separate property is not liable for her husband's debts.

A married woman may execute and deliver any instrument relating to her real property with the same effect as if she were unmarried, and any such instrument is valid without her husband's joinder or consent. However, no conveyance or act of such married woman can affect any estate or interest of her husband in such property. Either spouse may convey directly to the other real estate or any interest therein, and the conveyance is valid although the grantee spouse does not join in or acknowledge the same. Such conveyance extinguishes the dower or curtesy interest if specifically released. A conveyance by either spouse to himself or herself and the other spouse of real estate held in severalty shall be construed to vest an estate by the entirety in the husband and wife.

Marriage

Common-law marriages are not recognized.

Personal Property

Tenancy by the entirety in personal property is not recognized.

Real Property

Tenancy by the entirety in real property is recognized. A grant or devise to two or more persons creates a tenancy in common unless an intention to create a joint tenancy and not a tenancy in common is expressly stated in the instrument. (A grant or devise to trustees always creates a joint tenancy.) A grant or devise to a husband and wife creates a tenancy by the entirety unless it is otherwise expressly stated. Joint tenancy may be created by conveyance from a grantor to himself and others. An absolute divorce changes tenancy by the entirety to tenancy in common.

Taxation

An inheritance tax is imposed on the transfer of all real and tangible personal property situated in New Jersey and all intangible property wherever situated of resident decedents (and on certain property located in New Jersey of nonresident decedents) by will or intestate laws or in contemplation of death (within three years).

An estate tax is imposed in addition to an inheritance tax to equal the credit for state death taxes paid allowed on a federal return.

Wills

All rights of dower and curtesy are abolished as to real property acquired by married persons after May 28, 1980; but rights of dower and curtesy attached to real property acquired prior to that date are not affected.

A spouse to whom realty is devised takes the same in lieu of dower and curtesy, but he or she may file a written refusal renouncing such devise and is then entitled to dower or curtesy. There is no statutory provision as to the effect of a gift of personalty. If expressed in a will to be in lieu of dower or curtesy, the surviving spouse may instead elect to take the intestate share.

NEW MEXICO

Curtesy and Dower

Abolished.

Community Property

New Mexico follows the community property system.

Descent and Distribution

The surviving spouse owns one half of the couple's community property. The other one half can be disposed of by will. Community property is subject to community debts.

Dissolution of Marriage

The court has the power to make division of spouses' property. This may apply on permanent separation, even without dissolution of the marriage. Community property must be divided equally.

Husband and Wife

Separate property can include: property acquired by either spouse before marriage; property acquired by gift, devise, bequest, or descent; property designated as separate by written agreement of the parties; property held as co-tenants or in joint tenancy or tenancy in common; or property designated by a court as such, with all rents, issues, and profits from such property. Property acquired during marriage by the wife by an instrument in writing in her name alone (or in her name and name of another party not her husband) is presumed to be the wife's separate property if the instrument was executed prior to July 1, 1973.

Either spouse may convey his or her separate property without the other joining, or may dispose of it by will. As to community property, only one half can be disposed of by will; the surviving spouse owns one half.

All property acquired by either spouse after the marriage (except as listed above as "separate") is community property. A husband and wife may take title to realty as joint tenants. As to dealing with respect to her separate property, there is a conclusive presumption in favor of a person dealing in good faith and for valuable consideration with a married woman that she is the owner of the separate property.

As to community property, a husband and wife must join in all deeds of community real property (except from one spouse to the other). Either party may manage and control personal community property, unless one spouse is named in the document of title or in an agreement with a third party as having sole management and control. In the latter cases, only the spouse so named may manage or control that property. Where the document of title is in the names of both spouses (A *and* B), both must join in the transaction with regard to that property.

Marriage

Common-law marriages are not recognized.

Personal Property

Tenancy by the entirety is not specifically recognized by statute.

Real Property

Tenancy in common and joint tenancy are recognized. A grant or devise to two or more persons creates a tenancy in common unless it is expressly declared in the instrument that they take as joint tenants. Husband and wife may hold realty as joint tenants.

Taxation

There is no inheritance tax; there is an estate tax.

Wills

Upon the death of a spouse, the entire community property goes to the surviving spouse if the decedent did not exercise power of testamentary disposition over one half. An omitted spouse who married the testator after execution of the testator's will takes the intestate share unless omission was intentional or the testator made provision for the spouse by transfer outside the will with intent that such transfer would be in lieu of a testamentary provision.

NEW YORK

Curtesy and Dower

Abolished (since 1930).

Divorce

The court determines the respective rights of the parties in "separate" and "marital" property and orders disposition as follows: "Separate" property is to remain as such; "marital" property is to be distributed "equitably" between the parties, considering the facts and circumstances of the case.

Husband and Wife

A married woman has all rights with respect to real or personal property, including acquisition and disposition thereof, and to make contracts with regard to her property and be liable on such contracts (and upon judgments) as if she were unmarried. A husband and wife may agree in writing as to ownership or disposition of separate and matrimonial property, including testamentary provisions.

Marriage

Common-law marriages are prohibited but are recognized if entered into in New York before April 29, 1933, or if valid where created.

Personal Property

Tenancy by the entirety is not recognized.

Real Property

Tenancy by the entirety is recognized. A conveyance or devise to two or more persons (not husband and wife) creates a tenancy in common unless expressly declared to create a joint tenancy (except that estates vested in executors or trustees is held by them in joint tenancy). Conveyance to a husband and wife creates a tenancy by the entirety unless expressly declared to be a joint tenancy or a tenancy in common.

Taxation

There is no inheritance tax.

There is an estate tax. A New York gross estate consists of the federal gross estate, whether or not a federal return is required, excluding the value of real and tangible personal property situated outside New York whose amount is included in the federal gross estate. Gifts made within three years of a decedent's death are included in a New York gross estate.

A gift tax is imposed on the transfer of property by gift—it is modeled after the federal gift tax, but unification of estate and gift tax rates has not been adopted.

Wills

A surviving spouse has the right of election to take the intestate share.

NORTH CAROLINA

Curtesy and Dower

Abolished. After July 1, 1960, a surviving spouse may elect to take an interest similar to common law dower in the estate of deceased spouse in lieu of an intestate or testamentary share.

Divorce

Separation agreements are valid (but the court may exercise independent judgment regarding spouses' agreement as to the care and custody of child). In the absence of a separation agreement, either spouse may petition for an equitable distribution of marital property.

Husband and Wife

A married person may hold property free from the debts of his or her husband or wife. A married woman can contract and deal with regard to her separate real and personal property in the same manner as if she were unmarried. However, every conveyance or other instrument affecting the estate, right, or title of any married persons in lands or real estate is subject to the elective life estate of either the husband or wife. This right to elect may be waived by execution of the deed or by executing a valid separation agreement authorizing conveyance without the consent of the other spouse.

Certain conveyances are valid without joinder of the grantor's spouse. These are: (1) Conveyance by one spouse to the other; (2) conveyance by either spouse to both spouses (which creates tenancy by entireties unless a contrary intent is expressed in the conveyance); and (3) conveyance by one tenant in entirety to the other (which dissolves the estate by entireties in the property so conveyed).

Effective January 31, 1983, a husband and wife have equal right to the control of, use, income, and profits of real property held in tenancy by the entirety. Neither spouse may sell, lease, mortgage, or convey any property so held without a written joinder of the other spouse.

Personal Property

Tenancy by the entirety does not exist in personal property.

Real Property

Tenancy by the entirety does exist. Common law estates are recognized.

Taxation

There is an inheritance tax.

In addition to the inheritance tax, an estate tax is imposed on the transfer of the net estate of every decedent where an inheritance tax imposed is less than the maximum state death tax credit allowed by federal estate tax law so that the aggregate amount of tax due the State of North Carolina is equal to the maximum amount of credit allowed by federal law.

There is a gift tax, but charitable gifts are exempt. Also North Carolina follows federal law in allowing a $10,000 exclusion, including consent by spouses to each use his/her annual exclusion.

Gifts by nonresidents are taxable to the extent that the property given is located within the jurisdiction of North Carolina.

Wills

Any surviving spouse may, by timely election, dissent from the will of the decedent spouse and receive the same share he or she would have received had the deceased spouse died intestate, up to a maximum of one half of the deceased spouse's estate before deduction of estate taxes. There is an exception to this: Where the surviving spouse receives one half or more in value of all the property passing upon the death of the deceased spouse (including property passing under the will and property passing outside the will), there is no right of election.

NORTH DAKOTA

Curtesy and Dower

Abolished.

Divorce

When a divorce is granted, the court is to make an "equitable distribution" of real and personal property of the parties as may seem "just and proper." Either party may be required to provide the other with an allowance for support during life or for a shorter period, and the court may modify its orders from time to time. Where a husband or wife has a separate estate sufficient to provide proper support, the court, at its discretion, may withhold any allowance to that person out of the separate property of the other spouse. The court may assign the homestead to the innocent party either absolutely or for a limited time. The Supreme Court of North Dakota has held that, in determining the question of alimony or division of property, the court is to consider: ages of the parties; their earning ability; duration of the marriage and the conduct of each spouse during the marriage; their station in life; circumstances and necessities of each; the parties' health and physical condition; and their financial circumstances. As to the last-named criterion the court is to consider the property owned, its value and income-producing capacity, and whether it was accumulated or acquired before or after the marriage.

Husband and Wife

Separate property of either spouse is not liable for the debts of the other. Each is liable for his/her own debts contracted before or after marriage. The earnings of one spouse are not liable for the debts of the other. Husband and wife are jointly and severally liable for debts contracted by either while living together for certain necessary household expenses and education of minor children.

Marriage

Common-law marriages are invalid.

Real Property

Tenancies in common and joint tenancies are recognized. Tenancies by the entirety are not recognized.

Taxation

There is no inheritance tax or gift tax; there is an estate tax.

OHIO

Curtesy

Common law curtesy is abolished. A husband has dower interest the same as a wife.

Divorce

The court may grant permanent alimony payable in gross or in installments, in either real or personal property, and to either party. The court is to consider various factors prior to grant of alimony. The court also considers marital conduct. The court may grant alimony for the following causes: (1) Adultery; (2) any gross neglect of duty; (3) abandonment without good cause; (4) ill treatment; (5) habitual drunkenness; (6) sentence to and imprisonment in a penitentiary.

Ohio divides *marital* property.

Dower

A surviving spouse has a life estate in one third of all real property the decedent spouse owned during marriage. If the decedent spouse had encumbered the property, the surviving spouse's dower interest is computed on the basis of the amount of the encumbrance. The spouse of the owner of real property may be made a party to any action involving a judicial sale of real property to satisfy creditors' claims. A spouse's dower interest may be subject to sale without the spouse's consent, with the court determining the present value and priority of the dower interest. These provisions do not apply to a tax lien or sale for delinquent taxes. The dower interest of either spouse terminates upon granting of absolute divorce. Either spouse may release his/her dower right by joining the other spouse as a grantor in a deed, mortgage, etc., or by separate instrument.

Husband and Wife

Neither husband nor wife has any interest in the property of the other, except the right of support, dower, and to remain in the homestead after the death of either. Either spouse may receive, hold, or dispose of his/her separate property. No joinder is necessary, except to bar dower rights in real property.

Marriage

Common-law marriage is recognized.

Personal Property

Tenancy by the entirety does not exist.

Real Property

Tenancy by entireties may be created by language in a conveyance or grant.

Joint tenancy is not presumed, but express provisions in the instrument creating a joint tenancy will be given effect (otherwise, a tenancy in common is created).

Taxation

An inheritance tax only applies to estates of decedents who died before June 30, 1968.

There is no gift tax. An estate tax applies to gifts in contemplation of death or intended to take effect after death.

An estate tax applies to estates of residents dying on or after July 1, 1968. The value of a gross estate is similar to valuation for federal estate tax. A gross estate includes property transferred within three years of death (unless such transfer is shown not to be made in contemplation of death). There is a $10,000 per transferee per year gift exclusion. There is also a tax on a generation-skipping transfer in an amount equal to the credit allowed on a federal estate tax return for taxes paid to any state in respect to any property included in a generation-skipping transfer. The estate tax generally is intended to absorb the credit for state death taxes allowed by federal estate tax laws.

Wills

When a surviving spouse is the sole legatee or devisee under a will, no election is required, but one may be made. In all other cases, the surviving spouse must elect to take under the provisions of deceased spouse's will or under the statute of descent and distribution.

OKLAHOMA

Curtesy and Dower

Abolished.

Divorce

Permanent alimony may be awarded to either spouse for support. Alimony allowed by a divorce judgment must be based on the parties' circumstances at the time of divorce and constitutes a final determination; it is not to be modified by subsequent changes in condition.

Husband and Wife

Except as to the right of support, neither husband nor wife has any interest in the separate property of the other, although neither may be excluded from the other's residence. Husband and wife may hold property as joint tenants or tenants in common or as community property.

Personal Property

Tenancy by the entirety exists between husband and wife.

Real Property

Joint tenancy in real or personal property may be created by a single instrument, will, or transfer document when expressly declared that a joint tenancy is being created. Joint tenancy may be created by transfer to persons as joint tenants from an owner, or a joint owner to himself and one or more persons, or from tenants in common to themselves. Such an estate may be created by or for persons who have elected to become bound under any community property act now in existence or which may be enacted in the future. Tenancy by the entirety, in real or personal property, exists between husband and wife.

Taxation

There is no inheritance tax and, effective January 1, 1982, no gift tax.

An estate tax is levied on the transfer by will or intestate laws or any transfer taking effect at death (any transfer made within three years of death is deemed a transfer in contemplation of death unless shown to be otherwise).

Wills

If a married person attempts to devise or bequeath away from his or her spouse less in value than would be taken through succession by law, the surviving spouse may elect to take under the will or by succession.

OREGON

Curtesy and Dower

Abolished for the surviving spouse of person who dies after July 1, 1970.

Divorce

The term "alimony" is no longer used. Support, during divorce litigation and permanent, may be allowed. Permanent support may be ordered paid in a lump sum or in installments. A decree as to future support may be modified upon showing of changes in circumstances.

The marital property system of distribution prevails. The court may approve a voluntary property settlement agreement providing for support of a party. In distributing property by court, the court must consider the spouse's contribution as homemaker as a contribution to marital assets and the **tax** consequences and costs of sale of assets occurring in divorce property division. The court must also presume equal contribution (but that is rebuttable), and full disclosure of assets is required. Division of property by decree is not a taxable sale or exchange. Fault in causing dissolution of the marriage may not be considered.

Husband and Wife

Neither spouse is responsible for liabilities of the other spouse incurred before the marriage or incurred separately during the marriage (except for liabilities for expenses of the family or education of children).

Parties to an intended marriage may enter into prenuptial agreements in writing concerning their respective personal and real property holdings; these agreements will be binding on the parties and their heirs. Prenuptial agreements prohibiting alimony are enforced unless the spouse waiving alimony has no other reasonable means of support. Court approval of such an agreement can be modified if circumstances change.

Marriage

Common-law marriage cannot be entered into in Oregon but will be recognized if valid in the state where entered into.

Personal Property

Tenancy by the entirety does not exist in personal property. Oregon considers conveyance to a husband and wife with right of survivorship as creating concurrent life estates with contingent cross remainders. A joint tenancy in personal property may be created by written instrument. It does not negate the rights of creditors.

Real Property

Joint tenancy is abolished, and use of the term, without more, creates a tenancy in common. The right of survivorship, however, may be created by express agreement of the parties. Joint property rights may be created directly without the use of an intervening conveyance to a straw man. A husband and wife may own property as tenants by the entirety or as tenants in common.

Taxation

An inheritance tax is imposed on the right to receive beneficial interests in property by right of survivorship, will, or gift intended to take effect after the death of the decedent; also on the right to receive proceeds of insurance policies on the decedent's life if the decedent possessed incidents of ownership. A tax is also imposed on the transfer of property within three years of death (including the amount of any gift tax paid on such transfer). No tax is imposed on one half of jointly held property passing to a surviving spouse.

There is a gift tax but none is imposed on the creation or severance of a joint interest with right of survivorship by spouses (on severance each spouse receives an undivided one-half interest, thus becoming tenants in common).

Wills

A surviving spouse has the right to elect a percentage of the decedent's net estate and forfeits certain rights under the will of a decedent spouse.

PENNSYLVANIA

Curtesy

Curtesy in Pennsylvania is the share of the deceased wife's estate which is allotted to a surviving husband by the rules of intestate succession or by election against the will.

Divorce

The marital property system of distribution prevails. Upon request of either party in divorce or annulment proceedings, the court must equitably divide all marital property without regard to marital misconduct as the court deems just. Marital property is subject to division regardless of how title is held.

Dower

Dower in Pennsylvania is the share of the deceased husband's estate which is allotted to a surviving wife by the rules of intestate succession or by election against the will.

Husband and Wife

An 1893 act providing that a married woman could not convey real estate without her husband's joinder has been repealed. Married persons may convey to either husband or wife alone, and either alone may convey to both, as tenants by entireties.

For purpose of determining property subject to the elective share of a surviving spouse, a married person can convey title to individually owned real property without the necessity of the other spouse joining in the deed to the extent adequate consideration is received.

For the purpose of determining marital property in a divorce or annulment proceeding, real property conveyed or disposed of in good faith for adequate consideration before divorce proceedings is excluded from "marital property."

Marriage

Common-law marriages are recognized.

Personal Property

Pennsylvania recognizes tenancy by the entirety in personal property.

Real Property

A joint tenancy with right of survivorship may be created if such intention is expressed or can clearly be inferred from express directions. In the absence of a clear intention to create a joint tenancy with right of survivorship in the instrument of conveyance, such instrument would create a tenancy in common.

Unless a contrary intention is clearly stated, real estate in the name of a husband and wife creates a tenancy by the entirety.

Taxation

An inheritance tax is imposed on transfer of any property by will or by intestacy by a resident or nonresident and is also imposed on certain inter vivos transfers. Property held in joint tenancy with right of survivorship is taxable. The share of inheritance tax pertaining to each surviving joint tenant's ownership is determined by dividing the value of the whole property by the number of joint tenants in existence immediately prior to the death of the decedent. An exception to this is property held by husband and wife with right of survivorship (unless the co-ownership was created within one year of the death of a co-tenant).

In addition to the inheritance tax, an estate tax is imposed on estates of resident decedents (and on estates situated in Pennsylvania of decedents who resided elsewhere) in order to absorb the full credit allowed on a federal estate tax return.

There is no gift tax, but the inheritance tax applies to gifts made within one year of death (with a $3,000 exclusion).

Wills

A surviving spouse may elect to take against the will of a deceased spouse, and in such case is entitled to one third of the probate estate. The right to elect is personal to the spouse and may be exercised in whole or in part during his lifetime (or by his agent as power of attorney).

PUERTO RICO

Curtesy

Does not exist in Puerto Rico.

Divorce

The community property system prevails in Puerto Rico. Dissolution of marriage requires dissolution of the conjugal partnership and distribution of community property assets to the spouses. Upon filing a divorce action, neither spouse may contract debts or effect any settlements to be paid from community property without court approval.

Dower

Does not exist in Puerto Rico.

Husband and Wife

Separate property of spouses is: (1) Property brought into the marriage by either spouse as his or her own; (2) property acquired during the marriage by gift or inheritance; (3) property acquired by exchange for other separate property; and (4) property bought with money belonging exclusively to either the husband or wife. Each spouse has the right to manage and dispose of his or her separate property, but gifts between spouses (except "moderate" gifts on "festive" days) are void.

Community or conjugal property belongs in equal parts to both spouses. Such property is: (1) Property obtained by the earnings or wages of each spouse; (2) property purchased with money of the marriage partnership; and (3) the earnings obtained during marriage from the separate property of each spouse. Marriage partnership property does not include capital gains from the sale of private property of either spouse. Marriage is considered a co-partnership, but a prenuptial agreement may provide otherwise. Unless agreed to the contrary, both spouses are administrators of conjugal partnership property. Neither spouse may alienate or encumber community property without the written consent of the other spouse. The rules apply to immovable property in Puerto Rico (regardless of the place of marriage). When a marriage partnership is dissolved by death or divorce, property covered by it is divided equally between the spouses. Each spouse may by will dispose of one half of the couple's community property.

Marriage

Common-law marriages are not recognized in Puerto Rico.

Real Property

In Puerto Rico law, the term "real property" is unknown and instead the term "immovable" categorizes real property. Dominion title is roughly the same as fee simple. Common law estates of joint tenancy are unknown. Co-ownership is governed by contract.

Taxation

There is an estate tax patterned somewhat on the U.S. Internal Revenue Code. (Puerto Rico taxation involves a unique situation requiring special interpretation of U.S. law.)

A gift tax is imposed on gifts of property wherever situated if the donor is a resident of Puerto Rico. If the donor is a nonresident, the tax is imposed on gifts of property situated in Puerto Rico.

Wills

The surviving spouse has, in addition to half of all marriage partnership property, a life interest in a portion of the estate, varying according to the number of children (who have a share).

RHODE ISLAND

Curtesy and Dower

Common law estates of curtesy and dower are abolished. A surviving spouse is entitled to a life estate in realty owned by the deceased spouse at death, subject to encumbrances. The life estate takes precedence over any will provision or creditor's claim (except those secured by a lien) if the surviving spouse so elects. This life estate, by statute, replaced dower and curtesy; the right of spouse to a distributive share of the estate apparently does not bar a life estate in realty (which replaced dower and curtesy).

Divorce

The court may assign to either spouse (in addition to, or in lieu of, alimony) a portion of the estate of the other. Property held prior to the marriage is not assignable (but income from it is); property inherited before, during, or after the marriage may not be assigned. After a complaint for divorce is filed, the court may permit either party to sell or dispose of his/her separate real estate free of dower or curtesy.

Marriage

Common-law marriages are recognized.

Personal Property

Common law rule is presumed to govern the validity of tenancies by the entirety in personal property. There are no decisions.

Real Property

Common law estates in land are recognized, with statutory modifications. All transfers to two or more persons are deemed to create a tenancy in common and not a joint tenancy, unless the intent to create a joint tenancy is expressly declared. Joint heirs are deemed to be tenants in common. Tenancies by the entirety are recognized. Rhode Island also recognizes the common law estate of "fee tail." A devise in fee tail is limited to the first taker (lawful issue of the donee); after that it becomes an estate in fee simple. (This is a holdover of English law.)

Taxation

The inheritance tax was eliminated in 1980.

An estate tax is imposed on the estates of decedents dying on or after October 1, 1980. The tax is on transfers by will, by intestate succession, and inter vivos transfers in contemplation of (or to take effect at) death. Additional taxes are imposed to equal the amount of credit allowed under the Federal Revenue Act for state estate taxes.

Wills

Where a will fails to indicate an intention that provision for a surviving spouse is in lieu of the statutory life estate in real estate of the deceased, then the surviving spouse takes such statutory life estate in addition to such will provision.

SOUTH CAROLINA

Curtesy

Abolished.

Divorce

Family court settles legal and equitable rights of parties in real and personal property of the marriage. The title theory is the basis of distribution with property ordinarily set aside to the spouse with clear title. Exceptions to the title theory are recognized on the basis of other legal doctrines. For example, recent case law allows a wife to claim a contribution as a homemaker as the basis of "special equity."

Dower

Ruled unconstitutional as of May 22, 1984.

Husband and Wife

The real and personal property of a married woman, held by her at the time of marriage or acquired after marriage, is her separate property and not subject to her husband's debts. A married woman has all rights incident to her separate property as if she were unmarried "or a man."

Marriage

Common-law marriage is recognized.

Personal Property

Tenancy by the entirety does not exist in personal property. Joint tenancy with right of survivorship is recognized as to stocks and other securities.

Real Property

The estates recognized are fee simple, tenancy in common, joint tenancy (instrument must expressly provide for survivorship), and life estate.

Taxation

There is no inheritance tax. An estate tax is based on and similar to federal estate tax provisions in effect (but rates are different). The tax is assessed to absorb the federal estate tax credit for state death taxes. A gift tax is based on and similar to federal gift tax provisions.

SOUTH DAKOTA

Curtesy and Dower

Abolished.

Divorce

All property of spouses, including inherited property, regardless of which spouse holds title, is considered marital property and may be divided between spouses at the court's discretion. Factors to be considered by the court are: (1) Duration of the marriage; (2) value of the property; (3) ages of the spouses; (4) health of the spouses; (5) competency of the spouses to earn a living; (6) contribution of each spouse to the accumulation of property; and (7) the income-producing capacity of each spouse's assets. The court is not to take fault into account in awarding property unless fault is relevant to the acquisition of property during the marriage.

Husband and Wife

Neither husband nor wife has any interest in the property of the other, except as to the homestead, and neither can be excluded from the other's dwelling (if separate). Each has respective rights for support as provided by law.

Marriage

Common-law marriages are not permissible if initiated after July 1, 1959. Before that date, they were recognized and would be valid.

Personal Property

Joint tenancy is permitted in personal property. Tenancy by the entirety is not recognized.

Real Property

Tenancy by the entirety is not recognized. An interest in property created in favor of several persons is an interest in common unless expressly declared in the document to be an interest in joint tenancy. A joint tenancy is the only estate with survivorship rights. A creditor's rights are preserved against a surviving joint tenant. South Dakota law also specifically includes partnership interests as a type of joint ownership.

Taxation

An inheritance tax is imposed on all property of resident decedents passing by will or inheritance. It is also imposed on all property of nonresident decedents located in South Dakota and on all property transferred in contemplation of death.

An estate tax is imposed equal to the maximum allowable credit against federal estate taxes for state death taxes paid.

Wills

Unless there is a clear provision in the will requiring an election by the surviving spouse between the will provisions and homestead rights, the surviving spouse may take both.

TENNESSEE

Curtesy

Curtesy, unless vested, was abolished as of April 1, 1977.

Divorce

Tennessee is a marital property state. The court presiding over a divorce action is to equitably divide and distribute marital property, without regard to fault; it may divest and reinvest title where necessary or order a sale with proceeds to be divided between the parties. Guidelines provided are to be followed. The law does not affect the validity of an antenuptial agreement or preclude incorporation into the divorce decree of a property settlement agreement made by the parties themselves. The court may award the home and household effects to either party but must give special consideration to the parent with custody of the children.

Dower

Dower, unless vested, was abolished as of April 1, 1977.

Husband and Wife

A married woman may acquire, hold, manage, control, and dispose of all property, real or personal, as though "not married."

A married woman may contract with her husband or any other person. Husband and wife may transact business with each other. Antenuptial contracts and settlements regarding property must be registered. Such contracts are enforceable if entered into freely and in good faith. Postnuptial agreements regarding property are void as to existing creditors.

Marriage

Common-law marriages are not recognized but are considered valid if contracted in a state where such marriages are valid.

Personal Property

Personal property may be owned as tenants by the entirety.

Real Property

Tenancy by the entirety is recognized, as are all usual common law estates. Survivorship in joint tenancy has been abolished. Heirs of property jointly take as tenants in common. However, the right of survivorship may be created expressly and, if so created in the instrument, will be valid.

Taxation

There is an inheritance tax on the following: Transfer from a resident decedent of Tennessee of real property situated within the state, tangible personal property (unless it is outside the state), all intangible personal property, insurance proceeds, proceeds of certain employee benefit plans, and property in which the decedent had a "qualifying income interest for life," as defined by statute. When the transfer is from a nonresident decedent, a transfer of real property located within Tennessee is taxed as is tangible personal property located within the state. These transfers are taxed whether by will, by intestacy statutes, or by gift within three years of death. As to jointly held property, the rules are similar to the rules for federal estate taxation.

An estate tax is imposed to take full advantage of the credit for state death taxes allowed on a federal estate tax return.

There is a transfer tax on gifts of real property within the state and tangible personal property located within the state (even if the donor is a nonresident) and on gifts of intangible personal property where the donor is a resident.

Wills

A surviving spouse may elect to take one third of a decedent spouse's real and personal property after estate administration expenses.

TEXAS

Curtesy and Dower

Curtesy and dower do not exist in Texas.

Divorce

The court presiding in a divorce case may make division of property in such way as seems "just and right," having due regard for the rights of each party and their children. Texas is a community property jurisdiction.

Husband and Wife

Marriage creates certain responsibilities, duties, and privileges. There are no disabilities of married women. A married woman has full powers to make contracts and sue or be sued in her own name.

All property, real and personal, owned by either of the parties before marriage and that acquired afterward by gift, devise, or descent and increase in the same are the separate property of that individual. Separate property of a spouse is not subject to liabilities of the other spouse unless both spouses are legally liable. Rents and profits arising out of separate or community property are *community*. This includes cash dividends from stock and interest on bonds. However, bonus money and royalties payable with respect to oil and gas leases covering separate property are separate.

Persons about to marry or those already married may by written instrument partition between themselves all or part of their property, present or future, and set aside to each spouse separately such property, including the income from such property, provided such action is not taken to defraud pre-existing creditors. Spouses may create a joint tenancy with right of survivorship if property is partitioned into each spouse's separate property, but cannot create joint tenancy with right of survivorship with community property.

If one spouse makes a gift of property to the other spouse, the gift is presumed to include all income or property which might arise from that gift.

The Texas law gives management and control of separate property to each spouse and of community property to the spouse who would have owned it had both spouses been single. Property in a spouse's name is presumed to be subject to his or her management or control.

Each spouse has sole management, control, and disposition of his or her separate property, real and personal, and may convey or encumber the same without joinder of the other spouse. Community property may be conveyed by the spouse who would have owned it had both been single.

Parties intending to marry may enter into a marital property agreement concerning their property then existing or to be acquired listing such stipulations as they desire.

All property acquired by either a husband *or* wife during marriage is the common or community property of the husband *and* wife. The exceptions are: Property defined in the law as separate property and property contracted to be "separate" between the parties.

Marriage

Common-law marriages, both those contracted in Texas and out-of-state, are recognized.

Personal Property

Tenancy by the entirety is not recognized.

Real Property

Tenancy by the entirety is not recognized.

Taxation

The inheritance tax law was changed so that for estates of decedents who die after September 1, 1983, a tax will be imposed on the transfer at death of property of every resident of Texas (and on property within Texas of a nonresident) equal to the amount of the federal credit for state death transfer taxes.

There is no gift tax.

Wills

If the will of a husband or wife attempts, by explicit language, to dispose of the entire community property, or any part of the community property, the surviving spouse has a right to elect whether to take the provision in the will or to retain his or her right in the community property against the will. Election may be express or implied, by word or act, but must be made with a showing of knowledge that the right to elect exists. There is no right to elect between a testamentary provision (in a will) and a distributive share under the statute of descent and distribution (which applies when there is no will).

UTAH

Curtesy and Dower

There is no doctrine of curtesy in Utah. A wife does have certain dower rights.

Divorce

The equitable distribution theory applies. The court may make orders in relation to property "as may be equitable."

Husband and Wife

All disabilities of married women have been removed. Property acquired by a wife before marriage or acquired thereafter by purchase, gift, grant, inheritance, or devise remains her separate property, and she may deal with the same as though unmarried. A married woman is not liable for her husband's debts but is jointly liable with her husband for family expenses.

A wife must join in the deed of a husband in order to bar her statutory right of dower in the property conveyed. Because a husband has no curtesy right, it is not necessary that he join in his wife's deed of her property.

Personal Property

There is no statutory provision as to whether tenancy by the entirety is recognized in personal property.

Real Property

Tenancy by the entirety is recognized in real property. Every interest in real estate conveyed to two or more persons is deemed a tenancy in common unless expressly declared in the instrument to be otherwise. Joint tenancies (with survivorship right) may be created by express declaration.

Taxation

There is no inheritance tax.

There is an estate tax imposed on the transfer of property at death. It is based on the maximum amount of credit for estate state death taxes allowed on a federal return.

There is no gift tax, but the estate tax applies to gifts in contemplation of death or intended to take effect after the death of the donor.

Wills

Utah has adopted the Uniform Probate Code with modifications. There is a provision for an elective share for a surviving spouse who renounces a will. There is a provision for property to be applied first to satisfy such elective share before contributions due from other recipients or transferees are applied.

VERMONT

Curtesy

A widower is entitled to one third in value of all the real estate owned by his wife at death. If the wife left only one heir, who is the natural issue of that husband (or adopted child of both), the husband is entitled to half in value of such real estate.

Divorce

The court is to decree such disposition of property owned by the parties separately, jointly, or by the entirety, as is "just and equitable." The court is to consider the respective merits of the parties, the condition in which they will be left by such divorce, and the party through whom the property was acquired.

Dower

A widow is entitled to one third in value of all the real estate owned by her husband at his death. If the husband left only one heir, who is the natural issue of the widow (or adopted child of both), she is entitled to half the value of the real estate. Dower has preference over the claims of unsecured creditors of a deceased husband. Dower may be barred as follows: (1) By jointure (roughly means "widow's portion") settled on a wife by her husband or another person, or some monetary provision made for her before marriage (with or without her consent) or after marriage with her consent; or (2) by testamentary provision intended to be in lieu of dower (unless she elects to relinquish such provision); or (3) by election (if the husband left no children) to take the intestate share (as provided by statute if the deceased left no will) instead of dower.

Personal Property

Tenancy by the entirety exists in personal property.

Real Property

Tenancy by the entirety is recognized in real property. Unless specifically stated otherwise in a grant or deed, all property conveyed by such instrument to two or more persons, except to a husband and wife or in trust, is deemed to be owned by them as tenants in common.

Taxation

A Vermont taxable estate is the value of a Vermont gross estate (federal gross estate less the value of any property located outside Vermont at the time of death), reduced by certain allowable deductions and exemptions. (These deductions and exemptions bear the same proportion to the Vermont estate value as the Vermont gross estate bears to the value of the federal gross estate.) The gift tax is a ratio of the federal gift tax. There was a tax on "Vermont gifts," which are transfers by gift (except gifts of tangible personal property and real property having a situs outside Vermont) by a nonresident. The gift tax with respect to Vermont gifts made after December 31, 1979, was repealed effective January 1, 1980.

Wills

Where a testamentary provision is made for a surviving spouse in lieu of dower or curtesy, the surviving spouse may elect to relinquish such provision and take dower or curtesy. A surviving spouse may take curtesy or dower in lieu of the statutory distributive share of an estate (where there was no will).

VIRGINIA

Curtesy

A surviving husband is entitled to curtesy, in fee simple, in one third of the real estate owned by his wife during their marriage. This applies whether or not a child was born. A husband's joining in his wife's conveyance will bar curtesy.

Divorce

Division of property is by process of equitable distribution. The court may grant a monetary award, payable as lump sum or in installments. In determining the amount of award, the court is to consider both parties as having an interest in marital property. If all deposits to a joint savings account had been made from the husband's earnings, the divorce court does not have the power to equally divide such joint savings account at the conclusion of divorce proceedings. Contingent rights of either spouse in property of the other are extinguished by divorce. Tenancy with right of survivorship is terminated and becomes a tenancy in common.

Dower

A widow is entitled to one third of the real estate owned by her husband during their marriage. Dower may be barred by the wife joining in a conveyance with the husband or, if he has already conveyed, by her sole deed. There is also a provision in Virginia law for real or personal property intended to be in lieu of dower conveyed or bequeathed for jointure ("widow's portion") of the wife to take effect on her husband's death and to last for her life. A widow may waive "jointure" and demand dower. Dower may be assigned as at common law, or a widow may petition the court for payment of a sum in lieu of dower when it cannot be conveniently assigned in kind.

Marriage

Common-law marriages are void if contracted in Virginia but are recognized if contracted in a state where such marriages are valid.

Personal Property

Personal property may be held by a husband and wife as tenants by the entireties.

Real Property

Common law estates are recognized, including curtesy and dower. Tenancy by the entirety is recognized. There is no survivorship between joint tenants (other than tenants by the entireties) except where they hold as executors or trustees or the instrument creating a joint tenancy clearly shows the intent that there shall be survivorship.

Taxation

There are no statutory provisions for inheritance or gift taxes. An estate tax is imposed on Virginia residents in the amount of the federal credit for state death taxes allowable by Internal Revenue Code S 2011, with certain adjustments. Specific provisions cover the estate of a U.S. citizen who is not a resident of Virginia but had real property located in Virginia and/or tangible personal property having a situs in Virginia. Stock in a corporation organized under the laws of Virginia is deemed to be physically present within the state.

Wills

Whether or not provision is made for a husband or wife by will, a survivor may renounce and demand curtesy or dower and distributive rights. If renunciation is made, the surviving spouse takes one third of the decedent's estate if there are surviving children, or their descendants, otherwise one half (not all as in the case of intestacy).

VIRGIN ISLANDS

Curtesy and Dower

Abolished in 1957.

Divorce

There are no statutory provisions except that the court may divide the marital estate by just making a monetary award of alimony. Either party may institute a separate action for partition of property held as tenants in common. If one spouse has a particular equitable interest in property, a separate equity action may be maintained to realize that interest. A separation agreement between the parties may be helpful to a court in arriving at appropriate terms for alimony, but the court is not bound to accept the judgment or agreement of the parties on this issue.

Husband and Wife

Neither husband nor wife has an interest in the property of the other. Neither spouse is liable for debts or liabilities of the other incurred before marriage and neither is liable for separate debts of the other during marriage, nor is the rent or income of property of either liable for separate debts of the other. A conveyance, transfer, or lien executed by either husband or wife to or in favor of the other is valid to the same extent as between other persons.

Marriage

Common-law marriages are not recognized, but if valid in other jurisdictions, they will be recognized in the Virgin Islands.

Personal Property

There are no statutory provisions as to whether a tenancy by the entirety exists in personal property.

Real Property

A conveyance or devise to husband and wife creates an estate by the entirety unless otherwise provided in the deed or will. Upon divorce or annulment of a marriage, former spouses become tenants in common. A conveyance or devise of lands made to two or more persons (other than to executors and trustees or to husband and wife) creates a tenancy in common unless the instrument expressly declares that the grantees take as joint tenants.

Taxation

There is an inheritance tax, including a tax on inheritances between spouses (although the percentage is smaller than on inheritances received by more distant relatives).

A gift tax is imposed on transfers during a calendar year by a resident or nonresident of property located in the Virgin Islands.

The federal estate tax law is applicable.

Wills

There is a personal right of election given to a surviving spouse to take the share of the estate as in intestacy (as if there were no will), but this is limited to one half of the net estate of the decedent after the deduction of debts and administration expenses. A husband or wife may waive or release the right of election to take against a particular will.

WASHINGTON

Curtesy and Dower

Curtesy and dower have been abolished. Property rights of husband and wife are fixed by community property law.

Dissolution of Marriage

A court presiding over the dissolution of a marriage may make disposition of property as "just and equitable" without regard to marital misconduct. Relevant factors to consider are: The nature and extent of community and separate property; the duration of the marriage; the economic circumstances of each spouse at the time the division of property is effective.

Husband and Wife

All property, real and personal, owned by the wife or husband before marriage or afterwards acquired by gift, bequest, devise, or descent, or from the income and profits of such, is her or his separate property. Separate property of either is not subject to the separate debts of the other spouse. Either spouse may convey or encumber his or her separate real or personal property (other than the homestead) without the consent or joinder of the other spouse.

The community property law is in effect in the state of

Washington. Property acquired after marriage by either husband or wife, or both, is community property. Excepted from this is property acquired by gift or inheritance or from the sale or profits of separate property. Property acquired by a couple living together but unmarried is not community property. (See "Property of Cohabitants".) Community property is not owned by the community as a separate entity. Each spouse owns an equal undivided half interest in the whole. However, either spouse acting alone may manage and control all community property with the same power of disposition as a spouse has over his/her separate property. However, neither spouse may devise or bequeath by will more than one half of their community property; neither spouse may give community property without the consent of the other; neither spouse may sell, convey, or encumber community real property without the other spouse joining in the execution of the deed; any such deed must be acknowledged by both spouses; neither spouse may purchase or contract to purchase community real property without the other spouse joining in the transaction of purchase; neither spouse may acquire or sell assets, including real estate or the goodwill of a business where both spouses participate in its management, without the consent of the other (unless only one spouse manages the business); neither spouse may sell community household goods without the other spouse joining in the action.

On the death of one spouse, the surviving spouse is entitled to one half of the community property and takes the other half also if the deceased spouse did not dispose of the remaining half by will.

Marriage

Common-law marriage cannot be contracted in Washington, but common-law marriages consummated in a state that recognizes such marriages are valid in the state of Washington.

Property of Cohabitants

Based on case law, the following statement is made in the Washington law section of Martindale-Hubbell's digest of state laws: "In dividing property of cohabitants, court must examine relationship and property accumulations and, by analogy to community property laws, divide property justly and equitably."

Personal Property

Tenancy by the entirety may be permitted in personal property, but there is no right of survivorship.

Real Property

Washington has a "community property" system of property. Estates are recognized substantially as at common law. There are exceptions: Estates in dower and curtesy are abolished; the right of survivorship as an incident of tenancy by the entirety is abolished. Joint tenancies with incidents of survivorship and severability as at common law may be created only by express provision in a written instrument.

Taxation

Both inheritance and gift taxes have been repealed.

There is an estate tax. The tax is in an amount equal to the federal credit imposed on the transfer of a net estate of every resident. There is a tax imposed on the transfer of a nonresident's net estate *located* in Washington, also computed to absorb the federal tax credit for state death taxes.

Wills

There is no statute giving a surviving spouse a right to elect against a will. However, if a deceased spouse attempted to dispose of a surviving spouse's share of community property, the surviving spouse may take under the will or renounce it, taking instead his or her one-half community interest.

WEST VIRGINIA

Curtesy

Curtesy is abolished, but a surviving husband has a dower interest in his wife's estate.

Divorce

In the absence of a valid separation agreement, a court is to divide marital property of the parties equally between the parties, but may alter such distribution on consideration of the following: (1) The extent to which each party has contributed to the acquisition, preservation, and maintenance, or increase in value, of marital property by monetary contributions and by nonmonetary contributions, including child care services and homemaker services; (2) the extent to which each party expended his or her efforts during the marriage in a way that limited that party's earning ability or enhanced the income-earning ability of the other party (such as by direct contributions to education, forgoing employment, etc.); (3) the extent to which each party, during the marriage, acted in a manner that dissipated or depreciated the value of marital property. Except for economic considerations of the enumerated conduct, fault is not to be considered by the court in determining proper distribution of marital property. All rights of either party to dower are barred by a divorce order, but the court may compel a guilty party to compensate an innocent party for an inchoate right of dower [presumably "guilt" is defined within the above guidelines]. The court may restore to a spouse property in control of the other spouse.

Dower

A surviving husband or wife is entitled to dower, which consists of a life estate in one third of all the real estate the deceased spouse owned during the marriage. A court may award cash in lieu of dower in kind. Dower right is in addition to the right of inheritance. Dower may be barred by either spouse joining with the other spouse in a conveyance or a contract to convey or by a subsequent separate instrument executed by the spouse who is contingent dower owner. The concept of "jointure" exists in West Virginia. Real or personal property, intended to be in lieu of dower, conveyed or devised (by will) for the jointure (estate limited for the life of the holder) of the wife or husband bars dower. In some circumstances the surviving spouse may waive jointure and demand dower.

Husband and Wife

A married woman's rights with respect to property are the same as if she were single. Her separate property is not subject to disposal by the husband or liable for his debts. It is not necessary that either spouse consent or join in a conveyance or encumbrance of the other spouse of his or her real estate, except to bar dower. Consent to dower may be given separately after, but not before, a sale, conveyance, or agreement to convey by the other spouse. A husband or wife may convey real estate by deed directly to the other.

Marriage

Common-law marriage is not valid if contracted in West Virginia, but children of such a marriage are legitimate. A common-law marriage contracted in a state where it is valid will be recognized in West Virginia.

Personal Property

Tenancy in personal property is presumed to be a tenancy in common unless there are words in the instrument indicating that survivorship was intended or unless the instrument by use of the word "or" with regard to multiple owners indicates that joint tenancy is intended and not a tenancy in common.

Real Property

Common law estates are generally recognized, unless modified by statute. Joint tenancies and estates by entirety are abolished, with this exception: Where the instrument shows intention of conveying a survivorship interest among multiple owners, such as by use of the word "or," then ownership is as joint tenants with right of survivorship, unless expressly stated otherwise.

Taxation

There is an inheritance tax on all property transferred by will, or laws of descent and distribution (if there was no will), or by gift in contemplation of death. This relates to property—real, personal, or mixed—within the jurisdiction of the state. The inheritance tax applies to and is a lien on shares of corporate stock owned by a nonresident decedent when the shares are kept within the state and when the shares are those of a domestic corporation, wherever kept. The rates of tax are determined according to classification of beneficiaries and the amount or value of property transferred to each beneficiary.

There is no estate tax. However, the inheritance tax respecting resident decedents is at least equal to the allowable federal estate tax credit.

Wills

A surviving spouse may renounce a provision in a will in lieu of dower; and a provision in a will for a surviving wife or husband is in lieu of dower unless it clearly appears that the deceased intended otherwise. If there is no renunciation, the survivor takes real and personal property under the will. If there is no provision by will, or the surviving spouse renounces, the survivor takes real and personal property of the deceased as if the deceased spouse had died intestate (without a will) leaving children.

WISCONSIN

Curtesy

A surviving husband's curtesy right is replaced by dower. However, effective January 1, 1986, the Marital Property Act eliminates dower.

Divorce

Property shown to have been acquired by either party by gift, bequest, devise, or inheritance, or from funds so acquired, remains the property of such party unless the court finds that would create hardship. Other property is presumed to be divided equally, but the court may alter this distribution after considering various specified factors, but not marital misconduct.

Dower

A surviving spouse, whether widow or widower, has dower only in property which the decedent owned at death. Dower is limited to the right to elect a share of the estate. Divorce is a bar to dower. Effective January 1, 1986, the Marital Property Act eliminates dower.

Husband and Wife

The real and personal property of a married woman is her sole and separate estate and is not subject to debts of or disposal by her husband. She may receive, hold, convey, encumber, or devise her separate property as if she were sole; her earnings are not subject to her husband's control or debts. Joinder of a spouse in a deed, mortgage, or other conveyance is required only if the property is the homestead or if one spouse owns an interest in the property. A deed to husband and wife creates a joint tenancy, unless a contrary intent is expressed in the document.

Effective January 1, 1986, 1983 Wisconsin Act 186 (enacted in 1983), known as the Marital Property Act, will make Wisconsin a modified community property state. The act will have a significant impact on various chapters of the Wisconsin law on the statute books. Certain sections will be repealed and recreated.

Marriage

Common-law marriages are not recognized in Wisconsin. There is no authority as to the validity of common-law marriages contracted out of the state.

Personal Property

Tenancy by the entirety is not recognized.

Real Property

There is a general rule that all transfers to two or more persons are construed to create a joint tenancy. A husband and wife take as joint tenants unless the document expresses a different intent (trustees or personal representatives hold title to interests in property as joint tenants). Estates by the entirety are abolished. Any attempt to create such an estate in a husband and wife results in the creation of a joint tenancy.

Taxation

An inheritance tax is imposed on the transfer of all property within the jurisdiction of Wisconsin which is a transfer by will, by intestacy, or in contemplation of death (with a two-year presumption), and by survivorship of a joint tenancy. All property of a resident decedent is subject to the tax as is property of a nonresident decedent within the jursidiction of the state.

In addition to the inheritance tax, there is an estate tax to equal the maximum federal credit for state death taxes.

A gift tax is imposed at the same rates as the inheritance tax. Gifts to spouses after June 30, 1982, are fully exempt. Gifts after December 31, 1984, are excluded up to $10,000 per donee in a calendar year.

Wills

A surviving spouse, whether widow or widower, may elect to take one third of the value of the net probate estate (reduced by the value of any property given outright to the surviving spouse under the will). The spouse exercising such election forfeits the right to take under the will or by intestate succession. The right to elect may be barred by written agreement signed by both spouses before or after the marriage. The right is also barred if the surviving spouse receives at least one half of certain enumerated property. Note: Effective January 1, 1986, this section of the Wisconsin statute will be repealed by the Marital Property Act.

WYOMING

Curtesy and Dower

Abolished.

Divorce

In granting a divorce the court shall make such disposition of the property of the parties as appears just and equitable, having regard for: The respective merits of the parties and the condition in which they will be left by the divorce; the party through whom the property was acquired; burdens imposed on the property for the benefit of either party or the children. "Just and equitable" disposition is not always equated with quantitative equality. Broad authority has been granted the divorce court in determining "just and equitable" disposition of property. The court may decree to either party reasonable alimony out of the estate of the other, having regard for the ability of the party; and the court may order so much out of the real estate or rents and profits as is necessary to be assigned to either party for life, or may decree a specific sum to be paid by either party. The court may, on petition of either party, revise the decree with respect to the amount of alimony. There are no statutory provisions regarding separation agreements, but such agreements are recognized and enforced if they are incorporated in a divorce decree.

Husband and Wife

Husband and wife may own property, contract, and sue or be sued in general as though they were unmarried.

All property belonging to a married person as separate property which that person owns at the time of marriage or which is acquired separately by inheritance or otherwise, together with the profits and increase during marriage, is that person's sole and separate property and may be owned and enjoyed by that spouse the same as though he were single. Such property is not subject to disposal, control, or interference of his spouse and is exempt from execution or attachment for debts of his spouse (provided the property was not conveyed to him by his spouse in fraud of his creditors). Any married person may transfer his separate property in the same manner and to the same extent as if he were unmarried. [Note: The Wyoming statue uses the pronoun "he," but it is presumed the language means "he, she" or "his, her."]

All disabilities of married women have been removed.

Marriage

If entered into in Wyoming, common-law marriages are invalid, but if valid in the state where they are created, they are valid in Wyoming.

Personal Property

Tenancy by the entirety in personal property is recognized and may be established without the necessity of transfer to or through a third person.

Real Property

Common law estates are recognized, including joint tenancies, tenancy in common, and tenancies by the entirety. Joint tenancy or tenancy by the entirety may be created by the owner of property simply by designating in the instrument of conveyance or transfer the names of such tenants, including his own, without the necessity of conveyance to or through third persons.

Joint tenancies are *not* abolished nor is any presumption established by statute or decision in favor of tenancy in common, even where the intent to create a joint tenancy is not clear. A joint tenancy can be created in a husband and wife and may be terminated by one joint tenant's conveyance of his interest. Tenancies by the entirety for married persons are recognized. Tenancies by the entireties or joint tenancies may be terminated on the death of a joint tenant or of one spouse, by court procedure, or by simplified procedure by affidavit.

Taxation

Previous inheritance tax legislation is repealed (effective January 1, 1983). New statutory enactments are intended to take full advantage for Wyoming of the credit which is allowed as a deduction from federal estate tax liability for state death taxes. There is no gift tax.

Wills

A surviving spouse of a decedent domiciled in the state has the right to take against the net estate one half if there are no surviving children of a previous marriage; different percentages depending on other heirs. If a married decedent was not domiciled in Wyoming, the surviving spouse's right to election is governed by the state of the decedent's domicile. The contribution of the portion of other heirs is based on rules of equity and justice. Adjustment is made between a decedent's power to make a will and a spouse's right to elect against the will. Provisions of the will are to be disturbed as little as possible, and a loss caused by a spouse's election is to fall on all equally.

GLOSSARY

(Note: The words are given their meaning as used in the preceding text which is not necessarily the usual dictionary meaning.)

Alimony: Usually fixed, periodic payments established in a decree of divorce or legal separation issued by a court, or in a written settlement agreement, requiring one spouse to make the payments to the other spouse. Also sometimes called *spousal maintenance* or *support*.

Antenuptial Agreement: A contract or agreement made between a man and woman before marriage in contemplation and in consideration of marriage, in which the property rights of each party are fixed by the terms of the contract rather than by state law.

Basis: Usually the cost of an asset. *Adjusted basis* is basis after additions or subtractions required by the tax laws have been made. On the sale of the asset, the amount of taxable gain or loss is determined by the difference between basis (original or adjusted) and amount realized.

Beneficiary: One entitled to distribution of property from an estate if named in a will to receive a testamentary gift; one entitled to enjoy the benefit of property held in a trust; one named to receive life insurance proceeds or survivor benefits under a pension plan.

Capital Assets: In general, all property that you own. In the lexicon of taxation, capital assets are those the sale of which results in gain or loss taxed under special Internal Revenue Code rules. The rules differ when assets are held for business or investment, rather than personal, use.

Clifford Trust: A trust created during the grantor's life for the purpose of directing a trustee to pay the income from the trust property to beneficiaries other than the grantor for a period in excess of 10 years (or until the death of the beneficiary or beneficiaries even if less than 10 years), after which time the property reverts back to the grantor.

Provided the grantor does not retain elements of control and the trust is irrevocable for the stated period, the income is considered and taxed as the income of the beneficiary or beneficiaries. Also called a "short-term trust."

Cohabitation: The act of living together engaged in by two persons without any pretensions of being married.

Common Law: That law that this country received from England based on juristic theory, court decisions, and some early English statutes. Followed in a majority of American states.

Common-Law Marriage: A form of marriage not entered into in accordance with religious or civil requirements but with the intent to live together as husband and wife and a holding out to others of that relation. Elements required for a relation to be considered a common-law marriage vary among the states that recognize this status (many do not).

Community Property: A form of co-ownership of property by husband and wife in which each spouse owns an individual one-half interest in each item of community property from the moment of acquisition; assets acquired during the marriage are presumptively community property as well as assets acquired as a result of the efforts of either or both spouses during the marriage. The system prevails in: Arizona, California, Idaho, Louisiana, Nevada, New Mexico, Texas, Washington, and Puerto Rico.

Conservator: One appointed by a court to conserve and manage the affairs, particularly financial, of a person found by the court to be incompetent or incapable of managing his/her property.

Consideration: Anything of value (not necessarily money) which provides the inducement for entering into a contract.

Corpus: The property making up the principal of a trust, as distinguished from the income it produces.

Co-Tenancy: Co-ownership. See **joint tenancy, tenancy by the entireties,** and **tenancy in common** for definitions of various forms of co-ownership.

Curtesy: Estate allowed a surviving husband in the real property left by his wife, provided they had lawful issue. Now largely abolished or modified by state statutes.

Custodian: The term used in the Gifts to Minors Statutes to designate the fiduciary who receives the minor's property with power to use it for the minor until majority.

Decedent: One who has died.

Depreciation: An accounting concept describing an allowable deduction for income tax purposes in charging off the taxpayer's capital investments in equipment, buildings, etc., used in business, profession, or rental or other income-producing activities, according to specific provisions of the tax law.

Devise: Gift of land by will. **Devisee:** One who receives the gift.

Domicile: The place of one's permanent home. Estates are administered and wills probated in the state of decedent's legal domicile at the time of death.

Dower: The interest in the real property of the deceased husband which is given to the widow under the common law. Inchoate dower ripens into consummate dower on his death. In most states, dower has been abolished or modified by modern statute.

Elective Share: Share of a decedent's estate which a surviving spouse may elect to take after renouncing or dissenting from the decedent spouse's will. It is usually the same share designated by statute as that to which a surviving spouse is entitled if the decedent spouse died without a will.

Equitable Distribution: System of distribution of property by a court upon dissolution of a marriage based on fairness in consideration of certain factors, often specified by statute. State statutes define the court's authority and frequently provide guidelines for its action; these guidelines vary from state to state. Such statutes are in force in virtually all states.

Equitable Title: Beneficiaries of a trust are said to have "equitable title," while the trustee has "legal title." See **trust**.

Equity Sharing: Method of acquiring or owning real property by two or more people, whereby one purchaser occupies the property and pays proportionate rent to the other part owner.

Estate: The property or interest in property that is owned.

Exemption Equivalent: The value of property that may be transferred during life or at death without incurring any federal gift or estate taxes.

Fee Simple: The maximum ownership of property possible in law.

Feme Sole: A single woman; could be married but designated to have certain property ownership rights as "though she were a feme sole."

Generation-Skipping Transfer: A transfer, usually in trust, established for the benefit of two or more generations in succession. Properly constructed, it may avoid imposition of an estate tax on the death of a member of the older generation. To prevent that, a special tax, called the tax on generation-skipping transfers, was enacted by Congress.

Grantor: The one who establishes a trust. Also sometimes called settlor or trustor.

Heirs at Law: Those who are entitled to the property of one who has died intestate according to applicable state law. "Heir" is often loosely used to refer to one who inherits either by operation of law or by will.

Inheritance Tax: A tax imposed in some states on receipt of an inheritance. The rate applicable varies with the degree of the heir's relationship to the deceased.

Inter Vivos: During life.

Intestate: Description of a decedent who had not made a will. That decedent is said to have died "intestate." One who makes a will which fails to dispose of the entire estate dies partially intestate.

Joint Tenancy: One of the forms of co-ownership of property. It usually, though not inevitably, includes the right of survivorship, i.e., the enlargement of the surviving joint tenant's interest to include the share of a deceased joint tenant. JTRS is a convenient abbreviation for joint tenants with right of survivorship.

Legacy: A gift of money by will. The one who takes is a "legatee."

Life Estate: The right to use or receive the income from property during life.

Living Trust: A trust established during a person's lifetime. Also called an *inter vivos* trust. See **trust**.

Marital Deduction: A deduction allowed in computing federal gift tax or estate tax liability. It is available under the former for gifts inter vivos to a spouse and under the latter for transfers to a surviving spouse. The transfer must be in one of several possible forms that "qualify" for the deduction. Since 1981, there has been no ceiling on the amount of this deduction, resulting in transferability between spouses free of federal gift tax or estate tax.

Marital Property: This refers to property acquired by married individuals during the marriage except that acquired by gift to or inheritance of either party alone or traceable to property acquired by either party before marriage.

Partition: A court proceeding established by law in most states allowing a co-owner of property to petition for its division between the co-owners. Not available where property is held as tenants by the entireties, except upon divorce.

Personal Property: Tangible or intangible "movable" property; chattels; things; certain rights.

Power of Attorney: A form of agency. A power granting broad authority to the agent to act on behalf of the principal may be termed *general*. A power limited to particular specified acts may be termed *special*. **Durable Power of Attorney:** A power which by its terms will continue to confer authority on the agent although the principal may become incapacitated. Any action by the agent authorized under the terms of the power of attorney is legally binding on the principal.

Probate: The administration of a decedent's estate under supervision by a state court. *Probate estate* refers to the property subject to that administration, i.e., that owned outright by the decedent. Joint property that passes by right of survivorship is not administered by the probate court. The potentially *taxable estate* of a decedent might include everything the decedent owned, including nonprobatable assets.

Qualified Terminable Interest Property: One of the several forms of transfer which will qualify for the marital deduction under the federal estate tax law. The deceased spouse's executor must elect to claim the property on the decedent's estate tax return; the surviving spouse must be entitled to all of the income from the qualifying property for life; the deceased spouse's will may designate the recipient of the property after the surviving spouse's death; and the value of the property will be treated as transferred by the surviving spouse and taxed accordingly. Such terminable interest property "qualifies" for the 100 percent marital deduction.

Real Property: Land, including buildings and structures on the land with items permanently affixed to them. Ownership of real estate is transferred by deed signed by the transferor and identifying the transferee. Some states require a deed to be recorded in order to take effect.

Separate Property: Property owned by a married person in a community property state which is not community property. It includes property acquired before the marriage, property acquired during the marriage by gift or inheritance, and property acquired during the marriage traceable to proceeds of the sale of other separate property. It can also be used to describe similar property of married persons not residing in a community property state. State laws vary as to whether title alone determines ownership between spouses where the property was acquired during the marriage.

Settlor: One who establishes a trust. Also called *trustor* or *grantor*.

Short-Term Trust: See **Clifford Trust**.

Statutory Share: Shares of an estate taken by heirs of a decedent who died without having made a will. State laws establish the proportion of the estate taken by certain heirs, based on family relationship to the decedent. Also used to refer to the share a surviving spouse may elect to take (in some cases as specified in state law) when renouncing the share designated in the will of the decedent spouse. See **elective share**.

Stepped-Up Basis: Basis assigned to assets transferred at death. It is the date of death value (or value on a date six months thereafter, if elected by the executor). It is said to be "stepped up," but the term merely reflects the expected effect of inflation on assets in an estate. This benefits an heir because the "stepped-up basis" becomes the heir's basis for income tax purposes on a sale of the property when it is in the heir's hands.

Taxable Estate: The dollar value of a gross estate less all allowable deductions to which the rate structure is then applied to fix the federal estate tax due (before subtracting credits). *Gross estate* is the total inventory of property that can be taxed by an estate tax, as established in the Internal Revenue Code.

Tenants by the Entireties: A co-tenancy with right of survivorship, but the co-tenants must be husband and wife. Unlike the joint tenancy, one tenant cannot sever the co-tenancy alone. It will be changed only if both spouses act in concert or if there is a divorce. A divorce severs the "entirety."

Tenancy in Common: Co-ownership between two or more parties in which each co-owner holds a defined percentage of the whole and there is no right of survivorship between the co-owners, so that a deceased co-tenant's share passes through his or her estate.

Tentative Tax: Federal transfer tax on a gift or estate before the unified credit is applied. See **unified credit**.

Testamentary: Pertaining to transfer effective at death of the transferor. Testamentary gift is one made by terms of a will. A testamentary trust is one created in a will.

Title: Ownership in the name(s) of those who hold title and specifying the form of ownership, usually referring to ownership of real estate but not necessarily.

Transfer Tax: A tax levied by the federal government or a state on gratuitous transfers of property during life (inter vivos gift) or at death (testamentary gift).

Trust: A form of property holding in which ownership is divided between a trustee or trustees holding *legal title* and one or more beneficiaries who hold *equitable title*. The trustees have a fiduciary duty to manage and distribute the property or its earnings to or for the benefit of the beneficiaries.

Trustee: A person, persons, or institution appointed to carry out the terms of a document establishing a trust.

Unified Credit: A credit against the federal transfer taxes which would otherwise be payable on inter vivos gifts or death transfers. The credit is cumulative and may be used in part at different times.

Uniform Gifts to Minors Acts: Statutory authority for making gifts to a minor by delivery to a *custodian* empowered by state statutes to hold and use the property for the benefit of the minor until the age of majority according to state law. See **custodian**.

INDEX